A Young Girl's Diary

Sigmund Freud, et al.

A Young Girl's Diary

Copyright © 2021 Indo-European Publishing

The present edition is a reproduction of previous publication of this classic work. Minor typographical errors may have been corrected without note; however, for an authentic reading experience the spelling, punctuation, and capitalization have been retained from the original text.

ISBN: 978-1-64439-499-1

CONTENTS

PREFACE

THE best preface to this journal written by a young girl belonging to the upper middle class is a letter by Sigmund Freud dated April 27, 1915, a letter wherein the distinguished Viennese psychologist testifies to the permanent value of the document:

"This diary is a gem. Never before, I believe, has anything been written enabling us to see so clearly into the soul of a young girl, belonging to our social and cultural stratum, during the years of puberal development. We are shown how the sentiments pass from the simple egoism of childhood to attain maturity; how the relationships to parents and other members of the family first shape themselves, and how they gradually become more serious and more intimate; how friendships are formed and broken. We are shown the dawn of love, feeling out towards its first objects. Above all, we are shown how the mystery of the sexual life first presses itself vaguely on the attention, and then takes entire possession of the growing intelligence, so that the child suffers under the load of secret knowledge but gradually becomes enabled to shoulder the burden. Of all these things we have a description at once so charming, so serious, and so artless, that it cannot fail to be of supreme interest to educationists and psychologists.

"It is certainly incumbent on you to publish the diary. All students of my own writings will be grateful to you."

In preparing these pages for the press, the editor has toned down nothing, has added nothing, and has suppressed nothing. The only alterations she has made have been such as were essential to conceal the identity of the writer and of other persons mentioned in the document. Consequently, surnames, Christian names, and names of places, have been changed. These modifications have enabled the original author of the diary to allow me to place it at the free disposal of serious readers.

No attempt has been made to correct trifling faults in grammar and other inelegancies of style. For the most part, these must not be regarded as the expression of a child's incapacity for the control of language. Rather must they be looked upon as manifestations of affective trends, as errors in functioning brought about by the influence of the Unconscious.

THE EDITOR
VIENNA, Autumn, 1919

FIRST YEAR, AGE ELEVEN TO TWELVE

FIRST YEAR

July 12, 19 . . . Hella and I are writing a diary. We both agreed that when we went to the high school we would write a diary every day. Dora keeps a diary too, but she gets furious if I look at it. I call Helene "Hella," and she calls me "Rita;" Helene and Grete are so vulgar. Dora has taken to calling herself "Thea," but I go on calling her "Dora." She says that little children (she means me and Hella) ought not to keep a diary. She says they will write such a lot of nonsense. No more than in hers and Lizzi's.

July 13th. Really we were not to begin writing until after the holidays, but since we are both going away, we are beginning now. Then we shall know what we have been doing in the holidays.

The day before yesterday we had an entrance examination, it was very easy, in dictation I made only 1 mistake—writing ihn without h. The mistress said that didn't matter, I had only made a slip. That is quite true, for I know well enough that ihn has an h in it. We were both dressed in white with rose-coloured ribbons, and everyone believed we were sisters or at least cousins. It would be very nice to have a cousin. But it's still nicer to have a friend, for we can tell one another everything.

July 14th. The mistress was very kind. Because of her Hella and I are really sorry that we are not going to a middle school. Then every day before lessons began we could have had a talk with her in the class-room. But we're awfully pleased because of the other girls. One is more important when one goes to the high school instead of only to the middle school. That is why the girls are in such a rage. "They are bursting with pride" (that's what my sister says of me and Hella, but it is not true). "Our two students" said the mistress when we came away. She told us to write to her from the country. I shall.

July 15th. Lizzi, Hella's sister, is not so horrid as Dora, she is always so nice! To-day she gave each of us at least ten chocolate-creams. It's true Hella often says to me: "You don't know her, what a beast she can be. Your sister is generally very nice to me." Certainly it is very funny the way in which she always speaks of us as "the little ones" or "the children," as if she had never been a child herself, and indeed a much littler one than we are. Besides we're just the same as she is now. She is in the fourth class and we are in the first.

1

To-morrow we are going to Kaltenbach in Tyrol. I'm frightfully excited. Hella went away to-day to Hungary to her uncle and aunt with her mother and Lizzi. Her father is at manoeuvres.

July 19th. It's awfully hard to write every day in the holidays. Everything is so new and one has no time to write. We are living in a big house in the forest. Dora bagged the front veranda straight off for her own writing. At the back of the house there are such swarms of horrid little flies; everything is black with flies. I do hate flies and such things. I'm not going to put up with being driven out of the front veranda. I won't have it. Besides, Father said: "Don't quarrel, children!" (Children to her too!!) He's quite right. She puts on such airs because she'll be fourteen in October. "The verandas are common property," said Father. Father's always so just. He never lets Dora lord it over me, but Mother often makes a favourite of Dora. I'm writing to Hella to-day. She's not written to me yet.

July 21st. Hella has written to me, 4 pages, and such a jolly letter. I don't know what I should do without her! Perhaps she will come here in August or perhaps I shall go to stay with her. I think I would rather go to stay with her. I like paying long visits. Father said: "We'll see," and that means he'll let me go. When Father and Mother say We'll see it really means Yes; but they won't say "yes" so that if it does not come off one can't say that they haven't kept their word. Father really lets me do anything I like, but not Mother. Still, if I practice my piano regularly perhaps she'll let me go. I must go for a walk.

July 22nd. Hella wrote that I positively must write every day, for one must keep a promise and we swore to write every day. I. . . .

July 23rd. It's awful. One has no time. Yesterday when I wanted to write the room had to be cleaned and D. was in the arbour. Before that I had not written a single word and in the front veranda all my pages blew away. We write on loose pages. Hella thinks it's better because then one does not have to tear anything out. But we have promised one another to throw nothing away and not to tear anything up. Why should we? One can tell a friend everything. A pretty friend if one couldn't. Yesterday when I wanted to go into the arbour Dora glared at me savagely, saying What do you want? As if the arbour belonged to her, just as she wanted to bag the front veranda all for herself. She's too sickening.

Yesterday afternoon we were on the Kolber-Kogel. It was lovely. Father was awfully jolly and we pelted one another with pine-cones. It was jolly. I threw one at Dora and it hit her on her padded bust. She let out such a yell and I said out loud You couldn't feel it there. As she went by she said Pig! It doesn't matter, for I know she understood me and that what I said was true. I should like to know what she writes about every day to Erika and what she writes in her diary. Mother was out of sorts and stayed at home.

July 24th. To-day is Sunday. I do love Sundays. Father says: You children have Sundays every day. That's quite true in the holidays, but not at other times. The peasants and their wives and children are all very gay, wearing Tyrolese dresses, just like those I have seen in the theatre. We are wearing our white dresses to-day, and I have made a great cherrystain upon mine, not on purpose, but because I sat down upon some fallen cherries. So this afternoon when we go out walking I must wear my pink dress. All the better, for I don't care to be dressed exactly the same as Dora. I don't see why everyone should know that we are sisters. Let people think we are cousins. She does not like it either; I wish I knew why.

Oswald is coming in a week, and I am awfully pleased. He is older than Dora, but I can always get on with him. Hella writes that she finds it dull without me; so do I.

July 25th. I wrote to Fraulein Pruckl to-day. She is staying at Achensee. I should like to see her. Every afternoon we bathe and then go for a walk. But to-day it has been raining all day. Such a bore. I forgot to bring my paint-box and I'm not allowed to read all day. Mother says, if you gobble all your books up now you'll have nothing left to read. That's quite true, but I can't even go and swing.

Afternoon. I must write some more. I've had a frightful row with Dora. She says I've been fiddling with her things. It's all because she's so untidy. As if her things could interest me. Yesterday she left her letter to Erika lying about on the table, and all I read was: He's as handsome as a Greek god. I don't know who "he" was for she came in at that moment. It's probably Krail Rudi, with whom she is everlastingly playing tennis and carries on like anything. As for handsome—well, there's no accounting for tastes.

July 26th. It's a good thing I brought my dolls' portmanteau. Mother said: You'll be glad to have it on rainy days. Of course I'm much too old to play with dolls, but even though I'm 11 I can make dolls' clothes still. One learns something while one is doing it, and when I've finished something I do enjoy it so. Mother cut me out some things and I was tacking them together. Then Dora came into the room and said Hullo, the child is sewing things for her dolls. What cheek, as if she had never played with dolls. Besides, I don't really play with dolls any longer. When she sat down beside me I sewed so vigorously that I made a great scratch on her hand, and said: Oh, I'm so sorry, but you came too close. I hope she'll know why I really did it. Of course she'll go and sneak to Mother. Let her. What right has she to call me child. She's got a fine red scratch anyhow, and on her right hand where everyone can see.

3

July 27th. There's such a lot of fruit here. I eat raspberries and gooseberries all day and Mother says that is why I have no appetite for dinner. But Dr. Klein always says Fruit is so wholesome. But why should it be unwholesome all at once? Hella always says that when one likes anything awfully much one is always scolded about it until one gets perfectly sick of it. Hella often gets in such a temper with her mother, and then her mother says: We make such sacrifices for our children and they reward us with ingratitude. I should like to know what sacrifices they make. I think it's the children who make the sacrifices. When I want to eat gooseberries and am not allowed to, the sacrifice is mine not Mother's. I've written all this to Hella. Fraulein Pruckl has written to me. The address on her letter to me was splendid, "Fraulein Grete Lainer, Lyzealschulerin." Of course Dora had to know better than anyone else, and said that in the higher classes from the fourth upwards (because she is in the fourth) they write "Lyzeistin." She said: "Anyhow, in the holidays, before a girl has attended the first class she's not a Lyzealschulerin at all." Then Father chipped in, saying that we (I didn't begin it) really must stop this eternal wrangling; he really could not stand it. He's quite right, but what he said won't do any good, for Dora will go on just the same. Fraulein Pruckl wrote that she was delighted that I had written. As soon as I have time she wants me to write to her again. Great Scott, I've always time for her. I shall write to her again this evening after supper, so as not to keep her waiting.

July 29th. I simply could not write yesterday. The Warths have arrived, and I had to spend the whole day with Erna and Liesel, although it rained all day. We had a ripping time. They know a lot of round games and we played for sweets. I won 47, and I gave five of them to Dora. Robert is already more than a head taller than we are, I mean than Liesel and me; I think he is fifteen. He says Fraulein Grete and carried my cloak which Mother sent me because of the rain and he saw me home after supper.

To-morrow is my birthday and everyone has been invited and Mother has made strawberry cream and waffles. How spiffing.

July 30th. To-day is my birthday. Father gave me a splendid parasol with a flowered border and painting materials and Mother gave me a huge postcard album for 800 cards and stories for school girls, and Dora gave me a beautiful box of notepaper and Mother had made a chocolate-cream cake for dinner to-day as well as the strawberry cream. The first thing in the morning the Warths sent me three birthday cards. And Robert had written on his: With deepest respect your faithful R. It is glorious to have a birthday, everyone is so kind, even Dora. Oswald sent me a wooden paper-knife, the handle is a dragon and the blade shoots out of its mouth

4

instead of flame; or perhaps the blade is its tongue, one can't be quite sure. It has not rained yet on my birthday. Father says I was born under a lucky star. That suits me all right, tip top.

July 31st. Yesterday was heavenly. We laughed till our sides ached over Consequences. I was always being coupled with Robert and oh the things we did together, not really of course but only in writing: kissed, hugged, lost in the forest, bathed together; but I say, I wouldn't do that! quarrelled. That won't happen, it's quite impossible! Then we drank my health clinking glasses five times and Robert wanted to drink it in wine but Dora said that would never do! The real trouble was this. She always gets furious if she has to play second fiddle to me and yesterday I was certainly first fiddle.

Now I must write a word about to-day. We've had a splendid time. We were in Tiefengraben with the Warths where there are such a lot of wild strawberries. Robert picked all the best of them for me, to the great annoyance of Dora who had to pick them for herself. Really I would rather pick them for myself, but when some one else picks them for one for love (that's what Robert said) then one is quite glad to have them picked for one. Besides, I did pick some myself and gave most of them to Father and some to Mother. At afternoon tea which we had in Flischberg I had to sit beside Erna instead of Robert. Erna is rather dull. Mother says she is anemic; that sounds frightfully interesting, but I don't quite know what it means. Dora is always saying that she is anemic, but of course that is not true. And Father always says "Don't talk such stuff, you're as fit as a fiddle." That puts her in such a wax. Last year Lizzi was really anemic, so the doctor said, she was always having palpitation and had to take iron and drink Burgundy. I think that's where Dora got the idea.

August 1st. Hella is rather cross with me because I wrote and told her that I had spent the whole day with the W's. Still, she is really my only friend or I should not have written and told her. Every year in the country she has another friend too, but that doesn't put me out. I can't understand why she doesn't like Robert; she doesn't know anything about him except what I have written and certainly that was nothing but good. Of course she does know him for he is a cousin of the Sernigs and she met him once there. But one does not get to know a person from seeing them once. Anyhow she does not know him the way I do. Yesterday I was with the Warths all day. We played Place for the King and Robert caught me and I had to give him a kiss. And Erna said, that doesn't count, for I had let myself be caught. But Robert got savage and said: Erna is a perfect nuisance, she spoils everyone's pleasure. He's quite right, but there's some one else just as bad. But I do hope Erna has not told Dora about the kiss. If she has everyone will know and I shouldn't like that. I lay in wait for Erna with the sweets which Aunt Dora sent us. Robert and Liesel and I ate the rest. They were so good and nearly all large ones. At first Robert wanted to take quite a little one, but I said he must only have a big one. After that he always picked out the big ones. When I came home in the evening with the empty box Father laughed and said: There's nothing mean about our Gretel. Besides, Mother still has a great box full; I have no idea whether Dora still has a lot, but I expect so.

August 2nd. Oswald arrived this afternoon at 5. He's a great swell now; he's begun to grow a moustache. In the evening Father took him to the hotel to introduce him to some friends. He said it would be an awful bore, but he will certainly make a good impression especially in his new tourist getup and leather breeches. Grandmama and Grandpapa sent love to all. I've never seen them. They have sent a lot of cakes and sweets and Oswald grumbled no end because he had to bring them. Oswald is always smoking cigarettes and Father said to him: Come along old chap, we'll go to the inn and have a drink on the strength of your good report. It seems to me rather funny; no one wants to drink anything when Dora and I have a good report, at most they give us a present. Oswald has only Twos and Threes and very few Ones and in Greek nothing but Satisfactory, but I have nothing but Ones. He said something to Father in Latin and Father laughed heartily and said something I could not understand. I don't think it was Latin, but it may have been Magyar or English. Father knows nearly all languages, even Czech, but thank goodness he doesn't talk them unless he wants to tease us. Like that time at the station when Dora and I were so ashamed. Czech is horrid, Mother says so too. When Robert pretends to speak Czech it's screamingly funny.

August 3rd. I got a chill bathing the other day so now I am not allowed to bathe for a few days. Robert keeps me company. We are quite alone and he tells me all sorts of tales. He swings me so high that I positively yell. To-day he made me really angry, for he said: Oswald is a regular noodle. I said, that's not true, boys can never stand one another. Besides, it is not true that he lisps. Anyhow I like Oswald much better than Dora who always says "the children" when she is talking of me and of Hella and even of Robert. Then he said: Dora is just as big a goose as Erna. He's quite right there. Robert says he is never going to smoke, that it is so vulgar, that real gentlemen never smoke. But what about Father, I should like to know? He says, too, that he will never grow a beard but will shave every day and his wife will have to put everything straight to him.

6

But a beard suits Father and I can't imagine him without a beard. I know I won't marry a man without a beard.

August 5th. We go to the tennis ground every day. When we set off yesterday, Robert and I and Liesel and Erna and Rene, Dora called after us: The bridal pair in spee. She had picked up the phrase from Oswald. I think it means in a hundred years. She can wait a hundred years if she likes, we shan't. Mother scolded her like anything and said she mustn't say such stupid things. A good job too; in spee, in spee. Now we always talk of her as Inspee, but no one knows who we mean.

August 6th. Hella can't come here, for she is going to Klausenburg with her mother to stay with her other uncle who is district judge there or whatever they call a district judge in Hungary. Whenever I think of a district judge I think of District Judge T., such a hideous man. What a nose and his wife is so lovely; but her parents forced her into the marriage. I would not let anyone force me into such a marriage, I would much sooner not marry at all, besides she's awfully unhappy.

August 7th. There has been such a fearful row about Dora. Oswald told Father that she flirted so at the tennis court and he could not stand it. Father was in a towering rage and now we mayn't play tennis any more. What upset her more than anything was that Father said in front of me: This little chit of 14 is already encouraging people to make love to her. Her eyes were quite red and swollen and she couldn't eat anything at supper because she had such a headache!! We know all about her headaches. But I really can't see why I shouldn't go and play tennis.

August 8th. Oswald says that it wasn't the student's fault at all but only Dora's. I can quite believe that when I think of that time on the Southern Railway. Still, they won't let me play tennis any more, though I begged and begged Mother to ask Father to let me. She said it would do no good for Father was very angry and I mustn't spend whole days with the Warths any more. Whole days! I should like to know when I was a whole day there. When I went there naturally I had to stay to dinner at least. What have I got to do with Dora's love affairs? It's really too absurd. But grown-ups are always like that. When one person has done anything the others have to pay for it too.

August 9th. Thank goodness, I can play tennis once more; I begged and begged until Father let me go. Dora declares that nothing will induce her to ask! That's the old story of the fox and the grapes. She has been playing the invalid lately, won't bathe, and stays at home when she can instead of going for walks. I should like to know what's the matter with her. What I can't make out is why

Father lets her do it. As for Mother, she always spoils Dora; Dora is Mother's favourite, especially when Oswald is not on hand. I can understand her making a favourite of Oswald, but not of Dora. Father always says that parents have no favourites, but treat all their children alike. That's true enough as far as Father is concerned, although Dora declares that Father makes a favourite of me; but that's only her fancy. At Christmas and other times we always get the same sort of presents, and that's the real test. Rosa Plank always gets at least three times as much as the rest of the family, that's what it is to be a favourite.

August 12th. I can't write every day for I spend most of my time with the Warths. Oswald can't stand Robert, he says he is a cad and a greenhorn. What vulgar phrases. For three days I haven't spoken to Oswald except when I really had to. When I told Erna and Liesel about it, they said that brothers were always rude to their sisters. I said, I should like to know why. Besides, Robert is generally very nice to his sisters. They said, Yes before you, because he's on his best behaviour with you. Yesterday we laughed like anything when he told us what fun the boys make of their masters. That story about the cigarette ends was screamingly funny. They have a society called T. Au. M., that is in Latin Be Silent or Die in initial letters. No one may betray the society's secrets, and when they make a new member he has to strip off all his clothes and lie down naked and every one spits on his chest and rubs it and says: Be One of Us, but all in Latin. Then he has to go to the eldest and biggest who gives him two or three cuts with a cane and he has to swear that he will never betray anyone. Then everyone smokes a cigar and touches him with the lighted end on the arm or somewhere and says: Every act of treachery will burn you like that. And then the eldest, who has a special name which I can't remember, tattoos on him the word Taum, that is Be Silent or Die, and a heart with the name of a girl. Robert says that if he had known me sooner he would have chosen "Gretchen." I asked him what name he had tattooed on him, but he said he was not allowed to tell. I shall tell Oswald to look when they are bathing and to tell me. In this society they abuse the masters frightfully and the one who thinks of the best tricks to play on them is elected to the Rohon; to be a Rohon is a great distinction and the others must always carry out his orders. He said there was a lot more which he couldn't tell me because it's too tremendous. Then I had to swear that I would never tell anyone about the society and he wanted me to take the oath upon my knees, but I wouldn't do that and he nearly forced me to my knees. In the end I had to give him my hand on it and a kiss. I didn't mind giving him that, for a kiss is nothing, but nothing would induce me to kneel down. Still, I was in an awful fright, for we were quite alone in the garden and he took me by the throat and tried to force me to my knees. All that about the society he told me when we were quite alone for he said: I can't have your name tattooed on me because it's against our laws to have two names but now that you have sworn I can let you know what I really am and think in secret.

I couldn't sleep all night for I kept on dreaming of the society, wondering whether there are such societies in the high school and whether Dora is in a society and has a name tattooed on her. But it would be horrible to have to strip naked before all one's schoolfellows. Perhaps in the societies of the high-school girls that part is left out. But I shouldn't like to say for sure whether I'd have Robert's name tattooed on me.

August 15th. Yesterday Robert told me that there are some schoolboy societies where they do very improper things, but that never happened in their society. But he didn't say what. I said, the stripping naked seems to me awful; but he said, Oh, that's nothing, that must happen if we're to trust one another, it's all right as long as there's nothing improper. I wish I knew what. I wish I knew whether Oswald knows about it, and whether he is in such a society or in a proper one and whether Father was in one. If I could only find out. But I can't ask, for if I did I should betray Robert. When he sees me he always presses my left wrist without letting anyone see. He said that is the warning to me to be silent. But he needn't do that really, for I never would betray him whatever happened. He said: The pain is to bind you to me. When he says that his eyes grow dark, quite black, although his eyes are really grey and they get very large. Especially in the evening when we say goodbye, it frightens me. I'm always dreaming of him.

August 18th. Yesterday evening we had illuminations in honour of the emperor's birthday. We didn't get home until half past twelve. At first we went to a concert in the park and to the illuminations. They fired salutes from the hills and there were beacons flaring on the hill-tops; it was rather creepy although it was wonderful. My teeth chattered once or twice, I don't know whether I was afraid something would happen or why it was. Then R. came and talked such a lot. He is set on going into the army. For that he needn't learn so much, and what he's learning now is of no use to him. He says that doesn't matter, that knowledge will give him a great pull. I don't think he looks stupid, though Oswald says so to make me angry. All at once we found ourselves quite away from the others and so we sat on a bench to wait for them. Then I asked R. once more about the other societies, the ones in which they do such improper things. But he wouldn't tell me for he said he would not

9

rob me of my innocence. I thought that very stupid, and I said that perhaps he didn't know himself and it was all put on. All that happened, he said, was that anyone who joined the society was tickled until he couldn't stand it any longer. And once one of them got St. Vitus's dance, that is frightful convulsions and they were afraid that everything would come out. And since then in their society no more tickling had been allowed. Shall I tickle you a little? I don't understand you, I said, and anyhow you daren't.

He gave a great laugh and suddenly he seized me and tickled me under the arm. It made me want to laugh frightfully, but I stifled it for there were still lots of people going by. So he gave that up and tickled my hand. I liked it at first, but then I got angry and dragged my hand away. Just then Inspee went by with two other girls and directly they had passed us we followed close behind as if we had been walking like that all the time. It saved me a wigging from Mother, for she always wants us all to keep together. As we went along R. said: Look out, Gretel, I'm going to tickle you some day until you scream.—How absurd, I won't have it, it takes two to do that.

By the way, in the raffle I won a vase with 2 turtledoves and a bag of sweets and R. won a knife, fork and spoon. That annoyed him frightfully. Inspee won a fountain pen, just what I want, and a mirror which makes one look a perfect fright. A good job too, for she fancies herself such a lot.

August 29th. O dear, such an awful thing has happened. I have lost pages 30 to 34 from my diary. I must have left them in the garden, or else on the Louisenhohe. It's positively fiendish. If anyone was to find them. And I don't know exactly what there was on those pages. I was born to ill luck. If I hadn't promised Hella to write my diary every day I should like to give up the whole thing. Fancy if Mother were to get hold of it, or even Father. And it's raining so fearfully to-day that I can't even go into the garden and still less on the Louisenhohe above all not alone. I must have lost it the day before yesterday, for I didn't write anything yesterday or the day before. It would be dreadful if anyone were to find it. I am so much upset that I couldn't eat anything at dinner, although we had my favourite chocolate cream cake. And I'm so unhappy for Father was quite anxious and Mother too and they both asked what was the matter with me and I nearly burst out crying before everyone. We had dinner in the hotel to-day because Resi had gone away for 2 days. But I couldn't cry in the room before Father and Mother for that would have given the show away. My only hope is that no one will recognise my writing, for Hella and I use upright writing for our diary, first of all so that no one may recognise our writing and

10

secondly because upright writing doesn't use up so much paper as ordinary writing. I do hope it will be fine to-morrow so that I can hunt in the garden very early. I have been utterly in the dumps all day so that I didn't even get cross when Inspee said: "Have you been quarrelling with your future husband?"

August 30th. It's not in the garden. I begged Mother to let us go to Louisenhutte this afternoon. Mother was awfully nice and asked what I was so worried about, and whether anything had happened. Then I couldn't keep it in any longer and burst out crying. Mother said I must have lost something, and this gave me an awful fright. Mother thought it was Hella's letter, the one which came on Tuesday, so I said: No, much worse than that, my diary. Mother said: Oh well, that's not such a terrible loss, and will be of no interest to anyone. Oh yes, I said, for there are all sorts of things written in it about R. and his society. Look here, Gretel, said Mother, I don't like this way you talk about R.; I really don't like you to spend all your time with the Warths; they're really not our sort and R. is not a fit companion for you; now that you are going to the high school you are not a little girl any longer. Promise me that you'll not be eternally with the Warths.—All right, Mother, I will break it off gradually so that nobody will notice. She burst out laughing and kissed me on both cheeks and promised me to say nothing to Inspee about the diary for she needn't know everything. Mother is such a dear. Still 3 hours and perhaps the pages are still there.

Evening. Thank goodness! In front of the shelter I found 2 pages all pulped by the rain and the writing all run and one page was in the footpath quite torn. Someone must have trodden on it with the heel of his boot and 2 pages had been rolled into a spill and partly burned. So no one had read anything. I am so happy. And at supper Father said: I say, why are your eyes shining with delight? Have you won the big prize in the lottery? and I pressed Mother's foot with mine to remind her not to give me away and Father laughed like anything and said: Seems to me there's a conspiracy against me in my own house. And I said in a great hurry: Luckily we're not in our own house but in a hotel, and everyone laughed and now thank goodness it's all over. Live and learn. I won't let that happen again.

August 31st. Really I'm not so much with the W's and with R. I think he's offended. This afternoon, when I went there to tea, he seized me by the wrist and said: Your father is right, you're a witch. "You need a castigation." How rude of him. Besides, I didn't know what castigation meant. I asked Father and he told me and asked where I had picked up the word. I said I had passed 2 gentlemen and had heard one of them use it. What I really thought was that castigation meant tickling. But it is really horrid to have no one to talk to. Most of the people have gone already and we have only a week longer. About that castigation business. I don't like fibbing to Father, but I really had to. I couldn't say that R. wanted to give me a castigation when I didn't know what it meant. Dora tells a lot more lies than I do and I always love catching her in a lie for her lies are so obvious. I'm never caught. It only happened once when Frau Oberst von Stary was there. Father noticed that time, for he said: You little rogue, you tarradiddler!

September 3rd. Such a horrid thing has happened. I shall never speak to R. again. Oswald is quite right in calling him a cad. If I had really fallen out of the swing I might have broken my leg 4 days before we have to start from home. I can't make out how it all happened. It was frightful cheek of him to tickle me as he did, and I gave him such a kick. I think it was on his nose or his mouth. Then he actually dared to say: After all I'm well paid out, for what can one expect when one keeps company with such young monkeys, with such babies. Fine talk from him when he's not 14 himself yet. It was all humbug about his being 15 and he seems to be one of the idlest boys in the school, never anything but Satisfactory in his reports, and he's not in the fifth yet, but only in the fourth. Anyhow, we've settled our accounts. Cheeky devil. I shall never tell anyone about it, it will be my first and I hope my last secret from Hella.

September 6th. We are going home to-morrow. The last few days have been awfully dull. I saw R. once or twice but I always looked the other way. Father asked what was wrong between me and the Warths and R., so that our great friendship had been broken off. Of course I had to fib, for it was absolutely impossible to tell the truth. I said that R. found fault with everything I did, my writing, my reading aloud. (That's quite true, he did that once) and Father said: Well, well, you'll make it up when you say goodbye to-morrow. Father makes a great mistake. I'll never speak a word to him again.

For her birthday, although it's not come yet, Dora is to have a navy blue silk dustcloak. I don't think the colour suits her, and anyhow she's much too thin to wear a dustcloak.

September 14th. Hella came back the day before yesterday. She looks splendid and she says I do too. I'm so glad that she's back. After all I told her about R. She was very angry and said I ought to have given him 2 more; one for the tickling and one for the "baby" and one for the "young monkey." If we should happen to meet him, shan't we just glare at him.

September 17th. Inspee has really got the silk dustcloak but I think the tartan hood looks rather silly. Still, I didn't say so, but only that the cloak fitted beautifully. She has tried it on at least five times already. I don't know whether Father really wants to treat her as a grown-up lady or whether he is making fun of her. I believe he's only making fun. She doesn't really look like a grown-up lady. How could she when she's not 14 yet? Yesterday afternoon such a lot of girls were invited, and of course Hella was invited on my account and we had a grand talk. But most of them bragged frightfully about the country where they said they had been. We were 9 girls. But Hella is the only one I care about.

September 21st. School begins to-morrow. By the way, we have agreed to call it Liz [Lyzeum = High School] and not School. I'm frightfully curious.

September 22nd, 19—. School began to-day. Hella came to fetch me and we went along together. Inspee peached on us to Mother, saying we ran on in front of her. We don't want her as governess. There are 34 of us in the class. Our teachers are a Frau Doktor, 2 mistresses, one professor, and I think a drawing mistress as well. The Frau Doktor teaches German and writing. She put us together on the 3rd bench. Then she made a speech, then she told us what books to get, but we are not to buy them till Monday. We have 3 intervals, one long and 2 short. The long one is for games, the short ones to go out. I usen't to go out at the elementary school and now I don't need to. Mother always says that it's only a bad habit. Most of the girls went out, and even asked to leave the room during lesson time. To-day we hadn't any proper lessons. They are to begin to-morrow, but we don't know what. Then we came home.

September 23rd. To-day we had the mistress who teaches geography and history, she has no degree. Inspee says that she had her last year, but she could not stand her, she's so ugly. Father was angry and said to Inspee: You silly goose, don't fill her head with such stuff. Show what you are worth as elder sister. One can learn something from every mistress and every master if one likes. But I can't say, we're really fond of Fraulein Vischer and I don't much care for geography and history. Besides I'm not learning for her but for myself. Frau Dr. Mallburg is awfully nice and pretty. We shall always write Frau Dr. M. for short. When she laughs she has two dimples and a gold stopping. She is new at the school. I don't know if we are to have singing too. In French we have Madame Arnau, she is beautifully dressed, black lace. Hella has a lovely pen and pencil case; it's quite soft, we must have it soft so that it shan't make a row when it falls down during lesson time. I think it cost 7 crowns or 1.70 crowns, I don't know exactly. To-day lessons went on until 12, first German, then arithmetic, then religion for Catholics, and then we came away. Hella waited for me, for the Herr Pastor did not come.

September 24th. We thought the book shops would be open to-day but we were wrong. Hella's mother said, that's what happens when the chicks think themselves wiser than the hens. In the afternoon Hella came to our house and Inspee had been invited by the Fs. I don't go there, for it's so dull, they play the piano all day. I have enough piano at my lessons. My music lessons will begin when the school time-table has been fixed up. Perhaps on October 1st, then I must write to Frau B., she told me to write myself. She tells all her pupils to do that. I would rather have had Hella's music mistress. But she has no time to spare and I think she charges more. At least she wouldn't always be holding me up "Fraulein Dora" as a model. We are not all so musical as Fraulein Dora. In the evening Inspee was reading a great fat book until 10 or 12 o clock and she simply howled over it. She said she had not, but I heard her and she could hardly speak. She says she had a cold, liar.

September 25th. To-day they gave us the professors' time-table, but it won't work until the professors from the Gymnasium know exactly when they can come. Our Frau Doktor might be teaching in a Gymnasium, but since there is only one here she teaches in our school. To-morrow we are going to have a viva voce composition: Our Holidays. We may write 8 or 10 sentences at home before we come, but we must not look at what we have written in class. I've written mine already. But I've not said anything about Robert. He's not worth thinking about anyhow. I did not even tell Hella everything.

September 25th. We had the viva voce composition and Frau Doktor said, very good, what is your name? Grete Lainer I said and she said: And is that your chum next you? Now she must tell us how she spent her holidays. Hella did hers very well too and Frau Doktor said again, very good. Then the bell rang. In the long interval Frau Doktor played dodge with us. It was great fun. I was it six times. In the little intervals we were quite alone for the staff has such a lot to do drawing up the time-table. A pupil-teacher from the F. high school is in our class. She sits on the last bench for she is very tall. As tall as Frau Doktor.

September 26th. To-day we had Professor Riegel for the first time in natural history. He wears eye-glasses and never looks any of us in the face. And in French Madame A. said that my accent was the best. We've got an awful lot on and I don't know whether I shall be able to write every day. The younger girls say Professor Igel instead of Riegel and the Weinmann girl said Nikel.

14

September 30th. I've had simply no time to write. Hella hasn't written anything since the 24th. But I must write to-day for I met Robert in Schottengasse. Good morning, Miss, you needn't be so stuck up, he said as he went by. And when I turned round he had already passed, or I would have given him a piece of my mind. I must go to supper.

October 1st. I can't write, Oswald has come from S., he has sprained his ankle, but I'm not so sure because he can get about. He is awfully pale and doesn't say a word about the pain.

October 4th. To-day is a holiday, the emperor's birthday. Yesterday Resi told me something horrid. Oswald can't go back to S. He has been up to something, I wish I knew what, perhaps something in the closet. He always stays there such a long time, I noticed that when I was in the country. Or perhaps it may have been something in his society. Inspee pretends she knows what it is but of course it isn't true, for she doesn't know any more than I do. Father is furious and Mother's eyes are all red with crying. At dinner nobody says a word. If I could only find out what he's done. Father was shouting at him yesterday and both Dora and I heard what he said: You young scamp (then there was something we couldn't understand) and then he said, you attend to your school books and leave the girls and the married women alone you pitiful scoundrel. And Dora said. Ah, now I understand and I said: Please tell me, he is my brother as well as yours. But she said: "You wouldn't understand. It's not suitable for such young ears." Fancy that, it's suitable for her ears, but not mine though she's not quite three years older than I am, but because she no longer wears a short skirt she gives herself the airs of a grown-up lady. Such airs, and then she sneaks a great spoonful of jam so that her mouth is stuffed with it and she can't speak. Whenever I see her do this, I make a point of speaking to her so that she has to answer. She does get in such a wax.

October 9th. I know all about it now. . . That's how babies come. And that is what Robert really meant. Not for me, thank you, I simply won't marry. For if one marries one has to do it; it hurts frightfully and yet one has to. What a good thing that I know it in time. But I wish I knew exactly how, Hella says she doesn't know exactly herself. But perhaps her cousin who knows everything about it will tell her. It lasts nine months till the baby comes and then a lot of women die. It's horrible. Hella has known it for a long time but she didn't like to tell me. A girl told her last summer in the country. She wanted to talk about it to Lizzi her sister, really she only wanted to ask if it was all true and Lizzi ran off to her mother to tell her what Hella had said And her mother said; "These children are awful, a corrupt generation, don't you dare to repeat it to any other girl, to Grete Lainer, for instance," and she gave her a box on the ear. As if she could help it! That is why she didn't write to me for such a long time. Poor thing, poor thing, but now she can tell me all about it and we won't betray one another. And that deceitful cat Inspee has known all about it for ages and has never told me. But I don't understand why that time at the swing Robert said: You little fool, you wont get a baby simply from that. Perhaps Hella knows. When I go to the gymnastic lesson to-morrow I shall talk to her first and ask her about it. My goodness how curious I am to know.

October 10th. I'm in a great funk, I missed my gymnastic lesson yesterday. I was upstairs at Hella's and without meaning it I was so late I did not dare to go. And Hella said I had better stay with her that we would say that our sum was so difficult that we had not got it finished in time. Luckily we really had a sum to do. But I said nothing about it at home, for to-morrow Oswald is going to G. to Herr S's. I thought that I knew all about it but only now has Hella really told me everything. It's a horrible business this . . . I really can't write it. She says that of course Inspee has it already, had it when I wrote that Inspee wouldn't bathe, did not want to bathe; really she had it. Whatever happens one must always be anxious about it. Streams of blood says Hella. But then everything gets all bl . . . That's why in the country Inspee always switched off the light before she was quite undressed, so that I couldn't see. Ugh! Catch me looking! It begins at 14 and goes on for 20 years or more. Hella says that Berta Franke in our class knows all about it. In the arithmetic lesson she wrote a note: Do you know what being un . . . is? Hella wrote back, of course I've known it for a long time. Berta waited for her after class when the Catholics were having their religion lesson and they went home together. I remember quite well that I was very angry, for they're not chums. On Tuesday Berta came with us, for Hella had sent her a note in class saying that I knew everything and she needn't bother about me. Inspee suspects something, she's always spying about and sneering, perhaps she thinks that she's the only person who ought to know anything.

October 16th. To-morrow is Father's and Dora's birthday. Every year it annoys me that Dora should have her birthday on the same day as Father; What annoys me most of all is that she is so cocky about it, for, as Father always says, it's a mere chance. Besides, I don't think he really likes it. Everyone wants to have their own birthday on their own day, not to share it with someone else. And it's always nasty to be stuck up about a thing like that. Besides, it's not going to be a real birthday because of the row about Oswald.

Father is still furious and had to stay away from the office for 2 days because he had to go to G. to see about Oswald going there.

October 17th. It was much jollier to-day than I had expected. All the Bruckners came, so of course there was not much said about Oswald only that he has sprained his ankle, (I know quite well now that that's not true) and that he is probably going to G. Colonel B. said: The best thing for a boy is to send him to a military academy, that keeps him in order. In the evening Oswald said: That was awful rot what Hella's father said, for you can be expelled from a military academy just as easily as from the Gymnasium. That's what happened to Edgar Groller. Oswald gave himself away and Dora promptly said: Ah, so you have been expelled, and we believed you had sprained your ankle. Then he got in an awful wax and said: O you wretched flappers, I've gone and blabbed it all now, and he went away slamming the door, for Mother wasn't there.

October 19th. If we could only find out what Oswald really did. It must have been something with a girl. But we can't think what Father meant about a married woman. Perhaps a married woman complained of him to the head master or to the school committee and that's how it all came out. I feel awfully sorry for him, for I think how I should have felt myself if everything had come out about Robert and me. Of course I don't care now. But in the summer it would have been awful. Oswald hardly says a word, except that he has talks with Mother sometimes. He always pretends that he wants to read, but it's absurd, for with such a love trouble one can't really read. I have not told Berta Franke all about it, but only that my brother has had an unhappy love affair and that is why he is back in Vienna. Then she told us that this summer a cousin of hers shot himself because of her. They said in the newspapers that it was because of an actress, but really it was because of her. She is 14 already.

October 20th. We spend most of our time now with Berta Franke. She says she has had a tremendous lot of experience, but she can't tell us yet because we are not intimate enough. By and by she says. Perhaps she is afraid we shall give her away. She wants to marry when she is 16 at latest. That's in 2 years. Of course she won't have finished school by then, but she will have left the third class. She has three admirers, but she has not yet made up her mind which to choose. Hella says I mustn't believe all this, that the story about the three admirers at once is certainly a cram.

October 21st. Berta Franke says that when one is dark under the eyes one has it and that when one gets a baby then one doesn't have it any more until one gets another. She told us too how one gets it, but I didn't really believe what she said, for I thought she did

17

not know herself exactly. Then she got very cross and said: "All right, I won't tell you any more. If I don't know myself." But I can't believe what she said about husband and wife. She said it must happen every night, for if not they don't have a baby; if they miss a single night they don't have a baby. That's why they have their beds so close together. People call them marriage beds!!! And it hurts so frightfully that one can hardly bear it. But one has to for a husband can make his wife do it. I should like to know how he can make her. But I didn't dare to ask for I was afraid she would think I was making fun of her. Men have it too, but very seldom. We see a lot of Berta Franke now, she is an awfully nice girl, perhaps Mother will let me invite her here next Sunday.

October 23rd. Father took Oswald away to-day. Mother cried such a lot. When Oswald was leaving I whispered to him: I know what's the matter with you. But he did not understand me for he said: Silly duffer. Perhaps he only said that because of Father who was looking on with a fearful scowl.

October 27th. Everything seems to have gone wrong. Yesterday I got unsatisfactory in history, and in arithmetic to-day I couldn't get a single sum right. I'm frightfully worried about missing that gymnastic lesson. It will be all right if Mother gives me the money to-morrow, for if she goes herself she will certainly find out about it.

October 28th. To-day the head mistress was present at our French lesson and said awfully nice things about me. She said I was good enough in French to be in the Third and then she asked me whether I was as good in the other subjects. I didn't want to say either Yes or No, and all the other girls said Yes, she's good at everything. The head patted me on the shoulder and said: I'm glad to hear that. When she had gone I cried like anything and Madame Arnau asked: Why, what's the matter? and the other girls said: In arithmetic she had Unsatisfactory but she can really do her sums awfully well. Then Madame said: "You'll soon wipe off that Unsatisfactory."

October 30th. To-day I had a frightful bother with Fraulein Vischer in the history lesson. Yesterday when I got into the tram with Mother there was Fraulein V. I looked the other way so that Mother shouldn't see her and so that she should not tell Mother about me. When she came in to-day she said: Lainer, do you know the rules? I knew directly what she meant and said "I did bow to you in the tram but you didn't see me." "That's a fine thing to do, first you do wrong and then try to excuse yourself by telling a lie. Sit down!" I felt awful for all the girls looked at me. In the 11 interval Berta Franke said to me: Don't worry, she's got her knife into you

18

and will always find something to complain of. She must have spoken to Frau Doktor M., for in the German lesson the subject for viva voce composition was Good Manners. And all the girls looked at me again. She didn't say anything more. She's a perfect angel, my darling E. M., her name is Elisabeth; but she does not keep her name-day because she's a Protestant; that's an awful shame because November 19th is coming soon.

October 31st. I've been so lucky. Nothing's come out about the gymnastic lesson though Mother was there herself. And in mental arithmetic to-day I got a One. Fraulein Steiner is awfully nice too and she said: Why, L. what was the matter with you in your sums the other day, for you're so good at arithmetic? I didn't know what to do so I said: Oh I had such a headache the other day. Then Berta Franke nearly burst out laughing, it was horrid of her; I don't think she's quite to be trusted; I think she's rather a sneak. When the lesson was over she said she had laughed because "headache" means something quite different.

November 1st. To-day we began to work at the tablecloth for Father's Christmas present. Of course Inspee bagged the right side because that's easier to work at and I had to take the left side and then one has the whole caboodle on one's hand. For Mother I'm making an embroidered leather book cover, embroidered with silk and with a painted design; I can do the painting part at school in Fraulein H.'s lesson, she's awfully nice too. But I like Frau Doktor M. best of all. I'm not going to invite Berta Franke because of the way she laughed yesterday, and besides Mother doesn't like having strange girls to the house. November 2nd. I don't know all about things yet. Hella knows a lot more. We said we were going to go over our natural history lesson together and we went in to the drawing-room, and there she told me a lot more. Then Mali, our new servant, came in, and she told us something horrid. Resi is in a hospital because she's ill. Mali told us that all the Jews when they are quite little have to go through a very dangerous operation; it hurts frightfully and that's why they are so cruel. It's done so that they can have more children; but only little boys, not little girls. It's horrid, and I should not like to marry a Jew. Then we asked Mali whether it is true that it hurts so frightfully and she laughed and said: It can't be so bad as all that, for if it were you wouldn't find everyone doing it. Then Hella asked her: But have you done it already, you haven't got a husband? She said: Go on, Miss! One mustn't ask such questions it's not ladylike. We were in an awful funk, and begged her not to tell Mother. She promised not to.

November 5th. Everything has come out through that stupid waist band. Yesterday when I was tidying my drawers Mali came in to make the beds and saw my fringed waistband. "I say, she said, that is pretty!" You can have it if you like, I said, for I've given up wearing it. At dinner yesterday I noticed that Mother was looking at Mali and I blushed all over. After dinner Mother said, Gretel, did you give Mali that waistband? Yes, I said, she asked me for it. She came in at that moment to clear away and said: "No, I never asked for it, Fraulein Grete gave it to me herself." I don't know what happened after that, I'd gone back to my room when Mother came in and said: A fine lot of satisfaction one gets out of one's children. Mali has told me the sort of things you and Hella talk about. I ran straight off to the kitchen and said to Mali: How could you tell such tales of us? It was you who chipped in when we were talking. It was frightfully mean of you. In the evening she must needs go and complain of me to Father and he scolded me like anything and said: You're a fine lot, you children, I must say. You are not to see so much of Hella now, do you understand?

November 6th. A fine thing this, that I'm a silly fool now. When I gave Hella a nudge so that she should not go on talking before Mali, she laughed and said: What does it matter, Mali knows all about it, probably a great deal more than we do. It was only after that that Mali told us about the Jews. Now, if you please, I am a silly fool. All right, now that I know what I am, a silly fool. And that's what one's best friend calls one!

November 7th. Hella and I are very stand-offish. We walk together, but we only talk of everyday things, school and lessons, nothing else. We went skating to-day for the first time and we shall go whenever we have time, which is not very often. Mother is working at the table cloth. It's very hard work but she has not got as much to do as we have.

November 8th. There was such a lovely young lady skating to-day, and she skates so beautifully, inside and outside edge and figures of 8. I skated along behind her. When she went to the cloak room there was such a lovely scent. I wonder if she is going to be married soon and whether she knows all about everything. She is so lovely and she pushes back the hair from her forehead so prettily. I wish I were as pretty as she is. But I am dark and she is fair. I wish I could find out her name and where she lives. I must go skating again to-morrow; do my lessons in the evening.

November 9th. I'm so upset; she didn't come to skate. I'm afraid she may be ill.

November 10th. She didn't come to-day either. I waited two hours, but it was no good.

November 11th. She came to-day, at last! Oh how pretty she is.

November 12th. She has spoken to me. I was standing near

the entrance gate and suddenly I heard some one laughing behind me and I knew directly: That is she! So it was. She came up and said: Shall we skate together? Please, if I may, said I, and we went off together crossing arms. My heart was beating furiously, and I wanted to say something, but couldn't think of anything sensible to say. When we came back to the entrance a gentleman stood there and took off his hat and she bowed, and she said to me: Till next time. I said quickly: When? Tomorrow? Perhaps, she called back. . . . Only perhaps, perhaps, oh I wish it were to-morrow already.

November 13th. Inspee declares that her name is Anastasia Klastoschek. I'm sure it can't be true that she has such a name, she might be called Eugenie or Seraphine or Laura, but Anastasia, impossible. Why are there such horrid names? Fancy if she is really called that. Klastoschek, too, a Czech name, and she is supposed to come from Moravia and to be 26 already; 26, absurd, she's 18 at most. I'm sure she's not so much as 18. Dora says she lives in Phorusgasse, and that she doesn't think her particularly pretty. Of course that's rank jealousy; Dora thinks no one pretty except herself.

November 14th. I asked the woman at the pay box, her name really is Anastasia Klastoschek and she lives in the Phorusgasse; but the woman didn't know how old she is. She would not tell me at first but asked why I wanted to know and who had sent me to enquire. She wouldn't look into the book until I told her that it was only for myself that I wanted to know. Then she looked, for I knew the number of the cloak room locker: 36, a lovely number, I like it so much. I don't really know why, but when I hear anyone say that number it sounds to me like a squirrel jumping about in the wood.

November 20th. It's really impossible to write every day. Mother is ill in bed and the doctor comes every day, but I don't really know what's the matter with her. I'm not sure whether the doctor knows exactly. When Mother is ill everything at home is so uncomfortable and she always says: Whatever you do don't get ill, for it's such a nuisance. But I don't mind being ill; indeed I rather like being ill, for then everyone's so nice, when Father comes home he comes and sits by my bed and even Dora is rather nice and does things for me; that is she has to. Besides, when she had diptheria two years ago I did everything I could for her, she nearly died, her temperature went up to 107 and Mother was sick with crying. Father never cries. It must look funny when a man cries. When there was all that row about Oswald he cried, I think Father had given him a box on the ear. He said he hadn't but I think he had; certainly he cried, though he said he didn't. After all, why shouldn't he for he's not really grown up yet. I cry myself when I get frightfully annoyed. Still I shouldn't cry for a box on the ear.

November 21st. In the religion lesson to-day Lisel Schrotter who is the Herr Catechist's favourite, no we've got to call him Herr Professor, as she is the Herr Professor's favourite, well she went to him with the Bible and asked him what with child meant. That's what they say of Mary in the Bible. The Schrotter girl does not know anything yet and the other girls egged her on till she went and asked. The Herr Professor got quite red and said: If you don't know yet it does not matter. We shall come to that later, we're still in the Old Testament. I was so glad that Hella does not sit next me in the religion lesson, because she's a Protestant; we should certainly have both burst out laughing. Some of the girls giggled frightfully and the Herr Professor said to Lisel: You're a good girl, don't bother about the others. But Lisel positively howled. I would not have asked, even if I hadn't really known. With child is a stupid word anyhow, it doesn't mean anything really; only if one knows.

November 22nd. When I was coming away from the religion lesson with Berta Franke the other day, of course we began talking about it. She says that's why people marry, only because of it. I said I could not believe that people marry only for that. Lots of people marry and then have no children. That's all right said Berta, but it's quite true what I tell you. Then she told me a lot more but I really can't write it all down. It is too horrid, but I shan't forget. When I was sitting on Mother's bed to-day I suddenly realised that Father's bed is really quite close to Mother's. I had never thought about it before. But it's not really necessary now for we are all quite big. Still I suppose they've just left things as they were. Well dear, said Mother, what are you looking round so for? Of course I didn't let on, but said: I was only looking round and thinking that if your bed was where the washstand is you could see to read better when you are lying in bed. That would not do because the wall's all wrong said Mother. I said nothing more and she didn't either. I like much better to sleep on a sofa than in a bed, because I like to snuggle up against the back. I'm so glad Mother didn't notice anything. One has to be so frightfully careful not to give oneself away when one knows everything.

November 25th. I have just been reading a lovely story; it is called A True Heart and is about a girl whose betrothed has had to leave her because he has shot a man who was spying on him. But Rosa remains true to him till he comes back after 10 years and then they marry. It's simply splendid and frightfully sad at first. I do love these library books, but when we were at the elementary school I knew all the books they had and the mistress never knew what to give me and Hella. In the high school we get only one book a month, for the Frau Doktor says we have plenty of work to do, and that when we are not at work we ought to be out in the fresh air. I can't manage to go skating every day. I do love the Gold Fairy, that is my name for her, for I hate her real name. Inspee declares that they call her Stasi for short, but I don't believe that; most likely they call her Anna, but that's so common. Thank goodness Hella always calls me Rita, so at school I'm known as Rita. It's only at home that they will call me Gretl. The other day I said to Inspee: If you want me to call you Thea you must call me Rita; and anyhow I won't let you call me Gretl, that's what they call a little girl or a peasant girl. She said: I don't care tuppence what you call me. All right, then, she shall be Dora till the end of time.

November 27th. Father has been made Appeal Court Judge. He is awfully glad and so is Mother. The news came yesterday evening. Now he can become President of the Supreme Court, not directly, but in a few years. We shall probably move to a larger house in May. Inspee said to Mother that she hoped she would have her own room where she would not be disturbed. How absurd, who disturbs her, I suppose I do? Much more like she disturbs me, always watching while I'm writing my diary. Hella always says: "There really ought not to be any elder sisters;" she's jolly well right. It's a pity we can't alter things. Mother says we are really too big to keep St. Nicholas, but I don't see why one should ever be too big for that. Last year Inspee got something from St. Nicholas when she was 13 and I'm not 12 yet. All we get are chocolates and sweets and dates and that sort of thing, not proper presents. The girls want to give the Frau Doktor a great Krampus[1] to leave it on her desk. I think that's silly. It's not a proper present for a teacher one is really fond of, one doesn't want to waste sweets on a teacher one doesn't like, and to give an empty Krampus would be rude. Mother is really right and a Krampus is only suitable for children.

December 1st. We are giving everyone of the staff a Krampus, each of us is to subscribe a crown, I hope Father will give me the crown extra. Perhaps he'll give us more pocket money now, at least another crown, that would be splendid. We are going to give big Krampuses to the ones we like best, and: small ones to those we are not so fond of. We're afraid to give one to Professor J. But if he doesn't get one perhaps he'll be offended.

---

[1] Krampus=Ruprechtsknecht, i.e. a little Demon, who serves St. Nicholas, and is a bogey man to carry off naughty children An image of this Demon filled with sweets, is given as a present on the feast of St. Nicholas which inaugurates the Christmas season.—Translators' Note.

December 2nd. To-day we went to buy Krampuses for the staff. The one for Frau Doktor M. is the finest. When you open it the first thing you see is little books with Schiller, Goethe, and Fairy Tales written on the backs, and then underneath these are the sweets. That's exactly suited for her, for the Frau Doktor teaches German and in the Fourth in German they are reading these poets. Last month in the Fourth they had a Schiller festival and Frau Doktor made a splendid speech and some of the girls gave recitations. Besides Hella has shown me an awful poem by Schiller. There you can read: if only I could catch her in the bath, she would cry for mercy, for I would soon show the girl that I am a man. And then in another place: "To my mate in God's likeness I can show that which is the source of life." But you can only find that in the large editions of Schiller. I believe we've got some books of that sort in our bookcase, for when Inspee was rummaging there the other day Mother called from the next room: "Dora, what are you hunting for in the bookcase? I can tell you where it is." And she said: Oh, it's nothing, I was just looking for something, and shut the door quickly.

December 4th. The girls are so tiresome and have made such a muddle about the Krampuses for the staff. The money didn't come out right and Keller said that Markus had taken some but Markus said not taken only kept. Of course Markus complained to Frau Doktor and her father went to the head and complained too. Frau Doktor said we know quite well that collections are not allowed and that we must not give any one a Krampus. Now Keller has the five Krampuses and we don't know what to do about it. Mother says that sort of thing never turns out well but always ends in a quarrel.

December 5th. We are in such a funk: Hella and I and Edith Bergler have taken the Krampus which we bought for Frau Doktor M. and put it on her doorstep. Edith Bergler knew where she lived for she comes by there every day on her way to school. I wonder if she'll guess where the Krampus comes from. I did not know that Edith Bergler was such a nice girl, I always thought she must be deceitful because she wears spectacles. But now I'm quite certain she is not deceitful, so one sees how easy it is to make a mistake. To-morrow's our German lesson.

December 6th. Frau Doktor did not say anything at first. Then she gave out the subject for the essay: "Why once I could not go to sleep at night." The girls were all taken aback, and then Frau Doktor said: Now girls that's not so very difficult. One person cannot go to sleep because he's just going to be ill, another because he is excited by joy or fear. Another has an uneasy conscience because he has

24

done something which he has been forbidden to do; have not all of you experienced something of the kind? Then she looked frightfully hard at Edith Bergler and us two. She did not say anything more, so we don't really know if she suspects. I couldn't go to the ice carnival yesterday because I had such a bad cough, and Dora couldn't go either because she had a headache; I don't know whether it was a real headache or that kind of headache; but I expect it was that kind.

December 17th. I haven't managed to write anything for a whole week. The day before yesterday we had our Christmas reports: In history I had satisfactory, in Natural History good, in everything else very good. In diligence because of that stupid Vischer I had only a 2. Father was very angry; he says everyone can get a 1 in diligence. That's true enough, but if one has satisfactory in anything then one can't get a 1 for diligence. Inspee of course had only 1's, except a 2 in English. But then she's a frightful swot. Verbenowitsch is the best in our class, but we can't any of us bear her, she's so frantically conceited and Berta Franke says she's not to be trusted. Berta walks to school with her cousin who's in the seventh; she's nearly 14, and is awfully pretty. She didn't say what sort of a report she had, but I believe it was a very bad one.

December 18th. To-day at supper Dora fainted because she found a little chicken in her egg, not really a chicken yet, but one could make out the wings and the head, just a sketch of a chicken Father said. Still, I really can't see what there was to faint about. Afterwards she said it had made her feel quite creepy. And she'll never be able to eat another egg. At first Father was quite frightened and so was Mother, but then he laughed and said: What a fuss about nothing! She had to go and lie down at once and I stayed downstairs for a long time. When I came up to our room she was reading, that is I saw the light through the crack in the door; but when I opened the door it all dark and when I asked: Ah so you're still reading she didn't answer and she pretended to wake up when I switched on the light and said: What's the matter? I can't stand such humbug so I said: Shut up, you know quite well it's 9 o-clock. That's all. On our way to school to-day we didn't Speak a word to one another. Luckily after awhile we met a girl belonging to her class.

December 19th. I'm frightfully excited to know what I'm going to get for Christmas. What I've wished for is: A set of white furs, boa, muff, and velvet cap trimmed with the same fur, acme skates because mine are always working loose, German sagas, not Greek; no thank you, hair ribbons, openwork stockings, and if possible a gold pin like the one Hella got for a birthday present. But Father says that our Christ Child would find that rather too expensive.

25

Inspee wants a corset. But I don't think she'll get one because it's unhealthy. The tablecloth for Father is finished and is being trimmed, but Mother's book cover is not quite ready yet. I'm giving Dora a little manicure case. Oh, and I'd nearly forgotten what I want more than anything else, a lock-up box in which to keep my diary. Dora wants some openwork stockings too and three books. A frightful thing happened to me the other day. I left one of the pages of my diary lying about or lost one somehow or other. When I came home Inspee said: "you've lost this, haven't you? School notes I suppose?" I didn't notice what it was for a moment, but then I saw by the look of it and said: Yes, those are school notes. Hm-m-m, said Inspee, not exactly that are they? You can thank your stars that I've not shown them to Mother. Besides people who can't spell yet really ought not to keep diaries. It's not suitable for children. I was in a wax. In the closet I took a squint to see what mistakes I had made. There was only wenn with one n instead of double n and dass with short ss's, that's all. I was jolly glad that there was nothing about her on the page. She'd underlined the n and the short ss's with red, just as if she was a schoolmistress, infernal cheek! The best would be to have a book with a lock to it, which one could alway keep locked, then no one could read any of it and underline one's mistakes in red. I often write so fast that it's easy to make a slip now and again. As if she never made a mistake. The whole thing made me furious. But I can't say anything about it because of Mother, at least on the way to school; but no, if I say nothing at all then she always gets more waxy than ever. If I were to say much about it Mother might remember those 5 pages I lost in the country and I'd rather not thank you.

December 22nd. Aunt Dora came to-day. She's going to stay with us for a time till Mother is quite well again. I didn't remember her at all, for I was only four or five when she went away from Vienna. You dear little black beetle she said to me and gave me a kiss. I didn't like the black much, but Hella says that suits me, that it's piquant. Piquant is what the officers always say of her cousin in Krems, Father says she is a beauty, and she's dark like me. But I'd rather be fair, fair with brown eyes or better still with violet eyes. Shall I grow up a beauty? Oh I do hope I shall!

December 23rd. I am frightfully excited about to-morrow. I wonder what I shall get? Now I must go and decorate the Christmas tree. Inspee said: Hullo, is Gretl going to help decorate this year? She's never done it before! I should like to know why not. But Aunt Dora took my side. "Of course she'll help decorate too; but please don't stuff yourselves with sweets." "If Dora doesn't eat anything I shan't either," said I promptly.

Evening. Yesterday was our last day at school. The holidays are from the 23rd to January 2nd. It's glorious. I shall be able to go skating every day. Of course I had no time to-day and shan't have to—morrow. I wonder whether I should send the Gold Fairy a Christmas card. I wish she had a prettier name. Anastasia Klastoschek; it is so ugly. All Czech names are so ugly. Father knows a Count Wilczek, but a still worse name is Schafgotsch. Nothing would induce me to marry anyone called Schafgotsch or Wilczek even if he were a count and a millionaire. Yesterday we paid our respects to the staff, Verbenowitsch and I went to Frau Doktor because she is fondest of us, or is said to be. Nobody wanted to go to Professor Rigl, Igel, we always say Nikel, for when he has respects paid to him he always says: "Aw ri'." But it would have been rude to leave him out and so the monitors had to go. When Christmas was drawing near Frau Doktor told us that we were none of us to give presents to the staff. "I beg you, girls, to bear in mind what I am saying, for if you do not there will only be trouble. You remember what happened on St. Nicholas' day. And you must not send anything to the homes of the staff, nor must the Christ Child leave anything on any one's doorstep." As she said this she looked hard at me and Edith Bergler, so she knows who left the Krampus. I'm so tired I can't keep my eyes open. Hurrah, to-morrow is Christmas Eve!!!

December 24th. Christmas Eve afternoon is horrid. One does not know what to be at. I'm not allowed to go skating so the best thing is to write. Oswald came home yesterday. Everyone says he's looking splendid; I think he's awfully pale and he snorted when everyone said he had such a fine colour; of course, how can he look well when he has such a heartache. I wish I could tell him that I understand what he feels, but he's too proud to accept sympathy from me. He has wished for an army revolver for Christmas, but I don't think he'll get one for boys at the middle school are not allowed to have any firearms. Not long ago at a Gymnasium in Galicia one of the boys shot a master out of revenge; they said it was because the boy was getting on badly with his work, but really it was about a girl, although the master was 36 years old. This morg. I was in town with Oswald shopping; we met the Warths, Elli and . . . Robert. Oswald said that Elli was quite nice-looking but that Robert was an ugly beast. Besides, he can't stand him he said, because he glared at me so. If only he knew what happened in the summer! I was awfully condescending to Robert and that made him furious. If one could only save you girls from all the troubles which the world calls "Love," said Oswald on the way home. I was just going to say "I know that you're unhappy in love and I can feel for you," when Inspee came round the corner of the Bognergasse with her chum and 2 officers were following them, so none of them saw us. "Great Scott, Frieda's full-fledged now," said Oswald, "she's a little tart." I can't stand that sort of vulgarity so I did not say another word all the way home. He noticed and said to Mother: "Gretl's mouth has been frozen up from envy." That's all. But it was really disgusting of him and now I know what line to take.

Just a moment for a word or two. The whole Christmas Eve has gone to pot. A commissionaire came with a bouquet for Dora and Father is fuming. I wish I knew who sent it. I wonder if it was one of those 2 officers? Of course Inspee says she has not the ghost of an idea. What surprises me is that Oswald has not given her away. All he said was: I say, what a lark! But Father was down on him like anything, "You hold your jaw and think of your own beastly conduct." I didn't envy him; I don't think much of Dora's looks myself, but apparently she pleases someone. In the bouquet there was a poem and Dora got hold of it quickly before Father had seen it. It was awfully pretty, and it was signed: One for whom you have made Christmas beautiful! The heading is: "The Magic Season." I think Dora's splendid not to give herself away; even to me she declares she does not know who sent it; but of course that may be all humbug. I think it really comes from young Perathoner, with whom she's always skating.

December 28th. I've had absolutely no time to write. I got everything I wanted. Aunt Dora gave both of us an opera glass in mother-of-pearl in a plush case. We are going to all the school performances, Father's arranged it; he has subscribed to all the performances during the school year 19— to 19—. I am so delighted for Frau Doktor M. will come too. I do hope I shall sit next to her.

December 31st. To-day I wanted to read through all I have written, but I could not manage it but in the new year I really must write every day.

January 1st, 19—. I must write a few sentences at least. For the afternoon we had been invited to the Rydberg's the Warths were there and Edle von Wernhoff!! I was just the same as usual with Lisel but I would not say a word to R. They left before us, and then Heddy asked me what was wrong between me and R. He had said of me: Any one can have the black goose for me. Then he said that any one could take me in. I was so stupid that I would believe anything. I can't think what he meant, for he never took me in about anything. Anyhow I would not let him spoil new year's day for me. But Hella is quite right for if the first person one meets on January 1st is a

28

common person that's a bad beginning. The first thing this morning when I went out I met our old postman who's always so grumpy if he's kept waiting at the door. I looked the other way directly and across the street a fine young gentleman was passing, but it was no good for the common postman had really been the first.

January 12th. I am so angry. We mayn't go skating any more because Inspee has begun to complain again of her silly old ears and Mother imagines that she got her earache last year skating. It's all right to keep her at home; but why shouldn't I go? How can I help it when she gets a chill so easily? In most things Father is justice itself, but I really can't understand him this time. It's simply absurd, only it's too miserable to call it absurd. I'm in a perfect fury. Still, I don't say anything.

February 12th. I have not written for a whole month, I've been working so hard. To-day we got our reports. Although I've been working so frightfully hard, again I only got a 2 in Diligence. Frau Doktor M. made a splendid speech and said: As you sow, so you shall reap. But that's not always true. In Natural History I did not know my lesson twice but I got a 1, and in History I only did not know my lesson once and I got Satisfactory. Anyhow Fraulein V. does not like me because of that time when I did not bow to her in the tram. That is why in January, when Mother asked about me, she said: "She does not really put her back into her work." I overheard Father say: After all she's only a kid, but to-day he made a frightful row about the 2 in Diligence. He might have known why she gave me that. Dora, so she says, has only ones, but she has not shown me the report. I don't believe what I don't see. And Mother never gives her away to me.

February 15th. Father is furious because Oswald has an Unsatisfactory in Greek. Greek is really no use; for no one uses Greek, except the people who live in Greece and Oswald will never go there, if he is going to be a judge like Father. Of course Dora learns Latin; but not for me thank you. Hella's report is not particularly good and her father was in a perfect fury!!! He says she ought to have a better report than any one else. She does not bother much and says: One can't have everything. But if she doesn't get nothing but ones in the summer term she is not to stay at the high school and will have to go to the middle school. That'll make her sit up. Father's awfully funny too: What have you got history books for, if you don't read them? Yesterday when I was reading my album of stories, Father came in and said: You like a story book better than a history book, and shut the book up and took it away from me. I was in such a temper that I went to bed at 7 o'clock without any supper.

February 20th. I met the Gold Fairy to-day. She spoke to me

and asked why I did not come skating any more. The fancy dress Ice Carnival on the 24th was splendid she said. I said: Would you believe it, a year ago my sister had an earache, and for that reason they won't allow either of us to skate this year. She laughed like anything and said so exquisitely: Oh, what a wicked sister. She looked perfectly ravishing: A red-brown coat and skirt trimmed with fur, sable I believe, and a huge brown beaver hat with crepe-de-chine ribbons, lovely. And her eyes and mouth. I believe she will marry the man who is always going about with her. Next autumn, when we get new winter clothes, I shall have a fur trimmed red-brown. We must not always be dressed alike. Hella and Lizzi are never dressed alike.

March 8th. I shall never say another word to Berta Franker she's utterly false. I've such a frightful headache because I cried all through the lesson. She wrote to Hella and me in the arithmetic lesson: A Verhaltnis[2] means something quite different. Just at that moment the mistress looked across and said: To whom were you nodding? She said: To Lainer. Because she laughed at the word "Verhaltnis." It was not true. I had not thought about the word at all. It wasn't till I had read the note that it occurred to Hella and me what Verhaltnis means. After the lesson Fraulein St. called us down into the teachers' room and told Frau Doktor M. that Franke and I had laughed at the use of the word "Verhaltnis." Frau Doktor said: What was there to laugh at? Why did you not just do your sums? Fraulein St. said: You ought to be ashamed of yourselves, young girls in the first class shouldn't know anything about such things. I shall have to speak to your mothers. In the German lesson Frau Doktor M. told us to write an essay on the proverb: Pure the heart and true the word, clear the brow and free the eye, these are our safeguards, or something of that sort; I must get Hella to write it for me, for I was crying all through the lesson.

March 10th. To-day Berta Franke wanted to talk things out with us; but Hella and I told her we would not speak to her again. We told her to remember what sort of things she had said to us. She denied it all already. We shouldn't be such humbugs. It was mean of her. Really we didn't know anything and she told us all about it. Hella has told me again and again she wished we didn't know anything. She says she's always afraid of giving herself away and that she often thinks about that sort of thing when she ought to be learning her lessons. So do I. And one often dreams about such

---

[2] The German word Verhaltnis as used in the arithmetic lesson means ratio, proportion. The word is in common use in Germany for a love intimacy or liaison.—Translators' Note.

things at night when one has been talking about them in the afternoon. Still, it's better to know all about it.

March 22nd. I so seldom manage to write anything, first of all our lessons take such a lot of time, and second because I don't care about it any more since what Father said the other day. The last time I wrote was on Saturday afternoon, and Father came in and said: Come along children, we'll go to Schonbrunn. That will do you more good than scribbling diaries which you only go and lose when you've written them. So Mother told Father all about it in the holidays. I couldn't have believed it of Mother for I begged her to promise not to tell anyone. And she said: One doesn't promise about a thing like that; but I won't tell anyone. And now she must have told about it, although she said she wouldn't. Even Franke's deceitfulness was nothing to that for after all we've only known her since last autumn, but I could never have believed that Mother would do such a thing. I told Hella when we were having tea at the Tivoli and she said she would not altogether trust her mother, she'd rather trust her father. But if that had happened to her, her father would have boxed her ears with the diary. I did not want to show anything, but in the evening I only gave Mother quite a little kiss. And she said, what's the matter, dear? has anything happened? Then I could not keep it in and I cried like anything and said: You've betrayed me. And Mother said: "I?" Yes, you; you told Father about the diary though you promised me you wouldn't. At first Mother didn't remember anything about it, but soon she remembered and said: "But, little one, I tell Father everything. All you meant was that Dora was not to know." That's quite true, it's all right that Dora wasn't told; but still Father need not have been told either. And Mother was awfully sweet and nice and I didn't go to bed till 10 o'clock. But whatever happens I shan't tell her anything again and I don't care about the old diary any more. Hella says: Don't be stupid; I ought just to go on writing; but another time I should be careful not to lose anything, and besides I should not blab everything to Mother and Father. She says she no longer tells her mother anything since that time in the summer when her mother gave her a box on the ear because that other girl had told her all about everything. It's quite true, Hella is right, I'm just a child still in the way I run to Mother and tell her everything. And it's not nice of Father to tease me about my diary; I suppose he never kept one himself.

March 27th. Hurrah we're going to Hainfeld for Easter; I am so delighted. Mother has a friend there whose husband is doctor there, so she has to live there all the year round. Last year in the winter she and Ada stayed three days with us because her eyes were bad. Ada is really nearly as old as Dora, but Dora said, like her cheek: "Her intellectual level makes her much more suitable company for you than for me." Dora thinks herself cleverer than anyone else. They have 2 boys, but I don't know them very well for they are only 8 and 9. Mother's friend was in an asylum once, for she went off her head when her 2 year old baby died. I remember it quite well. It must have been more than 2 years ago when Father and Mother were always talking of poor Anna who had lost her child within 3 days. And I believed she had really lost it, and once I asked whether they had found it yet. I thought it had been lost in the forest, because there's such a great forest at Hainfeld. And since then I can't bear to hear people say lost when they mean dead, for it is so difficult to know which they really mean.

On the 8th of April the Easter holidays will begin and we shall go on the 11th, on Maundy Thursday.

April 6th. I don't know what to do about writing my diary. I don't want to take it with me and as for remembering everything and writing it down afterwards I know quite well I should never do that. Hella says I should only jot it down in outline, that's what Frau Doktor M. always says, and write it out properly after I come back from Hainfeld. That's what she does. They are going to the Brioni Islands. I've never seen the sea. Hella says there's nothing so wonderful about it. She's been there four times. Anyway she does not think so much of it as most people do. So it can't be anything so frightfully grand. Rather stupid I dare say.

April 12th. We got here yesterday. Ada is a darling but the two boys are awfully vulgar. Ernstl said to Ada: I shall give you a smack on the a—— if you don't give me my pistol directly. Ada is as tall as her mother. Their speech is rather countrified Even the doctor's. He drinks a frightful lot of beer; quarts I believe.

April 14th. Father came to-day. He's awfully fond of the doctor. They kissed one another. It did make me laugh. In the morning we were in the forest; but there are no violets yet, only a few snowdrops, but a tremendous lot of hellebores quite red.

April 15th. We got up at 4 yesterday morning. We did not go into the church for Mother was afraid that the smell of incense and boots would make Dora feel bad. What rot! It was lovely. This afternoon we are going to Ramsau, it's lovely there.

April 16th. Father went home to-day. We go home to-morrow. At Whitsuntide Ada's mother is going to bring her to be confirmed. They are all coming to stay with us. I got stuck in a bog on the bank of the Ramsau. It was awful. But the doctor pulled me out and then we did all laugh so when we saw what my shoes and stockings were like. Luckily I was able to catch hold of a tree stump or I should have sunk right in.

April 18th. Hella says it was splendid at the Brioni Islands. She is frightfully sunburned. I don't like that, so I shall never go to the south. Hella says that if one marries in winter one must spend one's honeymoon in the south. That would not suit me, I should just put off my marriage till the summer.

Ada is only 13 not 14 like Dora, and the parish priest makes a tremendous fuss because she's not confirmed yet. Her mother is going to bring her to be confirmed soon. We are not going to be confirmed because Father and Mother don't want to be bothered with it. Still I should like to be confirmed, for then one has to have a watch, and one can ask for something else at Christmas.

April 21st. Our lessons are something frightful just now. The school inspector is coming soon. It's always very disagreeable. Mme A. says: The inspection is for the staff not for the pupils. Still, it's horrid for the pupils too first of all because we get blamed at the time and secondly because the staff makes such a frightful row about it afterwards. Dora says that a bad inspection can make one's report 2 degrees worse. By the way, that reminds me that I have not yet written why Oswald did not come home at Easter. Although his reports were not at all good, he was allowed to go to Aunt Alma's at Pola, because this year Richard comes home for the holidays for the last time. After that he's going away for three years in the steamship "Ozean" to the East or Turkey or Persia, I don't quite know where. If Oswald likes he can go into the Navy too in two years.

May 9th. The school inspector came to-day, first of all in natural history, thank goodness I wasn't in for it that time, and then in German; I was in that, reading and in the table of contents of the Wandering Bells. Thank goodness I got through all right.

May 14th. It's Mother's birthday to-day. We've had simply no time to work anything for her, so we got a wonderful electric lamp for her bed table, the switch is a bunch of grapes and the stand is made of brass. She was so pleased with it. Yesterday Frau v. R. was here. She's a friend of Mother's and of Hella's mother. I should like to have music lessons from Frau v. R., she gives lessons since her husband who was a major died though she is quite well off.

May 15th. That must have been true about the inspection; in the interval to-day Professor Igel-Nikel said to the Herr Religionsprofessor: Well, he will go on coming all through the week and then we shall be all right for this year. We, of course that means the staff. But really the staff can't help it if the pupils are no good. Though Oswald says it's all the fault of the staff. I shall be glad too when the inspection is over. The staff is always quite different when the inspector is there, some are better, some are stricter, and Mme. A. says: I always feel quite ill with anxiety.

May 29th. At Whitsuntide Frau Doctor Haslinger came from Hainfeld with Ada and the two boys for the confirmation. On Whitsunday the doctor came too and in the evening they all went home again. Ada is very pretty, but she looks countrified. I'm not going to be confirmed anyhow. We had to wait 3 hours, though the Friday before Whitsunday was a very fine day. Dora did not come; only Mother and I and Ada and her mother. The women who were selling white favours all thought that I was one of the candidates because I wore a white dress too. Ada was rather put out about it. On Saturday we were in town in the morning and afternoon because Ada liked that better than the Kahlenberg; on Sunday morning we went to Schonbrunn and in the afternoon they went home. The watch they gave to Ada was a lovely one and Dora and I gave her a gold chain for a locket. She enjoyed herself immensely, except that on Sunday she had a frightful headache. Because she is not used to town noises.

May 31st. Ada knows a good deal already, but not everything. I told her a few things. In H. last winter a girl drowned herself because she was going to have a baby. It made a great sensation and her mother told her a little, but not everything. Ada once saw a bitch having her pups, but she didn't tell her mother about it; she thought that her mother might be very angry. Still, she could not help it, the dog belonged to their next door neighbour and she happened to see it in the out-house. Ada is expecting it to begin every day for she is nearly 14. In H. every grown-up girl has an admirer. Ada says she will have one as soon as she is 14; she knows who it will be.

June 3rd. Ada wrote to-day to thank Mother about the confirmation and she wrote to me as well. It is strange that she did not make friends with Dora but with me. I think that Dora won't talk about those things, at least only with her friends in the high school, especially with Frieda Ertl. That is why Ada made friends with me, though I am 2 years younger. She is really an awfully nice girl.

June 19th. One thing after another goes missing in our class, first it was Fleischer's galoshes, then my new gloves, three times money was missing, and today Fraulein Steiner's new vanity bag. There was a great enquiry. But nothing was found out. We all think it is Schmolka. But no one will tell. To-day we could none of us attend to our lessons especially when Sch. left the room at half past 11.

June 20th. In our closet the school servant found some beads on the floor but since she did not know anything she threw them

34

into the dustbin. Was it really Sch.? It would be a dirty trick. Frl. St. is frightfully upset because her betrothed gave her the vanity bag for a birthday present and his photo was in it. But I'm really sorry for Sch. Nobody will speak to her although nothing is proved yet. She is frightfully pale and her eyes are always full of tears. Hella thinks too that perhaps she didn't do it, for she is one of Frl. St.'s favourites and she is very fond of her herself. She always carries the copybooks home for her.

June 22nd. Our closet was stopped up and when the porter came to see what was the matter he found the vanity bag. But what use is it to Frl. now; she can't possibly use it any more. We giggled all through lessons whenever we caught one another's eye and the staff was in a frightful rage. Only Frau Doktor M. said: "Now please get through with your laughing over this extremely unsavoury affair, and then have done with it."

June 23rd. There was a frightful row to-day. Verbenowitsch was collecting the German copybooks and when Sch. wanted to hand up her copybook she said: Please give up your copybook yourself; I won't have anything to do with (then there was a long pause) you. We were all apalled and Sch. went as white as a sheet. At 10 o'clock she begged permission to leave the room because she felt bad. I'm sure her mother will come to speak about it to-morrow.

June 24th. Sch.'s mother did not come after all. Verbenowitsch said: Of course not! Sch. did not come either. Hella says she couldn't stand anything like that, she would rather drown herself. I don't know, one wants other reasons for drowning oneself. Still, I should tell Father so that he could speak about it at school. Franke said: Yes, that's all very well, because you didn't do it; but if one had done it one would not dare to say anything at home. Besides, Sch.'s father is an invalid, he's quite paralysed, has been bedridden for two years and can't speak.

June 27th. To-day Hella and I walked home with Frau Doktor M. Really she always goes home alone but Hella suddenly left me and went up to Frau Doktor in the street and said: Please excuse me Frau Doktor for bothering you in the street, we must speak to you. She got quite red. Then Frau Doktor said: "What's the matter?" And Hella said: "Isn't it possible to find out who took the vanity bag? If it wasn't Sch. the way the other girls treat her will make her quite ill, and if it was we can't stand having her among us any longer." Hella was really splendid and Frau Doktor M. made us tell her everything that had happened, including about Verbenowitsch and the copybooks; and we saw quite clearly she had tears in her eyes and she said: "The poor child! Children I promise I will do what I can for her." We both kissed her hand and my heart beat furiously. And

Hella said: "You are an angel." I could never have managed to say a thing like that.

June 28th. To-day Sch. was there again, but Frau Doktor M. did not say anything. Hella and I kept on looking at her and Hella cleared her throat three times and Frau Doktor said: Bruckner, do stop clearing your throat; it will only make your sore throat worse: But it seemed to me her eyes twinkled as she said it. So she hasn't forgotten. I wanted to speak to Sch., but Hella said: Wait a bit, we must give the Frau Doktor a chance. She's taken the matter in hand. To-morrow before 9 we'll walk up and down in front of her house till she comes out.

June 30th. Unluckily yesterday was a holiday and to-day Frau Doktor's first lesson began at 11. But she has already had a talk with Sch. only we don't know when and where; certainly it was not in the interval and she did not send for Sch. during lessons.

July 1st. To-day we walked to school with her She is such a dear. Children, she said, this is such a painful matter, and it is difficult to find a way out. Sch. insists that she did not do it, and whether she did it or not these days are burning themselves into her soul and Hella asked: "Please, Frau Doktor advise us what to do, speak to her or not?" Then she said: Children I think that after this affair she won't come back to us next year; you will be doing a good work if you make these last days bearable to her. You were never intimate with her, but to give her a friendly word or two will do you no harm and may help her. You 2 have a high standing in the class; your example will do good. We walked with her till we reached the school, and because we were there we could not kiss her hand but Hella said out loud: How sweet you are! She must have heard it. But Sch. was not at school. Father says he's glad that the term is nearly over, for I have been quite crazy about this affair. Still, he thinks that Hella and I should talk to Sch. So does Mother. But Dora said: Yes that's all right but you must not go too far.

July 5th. Sch. was not at school to-day. To-morrow we are to get our reports.

July 6th. We cried like anything I and Hella and Verbenowitsch because we shan't see Frau Doktor M. any more for nearly 3 months. I only had 2 in History and Natural History, but 1 in everything else. Franke says: Anyone who is not in Professor Igel-Nigl's good books can find out that he's cranky and stupid and he could never get a one. Father is quite pleased. Of course Dora has got only ones and Hella has three twos. Lizzi, I think, has 3 or 4. Father has given each of us a 2 crown piece, we can blow it, he says and Mother has given us a lace collar.

July 9th. We are going to Hainfeld this summer, its jolly, I'm awfully pleased; but not until the 20th because Father can't get away till then and Mother won't leave Father so long alone. It is only a few days anyhow. It's a pity Hella's gone already, she left early this morning for Parsch near Salzburg, what a horrid name and Hella too doesn't like saying it; I can't think how anyone can give a place such a nasty name. They have rented a house.

July 12th. It's shockingly dull. Nearly every day I have a quarrel with Dora because she's so conceited Oswald came home yesterday. He's fearfully smart nearly as tall as Father only about a quarter head shorter, but then Father's tremendously tall. And his voice is quite deep, it was not before. And he has parted his hair on one side, it suits him very well. He says his moustache is growing already but it isn't; one could see it if it were; five hairs don't make a moustache.

July 19th. Thank goodness we're going at last the day after to-morrow. Father wanted Mother to go away with us earlier, but she would not. It would have been nicer if she had.

July 24th. Our house is only 3 doors away from the Hs. Ada and I spend the whole day together. There happens to be a schoolfellow of Dora's here, one she gets on with quite well, Rosa Tilofsky Oswald says that Hainfeld bores him to death and that he shall get a friend to invite him somewhere. Nothing will induce him to spend the whole holidays here. His name for Ada is: "Country Simplicity." If he only knew how much she knows. Rosa T. he calls a "Pimple Complex" because she has two or three pimples. Oswald has some fault to find with every girl he comes across. He says of Dora: She is a green frog, for she always looks so pale and has cold hands, and he says of me: You can't say anything about her yet: "She is still nothing but an unripe embryo." Thank goodness I know from the natural history lessons what an embryo is, a little frog; "I got in a frightful wax and Father said: Don't you worry, he's still a long way from being a man or he would be more polite to his sisters and their lady friends." This annoyed him frightfully, and since then he never says a word when Ada and Rosa are with us. My birthday is coming soon, thank goodness I shall be 12 then, only 2 years more and I shall be 14; I am so glad. Hella wrote to me to-day for the second time. In August she is going to Hungary to stay with her uncle, he has a great estate and she will learn to ride there.

SECOND YEAR, AGE TWELVE TO THIRTEEN

SECOND YEAR

August 1st. It was awfully jolly on my birthday. We drove to Glashutte where it is lovely; there we cooked our own dinner in the inn for the landlady was ill and so was the cook. On one's birthday everyone is always so nice to one. What I like most of all is the Ebeseder paint-box, and the book too. But I never have any time to read. Hella sent me a lovely picture: Maternal Happiness, a dachshund with two puppies, simply sweet. When I go home I shall hang it up near the door over the bookcase. Ada gave me a silk purse which she had worked for me herself. Aunt Dora gave me a diary, but I can't use it because I prefer to write upon loose sheets. Grandfather and Grandmother at B. sent me a great piece of marzipan, splendid. Ada thinks it lovely; she didn't know marzipan before.

August 9th. When it's not holidays Ada goes to school in St. Polten staying there with her aunt and uncle, because the school in H. is not so good as the school in St. P. Perhaps next term she is coming to Vienna, for she has finished with the middle school and has to go on learning. But she has no near relations in Vienna where she could stay. She might come to live with us, Dora could have a room to herself as she always wants, and Ada and I could share a room. I would much rather share a room with her than with Dora who is always making such a fuss.

August 10th. I do really think! A boy can always get what he wants. Oswald is really going for a fortnight to Znaim to stay with his chum; only Oswald of course. I should like to see what would happen if Dora or I wanted to go anywhere. A boy has a fine time. It's the injustice of the thing which makes me furious. For we know for certain that he's had a bad report, even though he does not tell us anything about it. But of course that doesn't matter. They throw every 2 in our teeth and when he gets several Satisfactories he can go wherever he likes. His chum too; he only got to know Max Rozny this year and he's a chum already. Hella and I have been chums since we were in the second in the elementary school and Dora and Frieda Ertl since they went to the High School. We both gave him a piece of our mind about friendship. He laughed scornfully and said: That's all right, the friendships of men become closer as the years

38

pass, but the friendships of you girls go up in smoke as soon as the first admirer turns up. What cheek. Whatever happens Hella and I shall stick to one another till we're married, for we want to be married on the same day. Naturally she will probably get engaged before me but she must wait for me before she's married. That's simply her duty as a friend.

August 12th. Oswald went away yesterday and we had another scene just before he left because he wanted one of us to go with him to the station and help carry his luggage. As if we were his servants. Ada wanted to volunteer to carry it, but Dora gave her a nudge and luckily she understood directly. Sometimes, but only sometimes, when Dora gets in a wax she is rather like Hella. She thinks it's better that Oswald has gone away because otherwise there are always rows. That's because she always comes off second-best. For really he is cleverer than she is. And when he wants to make her really angry he says something to her in Latin which she can't understand. I think that's the real reason why she's learning Latin. I must say I would not bother myself so about a thing like that. I really wouldn't bother.

August 15th. To-day I posted the parcel to Hella, a silver-wire watchchain; I made it in four days. I hope she'll get it safely, one can never be sure in Hungary.

August 17th. We are so frightfully busy with Japanese lanterns and fir garlands. The people who have received birthday honours are illuminating and decorating their houses. While we were at work Ada told me a few things. She knows more than Hella and me, because her father is a doctor. He tells her mother a good deal and Ada overhears a lot of things though they generally stop talking when she comes in. Ada would like awfully to be an actress. I never thought of such a thing though I've been to the theatre often.

August 22nd. Hella is awfully pleased with the chain; she is wearing it. She is really learning to ride at her cousin's. It's a pity he's called Lajos. But Ludwig is not any better. He seems to be awfully nice and smart, but it's a pity he's 22 already.

August 25th. Ada is frightfully keen on the theatre. She has often been to the theatre in St. Polten and she is in love with an actor with whom all the ladies in St. Polten are in love. That is why she wants to be an actress and so that she can live free and unfettered. That is why she would like so much to come to Vienna. I wish she could come and live with us. She says she is pining away in H. for it's a dull hole. She says she can't stand these cramping conditions. In St. Polten she spent all her pocket money upon flowers for him. She always said that she had to buy such a lot of copybooks and things for school. That's where she's lucky not to be at home, for I could not easily take in Mother like that. It would not work. One always has too little pocket money anyhow, and when one lives at home one's parents know just what copybooks one has. I should like to go away from home for a few months. Ada says it is very good for one, for then one learns to know the world; at home, she says, one only grows musty and fusty. When she talks like that she really looks like an actress and she certainly has talent; her German master at school says so too. She can recite long poems and the girls are always asking the master to let her recite.

August 30th. To-day Ada recited Geibel's poem, The Death of Tiberius, it was splendid; she is a born actress and it's a horrid shame she can't go on the stage; she is to teach French or sewing. But she says she's going on the stage; I expect she will get her way somehow.

August 31st. Oswald's having a fine long fortnight; he's still there and can stay till September 4th!! If it had been Dora or me. There would have been a frightful hulabaloo. But Oswald may do anything. Ada says: We girls must take for ourselves what the world won't give us of its own free will.

September 5th. In the forest the other day I promised Ada to ask Mother to let her come and stay with us so that she could be trained for the stage. I asked Mother to-day, but she said it was quite out of the question. Ada's parents simply could not afford it. If she has talent, the thing comes of itself and she need only go to a school of Dramatic Art so that she could more easily get a good Theatre says Ada. So I don't see why it should be so frightfully expensive. I'm awfully sorry for Ada.

September 10th. Oh we have all been so excited. I've got to pack up my diary because we're going home to-morrow. I must write as quickly as I can. There have been some gypsies here for three days, and yesterday one of the women came into the garden through the back gate and looked at our hands and told our fortunes, mine and Ada's and Dora's. Of course we don't believe it, but she told Ada that she would have a great but short career after many difficult struggles. That fits in perfectly. But she made a frightful mess of it with me: Great happiness awaits me when I am as old again as I am now; a great passion and great wealth. Of course that must mean that I am to marry at 24. At 24! How absurd! Dora says that I look much younger than 12 so that she meant 20 or even 18. But that's just as silly, for Dr. H., who is a doctor and knows so many girls, says I look older than my age. So that it's impossible that the old gypsy woman could have thought I was only 10 or even 9. Dora's fortune was that in a few years she was to have much trouble and then happiness. And she told Ada that her line of life was broken!!

September 14th. Oswald left early this morning, Father kissed him on both cheeks and said: For God's sake be a good chap this last year at school. He has to matriculate this year, it's frightfully difficult. But he says that anyone who has cheek enough can get through all right. He says that cheek is often more help than a lot of swoting and grinding. I know he's right; but unfortunately at the moment it never occurs to me what I ought to do. I often think afterwards, you ought to have said this or that. Hella is really wonderful; and Franke too, though she's not particularly clever, can always make a smart answer. If only half of what Oswald says he says to the professors is true, then I can't understand why he is not expelled from every Gym. says Mother. Oswald says: If one only puts it in the right way no one can say anything. But that doesn't hold always.

September 16th. Hella is coming back to-day. That's why I'm writing in the morning, because she's coming here in the afternoon. I'm awfully glad. I have begged Mother to buy a lovely cake, one of the kind Hella and I are both so fond of.

September 20th. Only a word or two. School began again to-day. Thank goodness Frau Doktor M. still takes our class. Frl. Steiner took her doctor's degree at the end of the school year. In history we have a new Frau Doktor, but we don't know her name yet. The Vischer woman has been married in the holidays!!! It's enough to make one split with laughing that anyone should marry her!!! Dora says she wouldn't like to be her husband; but most likely he will soon get a divorce. Besides, spectacles in a woman are awful. I can put up with a pincenez for one does not wear them all the time. But spectacles! Dora says too that she can't understand how a man can marry a woman with spectacles. Hella often says it makes her feel quite sick when Vischer glares at her through her spectacles. We have a new natural history professor. I'm awfully glad that three of our mistresses have doctors degrees and that we have one or really 2 professors, for we have the Religionsprofessor too. In the Third they are frightfully annoyed because only one of their mistresses has a doctor's degree. Dora has 2 doctors and three professors.

September 25th. All the girls are madly in love with Professor Wilke the natural history professor. Hella and I walked behind him to-day all the way home. He is a splendid looking man, so tall that his head nearly touches the lamp when he stands up quickly, and a splendid fair beard like fire when the sun shines on it; a Sun God!

we call him S. G., but no one knows what it means and who we are talking about.

September 29th. Schmolka has left, I suppose because of Frl. St.'s vanity bag. Two other girls have left and three new one's have come, but neither I nor Hella like them.

October 1st. It was my turn in Natural History to-day I worked frightfully hard and He was splendid. We are to look after the pictures and the animals all through the term. How jolly. Hella and I always wear the same coloured hair ribbons and in the Nat. Hist. lesson we always put tissue paper of the same colour on the desk. He wants us to keep notebooks, observations on Nature. We have bound ours in lilac paper, exactly the same shade as his necktie. On Tuesdays and Fridays we have to come to school at half past 8 to get things ready. Oh how happy I am.

October 9th. He is a cousin of our gymnastic master, splendid! This is how we found it out. We, Hella and I, are always going past the Cafe Sick because he always has his afternoon coffee there. And on Thursday when we passed by there before the gymnastic lesson there was the gymnastic master sitting with him. Of course we bowed to them as we passed and in the gymnastic lesson Herr Baar said to us: So you two are tormented and pestered by my cousin in natural history? "Pestered" we said, o no, it's the most delightful lesson in the whole week. "Is that so?" said he, "I won't forget to let him know." Of course we begged and prayed him not to give us away, saying it would be awful. But we do hope he will.

October 20th. Frau Doktor Steiner's mother is dead. We are so sorry for her. Some of us are going to the funeral, I mayn't go, Mother says it is not suitable, and Hella is not allowed to go either, I wonder if He will go? I'm sure he will, for really he has to.

October 23rd. Frau Doktor St. looks frightfully pale. Franke says she will certainly get married soon now that both her parents are dead. Her fiance often fetches her from the Lyz, I mean he waits for her in L. Street. Hella thinks an awful lot of him of course, because he's an officer. I don't think much of him myself, he's too short and too fat. He's only a very little taller than Frl. St. I think a husband should be nearly a head taller than his wife, or at least half a head taller, like our Father and Mother.

October 29th. We have such a frightful lot of work to do that we're not taking season tickets this winter, but are going to pay each time when we go skating. I wish we knew whether He skates, and where. Hella thinks that with great caution we might find out from his cousin during the gymnastic lesson. They are often together in the Cafe. I should like to know what they talk about, they are always laughing such a lot, especially when we go by.

October 31st. Ada has written to me. She is awfully unhappy. She is back in St. P., in a continuation school. But the actor is not there any more. She writes that she yearns to throw off her chains which lie heavy on her soul. Poor darling. No one can help her. That is, her Mother could help her but she won't. It must be awful. Hella thinks that her parents will not allow her to go on the stage until she has tried to do herself a mischief; then things may be better. It's quite true, what can her mother be thinking of when she knows how fearfully unhappy Ada is. After all, why on earth shouldn't she go on the stage when she has so much talent? All her mistresses and masters at the middle school praised her reciting tremendously and one of them said in so many words that she had great dramatic talent. Masters don't flatter one; except . . .; first of all He is not just an ordinary master but a professor, and secondly He is quite, quite different from all others When he strokes his beard I become quite hot and cold with extasy. And the way he lifts up his coat tails as he sits down. It's lovely, I do want to kiss him. Hella and I take turns to put our penholder on his desk so that he can hallow it with his hand as he writes. Afterwards in the arithmetic lesson when I write with it, I keep looking at Hella and she looks back at me and we both know what the other is thinking of.

November 15th. It's a holiday to-day so at last I can write once more. We have such a frightful lot to do that I simply can't manage to write. Besides Mother is often ill. She has been laid up again for the last 4 days. It's awfully dull and dreary. Of course I had time to write those days, but then I didn't want to write. As soon as Mother is well again she's going to the Lyz to ask how we are getting on I'm awfully glad because of S.G.

November 28th. Mother came to school to-day and saw him too. I took her to him and he was heavenly. He said: I am very pleased with your daughter; she's very keen and clever. Then he turned over the pages of his notebook as if to look at his notes. But really he knows by heart how we all work. That is not all of course. That would be impossible with so many girls; and he teaches in the science school as well where there are even more boys than we are.

December 5th. Skating to-day I saw the Gold Fairy. She is awfully pretty, but I really don't think her so lovely as I did last year. Hella says she never could think what had happened to my eyes. "You were madly in love with her and you never noticed that she has a typical Bohemian nose," said Hella. Of course that's not true, but now my taste is quite different. Still, I said how d'you do to her and she was very nice. When she speaks she is really charming, and I do love her gold stoppings. Frau Doktor M. has two too and when she laughs its heavenly.

December 8th. I do wish Dora would keep her silly jokes to herself. When the Trobisch's were all here to-day they were talking about the school and she said: "Gretl has a fresh enthusiasm each year; last year it was Frau Doktor Malburg and this year it's Professor Wilke. Frau Doktor Malburg has fallen from grace now." If I had wanted to I could have begun about the two students on the ice. But I'm not like that so I merely looked at her with contempt and gave her a kick under the table. And she had the cheek to say: "What's the matter? Oh, of course these tender secrets of the heart must not be disclosed. Never mind Gretl, it does not matter at your age, for things don't cut deep." But she was rightly paid out: Frau von Tr. and Father roared with laughter and Frau v. Tr. said: "Why, grandmother, have you been looking at your white hair in the glass?" Oh, how I did laugh, and she was so frightfully put out that she blushed like fire, and in the evening she said to me that I was an ill-mannered pig. That's why I did not tell her that she'd left her composition book on the table and to-morrow she has to give it in. It's all the same to me, for I'm an ill-mannered pig.

December 9th. It's awful. At 2 o'clock this afternoon Hella was taken to the Low sanatorium and was operated on at once. Appendicitis. Her mother has just telephoned that the operation has been successful. But the doctors said that 2 hours later it would have been too late. My knees are trembling and my hand shakes as I write. She has not slept off the anisthetic yet.

December 10th. Hella is frightfully weak; no one can see her except her father and mother, not even Lizzi. On St. Nicholas Day we had such a jolly time and ate such a lot of sweets that we almost made ourselves sick. But its impossible that she got appendicitis from that. On Monday evening, when we were going home after the gym lesson, she said she did not feel at all well. The night before last she had a rigor and the first thing in the morning the doctor said that she must go to hospital at once for an operation.

December 11th. All the girls at school are frightfully excited about Hella, and Frau Dr. St. was awfully nice and put off mathematics till next Tuesday. On Sunday I am going to see Hella. She does want to see me so and so do I want to see her.

December 12th. She is still very weak and doesn't care about anything; I got her mother to take some roses and violets from me, she did like them so much.

December 14th. This afternoon I was with Hella from two until a quarter to 4. She is so pale and when I came in we both cried such a lot. I brought her some more flowers and I told her directly that when he sees me Prof. W. always asks after her. So do the other members of the staff especially Frau Doktor M. The girls want to

44

visit her but her mother won't let them. When anyone is lying in bed they look quite different, like strangers. I said so to Hella, and she said: We can never be strangers to one another, not even in death. Then I burst out crying again and both our mothers said I must go away because it was too exciting for Hella.

December 15th. I was with Hella again to-day. She passed me a little note asking me to get from her locker the parcel with the blotting-book for her father and the key basket for her mother and bring it to her because the things are not ready yet for Christmas.

December 16th. Hella's better to-day. I've got to paint the blotting-book for her father. Thank goodness I can. She'll be able to finish the key basket herself, that's nothing.

December 18th. The Bruckners are all frightfully unhappy for it won't be a real Christmas if Hella has to stay in hospital over Christmas. But perhaps she will for since yesterday she has not been so well, the doctors can't make out why she suddenly had fever once more. For she didn't let on that I had brought her some burnt almonds because she's so awfully fond of them. But now I'm so terribly frightened that she'll have to have another operation.

December 19th. Directly after school I went to see Hella again for I had been so anxious I could not sleep all night. Thank goodness she's better. One of the doctors said that if she'd been in a private house he would have felt sure it was an error in diet, but since she was in hospital that could be excluded. So it was from the burnt almonds and the two sticks of marzipan. Hella thinks it was the marzipan, for they were large ones at 20 hellers each because nuts lie heavy on the stomach. She had a pain already while I was still there, but she wouldn't say anything about it because it was her fault that I'd brought her the sweets. She can beg as much as she likes now, I shan't bring her anything but flowers, and they can't make her ill. Of course it would be different if it were true about the "Vengeance of Flowers." But that's all nonsense, and besides I don't bring any strong-scented flowers.

December 20th. I am so glad, to-morrow or Tuesday Hella can come home, in time for the Christmas tree. Now I know what to give her, a long chair, Father will let me, for I have not enough money myself but Father will give me as much as I want. Oh there's no one like Father! To-morrow he's going to take me to the Wahringerstrasse to buy one.

December 21st. I was only a very short time with Hella to-day because Father came to fetch me soon. At first she was a little hurt, but then she saw that we had important business so she said: All right as long as it is not anything made of marzipan. That nearly gave us both away. For when we were in the street Father asked me:

45

Why did Hella say that about marzipan? So I said quickly: Since she's been ill she has a perfect loathing for sweets. Thank goodness Father didn't notice anything. But I do hate having to tell fibs to Father. First of all I always feel that he'll see through it, and secondly anyhow I don't like telling fibs to him. The couch is lovely, a Turkish pattern with long tassels on the round bolster. Father wanted to pay for it altogether, but I said: No, then it would not be my present, and so I paid five crowns and Father 37. To-morrow early it will be sent to the Bruckners.

December 22nd. Hella is going home to-morrow. She has already been up a little, but she is still so weak that she has to lean on someone when she walks. She is awfully glad she is going home, for she says in a hospital one always feels as if one was going to die. She's quite right. The first time I went to see her I nearly burst out crying on the stairs. And afterwards we both really did cry frightfully. Her mother knows about the couch, but it has not been sent yet. I do hope they won't forget about it at the shop.

December 23rd. Hella went home to-day. Her father carried her upstairs while I held her hand. The two tenants in the mezzanin came out to congratulate her and the old privy councillor on the second story and his wife sent down a great pot of lilac. She was so tired that I came away at 5 o'clock so that she could rest. To-morrow I'm going to their Christmas tree first and then to ours. Because of Hella the Br's are going to have the present giving at 5 o'clock, we shall have ours as usual at 7.

December 26th. Yesterday and the day before I simply could not write a word. It was lovely here and at Hella's. I shan't write down all the things I got, because I've no time, and besides I know anyhow. Hella was awfully pleased with the couch, her father carried her into the room and laid her on the sofa. Her mother cried. It was touching. It's certainly awfully nice to have got through a bad illness, when everyone takes care of one, and when no one denies you the first place. I don't grudge it to Hella. She's such a darling. Yesterday I was there all day, and after dinner, when she had to go to sleep, she said: Open the drawer of my writing-table, the lowest one on the right, and you'll find my diary there if you want to read it. I shall never forget it! It's true that we agreed we would let one another read our diaries, but we've never done it yet; after all we're a little shy of one another, and besides after a long time one can't remember exactly what one has written. What she writes is always quite short, never more than half a page, but what she writes is always important. Of course she couldn't sleep but instead I had to read her a lot of things out of her diary, especially the holidays when she was in Hungary. She was made much of

46

there. By two cadets and her two cousins. We laughed so madly over some things that it hurt Hella's wound and I had to stop reading.

December 29th. We were put in such a frightful rage yesterday. This is how it happened. It is a long time since we both gave up playing with dolls and things of that sort but when I was rummaging in Hella's box I came across the dolls' things; they were quite at the bottom where Hella never looked at them. I took out the little Paris model and she said: Give it here and bring all the things that belong to it. I arranged them all on her bed and we were trying all sorts of things. Then Mother and Dora came. When they came in Dora gave such a spiteful look and said: Ah, at their favourite occupation: look, Lizzi, their cheeks are quite red with excitement over their play. Wasn't it impertinent. We playing with dolls! Even if we had been, what business was it of hers to make fun of us? Hella was in a frightful rage and to-day she said: "One is never safe from spies; please put all those things away in the box so that I shan't see them any more." It really is too stupid that one should always be reproached about dolls as if it was something disgraceful. After all, one doesn't really understand until later how all the things are made; when one is 7 or 8 or still more when one is quite a little girl and one first gets dolls, one does not understand whether they are pretty and nicely dressed or not. Still, to-day we've done with dolls for ever. A good day to turn over a new leaf, for the day after to-morrow is New Year's Day.

But what annoys me most of all was this piece of cheek of Dora's; she says that Lizzi said: "We used to delight in those things at one time," but I was in such a rage that I did not hear it. But to eat all the best things off the Christmas tree on the sly!!! I saw it myself, that is nothing. That's quite fit and proper for a girl of 15. After supper yesterday I asked: But what's become of the second marzipan sandwich, I'm sure there were two on the tree. And I looked at her steadily till she got quite red. And after a time I said: the big basket of vegetables is gone too. Then she said. Yes, I took it, I don't need to ask your permission. As for the sandwich, Oswald took that. I was in such a temper, and then Father said: Come, come, you little witch, cool your wrath with the second sandwich and wash it down with a sip of liqueur. For Grandfather sent Father a bottle of liqueur.

December 30th. This is a fine ending to the year. I've no interest in the school any longer. We're silly little fools, love-sick and forward minxes. That's all the thanks we get for having gone every Tuesday and Friday to the school at half past 8 to arrange everything and dust everything and then he can say a thing like that. I shall never write he with a big h again; he is not worthy of it. And I had to swallow it all, choke it down, for I simply must not excite Hella. It made me frightfully angry when Mother told me, but still I'm glad for I know what line to take now. Mother was paying a call yesterday and the sister of our gymnastic master, who is at the —— High School, happened to be there, and she told Mother that her cousin Dr. W. is so much annoyed because the girls in the high school are so forward. Such silly little fools, and the little minxes begin it already in the First Class. For that reason he prefers to teach boys, they are fond of him too but they don't make themselves such an infernal nuisance. Well, now that I know I shant make myself a nuisance to him any more. On Friday, when the next lesson is, I shall go there 2 minutes before nine and take the things into the class-room without saying a word. And I shall tell Kalinsky too that we're such an infernal nuisance to him. Just fancy, as if we were in the First Class!

January 1st, 19—. This business with Prof. W. makes me perfectly furious. Hella kept on asking yesterday what was the matter, said I seemed different somehow. But thank goodness I was able to keep it in. I must keep it in for the sake of her health, even if it makes me ill. Anyway what use is life now. Since people are so falsehearted. He always looked so awfully nice and charming; when I think of the way in which he asked how Hella was and all the time he was so false!!! If Hella only knew. Aha, to-morrow!

January 2nd. I treated him abominably. Knocked at the door—Good-morning, Herr Prof. please what do we want for the lesson to-day? He very civilly: Nothing particular to-day. Well, what sort of a Christmas did you have—I: Thank you, much as usual.—He turned round and stared at me: It does not seem to have been; to judge from your manner. —I: There are quite other reasons for that. He: O-o-h? He may well say O-o-h! For he has not the least idea that I know the way in which he speaks of us.

January 6th. To-day Hella was able to go out for her first drive. She's much better now and will come back to school by the middle of the month. I must tell her before that or she'll get a shock. Yesterday she asked: Does not S. C. ask about me any more?—Oh yes, I fibbed, but not so often as before. And she said: That's the way it goes, out of sight out of mind. What will happen when she learns the truth. Anyhow I shan't tell her until she's quite strong.

January 10th. I've had to tell Hella already. She was talking so enthusiastically about S. G. At first I said nothing. And then she said: What are you making such a face for? Are not you allowed to arrange the things any more?—I: Allowed? Of course I'm allowed, but I don't want to any more. I did not tell Hella how bad I feel about it; for I really was madly in love with him.

48

January 12th. Hella must have been madly in love with him too or rather must be in love with him still. On Sunday evening she was so much upset that her mother believed she was going to have a relapse. She had pains and diarrea at the same time. Thank goodness she's got over it like me. She said to-day: Don't let's bother ourselves about it any more. We wasted our feelings (not love!!) on an unworthy object. At such moments she is magnificent, especially now when she is still so pale. Besides in the holidays and now since she has been ill she has grown tremendously. Before I was a little taller and now she is a quarter head taller than me. Dora is frightfully annoyed because I am nearly as tall as she is. Thank goodness it makes me look older than 12 1/2.

Hella is not to come to school on January 15th, for her mother is going to take her to Tyrol for 2 or 3 weeks.

January 18th. It's horridly dull with Hella away. Only now do I realise, since her illness. I am always feeling as if she had fallen ill again. Her mother has taken her to Meran, they are coming back in the beginning of February.

January 24th. Since Hella has been ill, that is really since, she went away, I spend most of my time with Fritzi Hubner. She's awfully nice, though I did not know it last year. Till Hella comes back she and I sit together. For it's horrid to sit alone on a bench Fritzi knows a good deal already. She would not talk about it at first because it so often leads to trouble. Her brother has told her everything. He's rather a swell and is called Paul.

January 29th. Yesterday was the ice carnival and Dora and I were allowed to go. I skated with Fritzi and Paul most of the time and won 2 prizes, one of them with Paul. And one of them skating in a race with 5 other girls. Paul is awfully clever, he says he's going into the army, the flying corps. That's even more select than being on the general staff. Her father is a major and he, I mean Paul, ought to have gone to the military academy, but his grandfather would not allow it. He is to choose for himself. But of course he will become an officer. Most boys want to be what their father is. But Oswald is perhaps going into the Navy. I wish I knew what Father meant once when he said to Mother: Good God, I'm not doing it on my own account. I'm only doing it because of Oswald. The two girls won't get much out of it.

February 3rd. I've just been reading what I wrote about Father. I am wondering what it can be. I think that Father either wants to win the great prize in the lottery or is perhaps going to buy a house. But Dora and I would get something out of that, for it would not belong to Oswald only.

February 4th. Yesterday I asked Mother about it. But she said she didn't know; if it was anything which concerned us, Father would tell us. But it must be something, or Mother would not have told Father in the evening that I had asked. I can't endure these secrets. Why shouldn't we know that Father's going to buy a house. Fritzi's grandfather has a house in Brunn and another in Iglau. But Fritzi is very simply dressed and her mother too.

February 9th. Thank goodness Hella is coming back to-morrow, just before her birthday. Luckily she can eat everything again so I am giving her a huge bag of Viktor Schmid's sweets with a silver sugar tongs. Mother and I are going to meet Hella at the station. They are coming by the 8.20.

February 10th. I am so glad Hella is coming to-day. I nearly could not meet her because Mother is not very well to-day. But Father's going to take me. Fritzi wanted to come and see Hella to-morrow afternoon, but she can't. She's an awfully nice girl and her brother is too, but on the first day Hella is back we must be alone together. She said so too in the last letter she wrote me. She's been away more than 3 weeks. It's a frightfully long time when you are fond of one another.

February 15th. I simply can't write my diary because Hella and I spend all our free time together. Yesterday we got our reports. Of course Hella has not got one. Except in Geography and History I have nothing but Ones, even in Natural History although since New Year I have not done any work in that subject. I detest Natural History. When Hella comes back to school we are going to ask the sometime S. G. to relieve us from the labours of looking after the things. Hella is still too weak to do it. Hella is 13 already and Father says she is going to be wonderfully pretty. Going to be, Father says; but she's lovely already. She's been burned as brown as a berry by the warm southern sun, and it really suits her, though only her. I can't stand other people when they are sun-burned. But really everything suits Hella; when she was so pale in hospital, she was lovely; and now she is just as lovely, only in quite a different way. Oswald is quite right when he says: You can measure a girl's beauty by the degree in which she bears being sunburned without losing her good looks. He really used to say that in the holidays simply to annoy Dora and me, but he's quite right all the same.

February 20th. The second half-year began yesterday. They were all awfully nice to Hella, and Frau Doktor M. stroked her cheeks and put her arm round her so affectionately. Now for the chief thing. Today was the Natural History lesson. We knocked at the door and when we went in Prof. W. said: Ah I'm glad to see you Bruckner; take care that you don't give us all another fright. How

50

are you? Hella said: "Quite well, thank you, Herr Prof." And as I looked at her she put on a frightfully serious face and he said: It seems to me that you've caught your friend's ill humour.—Hella: "Herr Prof., you are really too kind, but we don't want to trouble you. What things have we to take to the class-room? And then we beg leave to resign our posts, for I don't feel strong enough for the work." She said this in quite a soldierly way, the way she is used to hear her father speak. It sounded most distinguished. He looked at us and said: "All right, two of the other pupils will take it over." We don't know whether he really noticed nothing or simply did not wish to show that he had noticed. But as we shut the door I felt so awfully sorry; for it was the last time, the very last time.

February 27th. In Natural History to-day I got Unsatisfactory. I was not being questioned, but when Klaiber could not answer anything I laughed, and he said: Very well, Lainer, you correct her mistake. But since I had been thinking of something quite different I did not know what it was all about, and so I got an Unsatisfactory. Before of course that would not have mattered; but now since . . . Hella and Franke did all they could to console me and said: "That does not matter, it wasn't an examination; he'll have to examine you properly later." Anyhow Franke thinks that however hard I learn, I shall be well off if he gives me a Satisfactory. She says no professor can forget such a defeat. For we told her about the silly little fools. She said, indeed, that we had made it too obvious. That's not really true. But now she takes our side, for she sees that we were in the right. Verbenowitsch and Bennari bring in the things now. They are much better suited for it. Hella's father did not like her doing it anyhow; he says: The porter or the maidservant are there for that— we never see them all the year round, that's a fine thing.

March 8th. Easter does not come this year until April 16th. I am going with the Bruckners to Cilli, outside the town there they have a vineyard with a country house. Hella needs a change. I am awfully glad. All the flowers begin to come out there at the end of March or beginning of April.

March 12th. Hella is not straightforward. We met a gentleman to-day, very fashionably dressed with gold-rimmed eyeglasses and a fair moustache. Hella blushed furiously, and the gentleman took off his hat and said: Ah, Fraulein Helenchen, you are looking very well. How are you? He never looked at me, and when he had gone she said: "That was Dr. Fekete, who assisted at my operation."—"And you tell me that now for the first time?" Then she put on an innocent air and said: "Of course, we've never met him before," but I said: "I don't mean that. If you knew how red you got you would not tell me a lie." Then she said: "What am I telling you a lie about?

Do you think I'm in love with him? Not in the very least."—But when one is not in love one does not blush like that. Anyhow I shan't tell everything now either; I can hold my tongue too.

March 14th. Yesterday we did not talk to one another so much as usual; I especially was very silent. When the bell rang at 5 and I had just been doing the translation Hella came and begged my pardon and brought me some lovely violets, so of course I forgave her. This is really the first time we've ever quarrelled. First she wanted to bring me some sweets, but then she decided upon violets, and I think that was much more graceful. One gives sweets to a little child when it has hurt itself or been in a temper. But flowers are not for a child.

March 19th. Frieda Belay is dead. We are all terribly upset. None of us were very intimate with her, but now that she is dead we all remember that she was a schoolfellow. She died of heart failure following rheumatic fever. We all attended her funeral, except Hella who was not allowed to come. Her mother cried like anything and her grandmother still more; her father cried too. We sent a wreath of white roses with a lovely inscription: Death has snatched you away in the flower of your youth—Your Schoolfellows.

I have no pleasure in anything to-day. I did not see Frieda Belay after she was dead, but Franke was there yesterday and saw her in her coffin. She says she will never forget it, it gave her such a pang. In the church Lampl had a fit of hysterics, for her mother was buried only a month ago and now she was reminded of it all and was frightfully upset. I cried a lot too when I was with Hella. She fancied it was because I was thinking she might have died last Dec. But that wasn't it, I don't think about that sort of thing. But when anyone dies it is so awfully sad.

March 24th. I never heard of such a thing. I can't go to Cilli with Hella. Her mother was at her cousin's, and when she heard that she was going to Cilli at Easter she asked her to take Melanie with her. That is, she didn't ask straight out, but kept on hinting until Hella's mother said: Let Melanie come with us, it will help to set her up after her illness. In the winter she had congestion of the lung. Hella and I can't bear her because she's always spying on us and is so utterly false. So of course I can't go. Hella says too she's frightfully sorry, but when she is about we could never say a word about anything, it would drive us crazy. She quite agrees that I had better not come. But oh I'm so annoyed for first of all I do so like going away with Hella and secondly I should like to go away in the holidays anyhow for nearly all the girls in our class are going away. Still, there's nothing to be done. Hella's mother says she can't see why we can't all 3 go though it simply would not work. But we can't

52

explain it to her. Hella is so poetical and she says "A beautiful dream vanished."

In Hella's mouth such fine words sound magnificent, but when Dora uses such expressions they annoy me frightfully because they don't come from her heart.

March 26th. The school performances finish today with Waves of the Sea and Waves of Love. I'm awfully fond of the theatre, but I never write anything about that. For anyhow the play is written by a poet and one can read it if one wants to, and one just sees the rest anyhow. I can't make out what Dora finds such a lot to scribble about always the day after we've been to the theatre. I expect she's in love with one of the actors and that's why she writes such a lot. Besides we in the second class did not get tickets for all the performances, but only the girls from the Fourth upwards. Still, it did not matter much to me anyhow for we often go in the evening and on Sunday afternoons. But unfortunately I mayn't go in the evening as a rule.

March 29th. To-day something horrible happened to Dora and me. I simply can't write it down. She was awfully nice and said: Two years ago on the Metropolitan Railway the same thing had happened when she was travelling with Mother on February 15th, she can never forget the date, to Hietzing to see Frau v. Martini. Besides her and Mother there was only one gentleman in the carriage, Mother always travels second class. She and Mother were sitting together and the gentleman was standing farther down the carriage where Mother could not see him but Dora could. And as Dora was looking he opened his cloak and − − −! just what the man did to-day at the house door. And when they got out of the train Dora's boa got stuck in the door and she had to turn round though she did not want to, and then she saw again − − −! She simply could not sleep for a whole month afterwards. I remember that time when she could not sleep but I did not know why it was. She never told anyone except Erika and the same thing happened to her once. Dora says that happens at least once to nearly every girl; and that such men are "abnormal." I don't really know what that means, but I did not like to ask. Perhaps Hella will know. Of course I did not really look, but Dora shivered and said: "And that is what one has to endure." And then, when we were talking it over she said to me that that was why Mother was ill and because she has had five children; Then I was very silly and said: "But how from that? one does not get children from that?" "Of course," she said, "I thought you knew that already. That time there was such a row with Mali about the waistband, I thought you and Hella had heard all about everything." Then I was silly again, really frightfully stupid; for

53

instead of telling her what I really knew I said: "Oh, yes, I knew all about it except just that." Then she burst out laughing and said: "After all, what you and Hella know doesn't amount to much." And in the end she told me a little. If it's really as Dora says, then she is right when she says it is better not to marry. One can fall in love, one must fall in love, but one can just break off the engagement. Well, that's the best way out of the difficulty for then no one can say that you've never had a man in love with you. We walked up and down in front of the school for such a long time that we were very nearly late and only got in just as the bell rang. On the way home I told Hella the awful thing we'd seen the man do. She does not know either what "abnormal" really means as far as this is concerned. But now we shall use it as an expression for something horrible. Of course no one will understand us. And then Hella told me about a drunken man who in Nagy K. . . . was walking through the streets like that and was arrested. She says too that one can never forget seeing anything like that. Perhaps the man this morning was drunk too. But he didn't look as if he were drunk. And if he hadn't done that one would really have taken him for a fine gentleman. Hella knows too that it is from that that one gets children. She explained it all to me and now I can quite understand that that must make one ill. Yesterday it was after 11 at night and so I'm finishing to-day. Hella says: That is the original sin, and that is the sin which Adam and Eve committed. Before I had always believed the original sin was something quite different. But that—that. Since yesterday I've been so upset I always seem to be seeing that; really I did not look at all, but I must have seen it all the same.

March 30th. I don't know why, but in the history lesson to-day it all came into my head once more what Dora had said of Father. But I really can't believe it. Because of Father I'm really sorry that I know it. Perhaps it does not all happen the way Dora and Hella say. Generally I can trust Hella, but of course she may be mistaken.

April 1st. To-day Dora told me a lot more. She is quite different now from what she used to be. One does not say P[eriod], but M[enstruation]. Only common people say P—. Or one can say one's like that. Dora has had M— since August before last, and it is horribly disagreeable, because men always know. That is why at the High School we have only three men professors and all the other teachers are women. Now Dora often does not have M— and then sometimes it's awfully bad, and that's why she's anemic. That men always know, that's frightfully interesting.

April 4th. We talk a lot about such things now. Dora certainly knows more than I do, that is not more but better. But she isn't

54

quite straightforward all the same. When I asked her how she got to know about it all, whether Erika told her or Frieda, she said: "Oh, I don't know; one finds it all out somehow; one need only use one's eyes and one's ears, and then one can reason things out a little." But seeing and hearing don't take one very far. I've always kept my eyes open and I'm not so stupid as all that. One must be told by some one, one can't just happen upon it by oneself.

April 6th. I don't care about paying visits now. We used always to like going to see the Richters, but to-day I found it dull. Now I know why Dora hates going second class on the Metropolitan. I always thought it was only to spite me because I like travelling second. She never likes going second since that happened. It seems one is often unjust to people who never meant what one thought. But why did she not tell me the truth? She says because I was still a child then. That's all right, but what about this winter when I was cross because we went Third class to Schonbrunn; I really believed she did it to annoy me, for I could not believe she was afraid that in the second class, where one is often alone, somebody would suddenly attack her with a knife. But now I understand quite well, for of course she could not tell Mother the truth and Father still less. And in winter and spring there are really often no passengers to speak of on the Metropolitan, especially on the Outer Circle.

April 7th. Mother said to-day that at the Richters yesterday we, especially I, had been frightfully dull and stupid. Why had we kept on exchanging glances? We had been most unmannerly. If she had only known what we were thinking of when Frau Richter said, the weather to-day is certainly quite abnormal; we have not had such abnormal heat for years. And then when Herr Richter came home and spoke about his brother who had spent the whole winter at Hochschneeberg and said: Oh, my brother is a little abnormal, I think he's got a tile loose in the upper storey, I really thought I should burst. Luckily Frau R. helped us once more to a tremendous lot of cake and I was able to lean well forward over my plate. And Mother said that I ate like a little glutton and just as if I never had any cake at home. So Mother was very unjust to me, for the cake had nothing at all to do with it. Dora says too that I must learn to control myself better, that if I only watch her I'll soon learn. That's all very well, but why should one have to bother? If people did not use words that really mean something quite different then other people would not have to control themselves. Still, I must learn to do it somehow.

April 8th. We were terribly alarmed to-day; quite early, at half past 8, they telephoned from the school that Dora had suddenly been taken ill in the Latin lesson and must be fetched in a carriage. Mother drove down directly in a taxi and I went with her because anyhow my lessons began at 9 and we found Dora on the sofa in the office with the head sitting by her and the head's friend, Frau Doktor Preisky, who is a medical doctor, and they had loosened her dress and put a cold compress on her head for she had suddenly fainted in the Latin lesson. That's the third time this year, so she must really have anemia. I wanted to drive home with her, but Mother and Frau Dr. P. said I'd better just go to my lessons. And as I went out I heard Frau Dr. P. say: "That's a fine healthy girl, a jolly little fellow." Really one should only use that word of boys and men, but I suppose she has got into the way of using it through being with men so much. If one studies medicine one has to learn all about that and to look at everything. It must be really horrid.

Dora is kept in bed to-day and our Doctor says too that she's anemic. To-morrow or the day after Mother is going to take her to see a specialist. Dora says it's a lovely feeling to faint. Suddenly one can't hear what people are saying and one feels quite weak and then one does not know anything more. I wonder if I shall ever faint? Very likely when — — — We talked a lot about everything we are interested in. In the afternoon Hella came to ask after Dora, and she thinks she looks awfully pretty in bed, an interesting invalid and at the same time so distinguished looking. It's quite true, we all look distinguished.

April 9th. To-day is Father and Mother's wedding day. Now I know what that really means. Dora says it can't really be true that it is the most lovely day in one's life, as everyone says it is, especially the poets. She thinks that one must feel frightfully embarrassed because after all everyone knows. . . . That's quite true, but after all one need not tell anyone which one's wedding day is. Dora says she will never tell her children which her wedding day is. But it would be a great pity if parents always did that for then in every family there would be one anniversary the less. And the more anniversaries there are, the jollier it is.

April 10th. To-morrow I'm going with Father to Salzburg. Dora can't come, for they think she might faint in the train. I'm rather glad really, though I've nothing against her and I'm sorry for her, but it's much nicer to go with Father alone. It's a long time since I was in Salzburg. I'm so awfully glad to go. Our spring coats and skirts are so pretty, dark green with a silk lining striped green and gold-brown, and light brown straw hats with daisies for the spring and later we shall have cherries or roses. I'm taking my diary so that I can write everything which interests me.

April 12th. I slept all the way in the train. Father says I ground

56

my teeth frightfully and was very restless: but I did not know anything about it. We had a compartment by ourselves, except just at first when there was a gentleman there. Hella did not come with us, because her aunt, who has just been married, is coming to visit them. Really I'm quite glad, for I like so much being with Father quite alone. This afternoon we were in Hellbrunn and at the Rock Theatre. It is wonderful.

April 13th. Father always calls me: Little Witch! But I don't much like it when other people are there. To-day we went up the Gaisberg. The weather was lovely and the view magnificent. When I see so extensive a view it always makes me feel sad. Because there are so many people one does not know who perhaps are very nice. I should like to be always travelling. It would be splendid.

April 14th. I nearly got lost to-day. Father was writing a letter to Mother and he let me go to see the salt works; I don't know how it happened, but suddenly I found myself a long way from anywhere, in a place I did not know. Then an old gentleman asked me what I was looking for; because I had walked past the same place 3 times and I said we were staying in the "Zur Post Hotel" and I did not know how to find my way back. So he came with me to show me and as we were talking it came out that he had known Father at the university. So he came in with me and Father was awfully glad to see him. He is a barrister in Salzburg but he has a grey beard already. As he was going away he said in an undertone to Father: "I congratulate you old chap on your daughter; she'll be something quite out of the ordinary!" He whispered it really, but I heard all the same. We spent all the afternoon with him at the Kapuzinerberg. There was a splendid military band; two young officers in the Yagers who were sitting at the next table to ours kept on looking our way; one was particularly handsome. My new summer coat and skirt is awfully becoming everyone says. Father says too: "I say, you'll soon be a young lady! But don't grow up too quickly!" I can't make out why he said that; I should like to be quite grown up; but it will be a long time yet.

April 14th. It's been raining all day. How horrid. One can't go anywhere. All the morning we were walking about the town and saw several churches. Then we were at the pastrycook's, where I ate 4 chocolate eclairs and 2 tartlets. So I had no appetite for dinner.

April 15th. Just as I was writing yesterday Dr. Gratzl sent up the hotel clerk to ask us to dinner. We went, they live in the Hellbrunnerstrasse. He has 4 daughters and 2 sons and the mother died three years ago. One of the sons is a student in Graz and the other is a lieutenant in the army; he is engaged to be married. The daughters are quite old already; one of them is 27 and is engaged. I think that is horrid. The youngest (!!!) is 24. It is so funny to say "the youngest" and then she is 24. Father says she is very pretty and will certainly get married At 24!! when she's not even engaged yet; I don't believe she will. They have a large garden, 3 dogs and 2 cats, which get on very well together. There are steps leading up and down from room to room, it is lovely, and all the windows are bow-windows. Everything is so old-fashioned, even the furniture I do think it's all so pretty. The hall is round like a church. After tea we had candied fruits, stewed fruit, and pastries. I had a huge go of stewed fruit. They have a gramaphone and then Leni and I played the piano. Just as we were going away Fritz, the student, came in; he got quite red and in the hall Dr. Gratzl said to me: "You've made a conquest to-day." I don't really believe I have, but I do like hearing it said. I'm sorry to say we are going away to-morrow, for we are going to stay 2 days in Linz with Uncle Theodor whom I don't know.

April 17th. Uncle Theodor is 60 already and Aunt Lina is old too. Still, they are both awfully nice. I did not know them before. We are staying with them. In the evening their son and his wife came. They are my cousins, and they brought their little girl with them; I am really a sort of aunt of hers. It's awfully funny to be an aunt when one is only 12 and 3/4 and when one's niece is 9. To-day we went walking along the Danube. It only rained very gently and not all the time.

April 18th. We are going home to-day. Of course we have sent a lot of picture postcards to Mother and Dora and Hella; we sent one to Oswald too. He came home for Easter. I don't know whether he will still be there to-morrow.

April 22nd. We've begun school again. Dora and I generally walk to school together since she does not go to the Latin lesson now because it was too great a strain for her. The specialist Mother took her to see wanted her to give up studying altogether, but she absolutely refuses to do that. But I'm very furious with her; she's learning Latin in secret. When I came into the room the day before yesterday she was writing out words and she shut her book quickly instead of saying openly and honestly: Rita, don't tell Father and Mother that I'm still studying in the evening: "I trust your word." She could trust me perfectly well. There are plenty of things I could tell if I liked! Perhaps she fancies that I don't see that the tall fair man always follows us to school in the morning. Hella has noticed him too, besides he is frightfully bald and must be at least 30. And I'm certain she would not talk as much as she does to Hella and me if it were not that she wants to talk about that. But this deceitfulness annoys me frightfully. Otherwise we are now quite intimate with one another.

58

April 24th. We went to confession and communion to-day. I do hate confession; though it's never happened to me what many girls have told me, even girls in the Fifth. No priest has ever asked me about the 6th commandment; all they've asked is: In thought, word, or deed? Still, I do hate going to confession, and so does Dora. It's much nicer for Hella as a Protestant for they have no confession. And at communion I'm always terrified that the host might drop out of my mouth. That would be awful. I expect one would be immediately excommunicated as a heretic. Dora was not allowed to come to confession and com., Father would not let her. She must not go out without her breakfast.

April 26th. In the Third there really is a girl who dropped the host out of her mouth. There was a frightful row about it. She said it was not her fault the priest's hand shook so. It's quite true, he was very old, and that is why I'm always afraid it will happen to me. It's much better when the priest is young, because then that can never happen. Father says that the girl won't be excommunicated for this, and luckily one of her uncles is a distinguished prelate. He is her guardian too. That will help her out.

April 27th. To-day we got to know this girl in the interval. She is awfully nice and she says she really did not do it on purpose for she is frightfully pious and perhaps she's going to be a nun. I am pious too, we go to church nearly every Sunday, but I would not go into a convent, not I. Dora says people generally do that when they've been crossed in love, because then the world seems empty and hateful. She looked so frightfully sentimental that I said: Seems to me you've a fancy that way yourself? Then she said: "No, thank goodness, I've no reason for that." Of course what she meant was that she was not crossed in love but the other way. No doubt the tall man in the mornings. I looked hard at her for a long time and said: "I congratulate you on your good fortune. But Hella and I wish he was not bald," then she said with an astonished air: "Bald? What are you talking about, he has the lofty brow of a thinker."

27th. To-day Mademoiselle came for the first time. I have forgotten to say that Dora has to go out every day for two hours to sit and walk in the sunshine. Since Mother is not very well and can't walk much, we've engaged the Mad. Father says that when I have time I must go too "as a precautionary measure." I don't like the idea at all, it's much too dull; besides I have simply no time. Mad. is coming 3 times a week, Mondays, Wednesdays, and Fridays, and on Mondays, Thursdays, and Saturdays I have my music lesson, so I can't go; so Finis and Jubilation! That's what Oswald always says at the end of the year and at the end of term. Still, she's very pretty, has fair curly hair, huge grey eyes with black lashes and eyebrows, but she speaks so fast that I can't understand all she says. On the other 3 days an Englishwoman is to come, but we have not got one yet, they are all so expensive. It does seem funny to me to get a salary for going out with grown up girls, that's only an amusement. With regular tomboys, such as we saw last year in Rathaus Park, it would be different. As for the French or English conversation! If they did not want to talk what would it matter? And besides why should one want to talk either French or English, it's so stupid.

April 28th. The Richters were here to-day, and the eldest son came too, the lieutenant from Lemberg; he is awfully handsome and made hot love to Dora; Walter is very nice too, he is at the School of Forestry in Modling; to-morrow the lieutenant is going to bring Dora one of Tolstoi's books to read. Then they will do some music together, she piano and he violin; it's a pity I can't play as well as Dora yet. At Whitsuntide Walter is coming too and Viktor (that means conqueror) is on furlough for 6 months, because he's ill, or because he is said to be ill; for one does not look like that when one is really ill.

May 4th. Lieutenant R. is always coming here, he must be frightfully smitten with Dora. But Father won't have it at any price. He said to Dora to-day:

"You get this gay young spark out of your head; he is no good. But at sight of a uniform there is no holding you girls. I've no objection to you doing music together for an hour or two; but this perpetual running to and fro with books and notes is all humbug."

May 6th. Lieutenant R. walks with us, that is with Dora, to school every day. He is supposed to lie in bed late every morning, for he is really ill but for Dora's sake he gets up frightfully early and comes over from Heitzing and waits in —— Street. Of course I go on alone with Hella and we all meet In —— Street, so that no one shall notice anything at school.

May 13th. To-morrow is Mother's birthday and Viktor (when I am talking about him to Dora I always speak of him as V.) brought her some lovely roses and invited us all to go there next Sunday. In the hall he called me "the Guardian Angel of our Love." Yes, that is what I am and always shall be; for he really deserves it and Dora too is quite different from what she used to be. Hella says one can see for oneself that love ennobles; up till now she has always thought that to be mere poetical fiction.

May 15th. Father said: I don't care much about these visits to the Richters as long as that young jackanapes is still there, but Mother can't very well refuse. We shall wear our green coats and skirts with the white blouses with the little green silk leaves for Dora does not like to wear all white except in summer. And because the leaves on the blouses are clover leaves, that is because of their meaning. We are looking forward to it tremendously. I do hope Mother will be all right, for she is in bed to-day. It's horrid being ill anyhow, but when being ill interferes with other people's pleasure it's simply frightful.

May 16th. The day before yesterday was Mother's birthday; but it was not so jolly as usual because Mother is so often ill; for a birthday present I painted her a box with a spray of clematis, which looks awfully chic. Dora gave her a book cover embroidered with a spray of Japanese cherries, I don't know what Father gave her, money I think, because on her birthday and name day he always hands her an envelope. But since Mother is not well we were not very cheerful, and when we drank her health at dinner she wiped her eyes when she thought we were not looking. Still, it's not so dangerous as all that; she is able to go out and doesn't look bad. I think Mother's awfully smart, she looks just as well in her dressing gown as when she's dressed up to go out. Dora says that if she had been made ill by her husband she would hate him and would never let her daughters marry. That's all very well, but one ought to be quite sure that that is why one has become ill. They say that is why Aunt Dora doesn't like Father. Certainly Father is not so nice to her as to other relations or to the ladies who some to see Mother. But after all, Aunt Dora has no right to make scenes about it to Father, as Dora says she does. Mother's the only person with any right to do that. Dora says she is afraid that it will come to Mother's having to have an operation. Nothing would ever induce me to undergo an operation, it must be horrible, I know because of Hella and the appendicitis. But Dora says: "Anyone who's had five children must be used to that sort of thing." I shall pray every night that Mother may get well without an operation. I expect we shan't all go away together at Whitsuntide this year, for Mother and Dora are to go to a health resort, most likely to Franzensbad.

May 18th. It was lovely at the Richters; Walter was there from Modling, he was awfully nice, and said I was so like my sister that it was difficult to tell us apart. That's a frightful cram, but I know what he really meant. He plays the flute splendidly, and the three played a trio, so that I was frightfully annoyed with myself for not having worked harder at my music. From to-morrow on I shall practice 2 hours every day, if I can possibly find time. Next winter Viktor is going to found a private dramatic club, so he must be going to stay more than six months in Vienna. Walter thinks Dora awfully charming, and when I said: "The great pity is that she's got such frightful anemia," he said: In a man's eyes that is no drawback whatever, as you can see in my brother. Moreover, that illness is not

61

a real illness, but often makes a girl more charming than ever, as you can see in your sister.

Day before yesterday Miss Maggie Lundy came for the first time; anybody can have her for me. She wears false hair, flaxen. She says she is engaged, but Dora says, has been. I simply don't believe it. V. says Mad. is awfully pretty. When I asked Dora if she was not jealous, she said she didn't care, she was quite sure of his love. He means to leave the army and go into the civil service, and then he will be able to marry. But Dora said, there's plenty of time for that, a secret engagement is much nicer. Then she noticed she'd given herself away, and she blushed like anything and said: You naturally must be engaged before you are married, mustn't you?—of course she is secretly engaged, but she won't tell me about it. What's the good of my being the "Guardian Angel of their Love?" If he only knew.

May 19th. I really ought to practice to-day, but I simply have no time, first of all I had my lesson anyhow, and secondly something awful happened to Dora. She left her diary lying about in the school; and because we have our religion lesson in the Fifth I saw a green bound book lying under the third bench. Great Scott, I thought, that looks like Dora's diary. I went up as quickly as I could and put my satchel over it. Later in the lesson I picked it up. When I got home at 1 o'clock I did not say anything at first. After dinner she began rummaging all over the place, but without saying anything to me, and then I said quite quietly: "Do you hap—pen to be look—ing for your di—ar—y? Here it is; you—left—it in—the—fifth—class—un—der—the—third—bench." (I kept her on tenter hooks that way.) She got as white as a sheet and said: "You are an angel. If any one else had found it, I should have been expelled and Mad. would have had to drown herself." "Oh, it can't be as bad as all that," I said, for what she said about Mad. was frightfully exciting. In class I had looked chiefly at what she had written about V. But I could not read it there, because it was written very small and close together and was several pages, but I had not looked much at what she had written about Mad. "Did you read it?" "No, only where it happened to come open because there's a page torn out." "About V. or about Mad?" "A little about Mad; but tell me all about it; I shan't tell anyone. For if I'd wanted to betray you, you know quite well. . . ." And then she told me all about Mad. But first I had to promise that I would not even tell Hella. Mad. is secretly engaged to a man to whom she has given "the utmost gifts of love," that is to say she has . . . . She is madly in love with him, and they would marry directly but he is a lieutenant too, and they have not enough money for the security. She says that when one really loves a man one can bear everything for his sake. She has often been to his rooms, but she has to be frightfully careful for her father would kill her if he found out. Dora has seen the lieutenant and says he is very handsome, but that V. is much handsomer. Mad. says that you can't trust men as a rule, but that her lover is quite different, that he is true as steel. I am sure V. is too.

May 21st. When Mad. came to-day I simply could not look at her while Mother was there and Dora says I made an awful fool of myself. For I went out walking with them to-day, and when we met a smart-looking officer I hemmed and looked at Dora. But she didn't know why. Mad. is the daughter of a high official in the French military service and she only took her teacher's degree in order to get free from her Mother's "tyranny;" she nagged at her frightfully and until she began to give lessons she was never allowed to go out alone. Dora says she is very refined in her speech, especially when she is talking about these things. Of course about them she always speaks German, for it's much more difficult to say it in French, and probably Dora would not understand it and then Mad. would only have to translate it. She is called Sylvia and he calls her Sylvette. Mad. says that if one is madly in love with a man one does whatever he asks. But I don't see that one need do that, for he might ask the most idiotic things; he might ask you to get the moon out of the skies, or to pull out a tooth for his sake. Dora says she can understand it quite well; that I still lack the true inwardness of thought and feeling. It looks like utter nonsense. But since it sounds fine I've written it down, and perhaps I shall find a use for it some day when I'm talking to Walter. Mad. is always frightfully anxious lest she should get a baby. If she did she's sure her father would kill her. The lieutenant is in the flying corps. He hopes he's going to invent a new aeroplane, and that he will make a lot of money out of it. Then he will be able to marry Mad. But it would be awful if something happened and she got a baby already.

May 22nd. Dora asked me to-day how it was I knew all about these things, whether Hella had told me. I did not want to give Hella away, so I said quite casually: "Oh, one can read all about that in the encyclopedia." But Dora laughed and said: "You are quite on the wrong scent; you can't find a tenth of all those things in the encyclopedia, and what you do find is no good. In these matters it is absolutely no good depending on books." First of all she would not tell me any more, but after a time she told me a good deal, especially the names of certain parts, and about fertilisation, and about the microscopic baby which really comes from the husband, and not as Hella and I had thought, from the wife. And how one knows whether a woman is fruitful. That is really an awful word. In fact almost every word has a second meaning of that sort, and what Dora says is quite true, one must be fearfully careful when one is talking. Dora thinks it would be best to make a list of all such words, but there are such a frightful lot of them that one never could. The only thing one can do is to be awfully careful; but one soon gets used to it. Still it happened to Dora the other day that she said to V.: I don't want any intercourse. And that really means "the utmost gifts of love," so Mad. told her. But V. was so well-mannered that he did not show that he noticed anything; and it did not occur to Dora until afterwards what she had said. It's really awfully stupid that every ordinary word should have such a meaning. I shall be so frightfully careful what I say now, so that I shan't use any word with two meanings. Mad. says it's just the same in French. We don't know whether it is the same in English and we could never dream of asking that awful fright, Miss Lundy. Very likely she does not know the first thing about it anyhow. I know a great deal more than Hella now, but I can't tell her because of betraying Dora and Mad. Perhaps I can give her a hint to be more careful in what she says, so as not to use any word with two meanings. That is really my duty as a friend.

May 23rd. I quite forgot. Last week Oswald had his written matriculation exam, he wrote a postcard every day and Mother was frightfully annoyed because he made such silly jokes all the time that we could not really tell how he got on. Dora and I are awfully excited because next Monday we are going to the aerodome with Frau Richter and her niece who is at the conservatoire. Lieutenant Streinz is going to fly too. Of course we'll motor out because the railway is not convenient. Of course Viktor will be there, but he is motoring over with some other officers. It's a great pity, for it would have been lovely if he'd been in our car. By the way, I saved the class to-day, the school inspector has been this week and examined our class first in History and then in German, and I was the only one who knew all that Frau Doktor M. had told us about the Origin of Fable. The insp. was very complimentary and afterwards Frau Doktor M. said: its quite true one can always depend upon Lainer; she's got a trustworthy memory. When we were walking home she was awfully nice: "Do you know, Lainer, I feel that I really must ask your pardon." I was quite puzzled and Hella asked: But why? She said: "It seemed to me this year that you were not taking quite so much interest in your German lessons as you did last year; but now you've reinstated yourself in my good opinion." Afterwards Hella said: I say you know, Frau Doktor M. is not so far wrong when I think of all that we used to read last year so that we might know everything when the lesson came, and when I think of what we do this year!!! You know very well — — — —. Hella is quite right, but still one can learn in spite of those things, one can't be always talking about them. And then it's quite easy to learn for such an angel as Frau Doktor M. Hella says that I got as red as a turkey cock from pride because I could say it all in the very words of Frau Doktor M., but it was not so, for first of all I was not a bit puffed up about it, and secondly I really don't know myself how I managed to say it all. I only felt that Frau Doktor M. is so annoyed when no one offers to answer a question, and so I took it on.

May 25th. Confound it, I could slap myself a hundred times. How could I be so stupid! Now we're not allowed to go to the aerodome. Father only let us go because Viktor is in Linz and Father believed he was going to stay there another fortnight. And at dinner to-day I made a slip and said: "It is a pity there's no room for five in our car. If Fraulein Else were not coming Lieutenant Richter could come with us." Dora kicked me under the table and I tried to brazen it out, but Father was so angry and said. "Hullo, is the flying man coming? No, no, children, nothing doing. I shall make your excuses to Frau Richter directly. I'm not having any, did not I tell you you weren't to see the fellow any more?" Of course this last was to Dora. Dora did not say anything but she did not eat any pudding or fruit, and as soon as we were back in our room she gave it me hot, saying: You did that on purpose, you little beast, but really you are only a child whom I never ought to have trusted, and so on. It's really too bad to say I did it on purpose, as if I envied her. Besides it's bad for me as well as for her, for I like him very much too, for he makes no difference between us and treats me exactly like Dora. Of course we are not on speaking terms now, and what infuriated me more than anything was that she said she grudged every word she had said to me in this connection: "Pearls before Swine." What a rude thing to say. So I am an S. But I should like to know who told most. I forsooth? Anyhow I'm quite sure that I shall never talk to her again about anything of that sort. Thank goodness I have a friend in Hella. She would never say or think anything of the kind of me.

May 26th. Neither of us could sleep a wink all night; Dora cried frightfully, I heard her though she tried to stifle it, and I cried too, for I was thinking all the time what I could do to prevent Viktor from thinking unkindly of me. That would be awful. Then I thought of something, and chance or I ought to say luck helped me. Viktor does not walk to school with us any longer, because the girls of the Fifth have seen us several times, but he comes to meet Dora when she comes away at 1 o'clock. So quite early I telephoned to him at a public telephone call office, for I did not dare to do it at home. Dora was so bad that she could not go to school so I was going alone with Hella. I telephoned saying a friend was ringing him up, that was when the maid answered the telephone, and then she called him. I told him: that whatever happened he was not to think unkindly of me and I must see him at 1 o'clock because Dora was ill. He must wait at the corner of —— Street. All through lessons I was so upset that I don't in the least know what we did. And at 1 o'clock he was there all right, and I told him all about it and he was so awfully kind and he consoled me; he consoled me. That's quite different from the way Dora behaved. I was so much upset that I nearly cried, and then he drew me into a doorway and put his arm round me and with his own handkerchief wiped away my tears. I shall never tell Dora about that. Then he asked me to be awfully kind to Dora because she had such a lot to bear. I don't really know what she has to bear, but still, for his sake, because it's really worth doing it for that, after dinner I put a note upon her desk, saying: V. sends oceans of love to you and hopes you will be all right again by Monday. At the same time his best thanks for the book. I put the note in Heidepeter's Gabriel, which she had lent to me to read and put it down very significantly. When she read it she flushed up, swallowed a few times and said: "Have you seen him? Where was it and when?" Then I told her all about it and she was frightfully touched and said: "You really are a good girl, only frightfully undependable." What do you mean, undependable? She said: Yes undependable, for one simply must not blurt out things in that way; never mind, I will try to forget. Have you finished Heidepeter's Gabriel yet? "No," I said, "I'm not going to read anyone's book with whom I'm angry." In the end we made it up, but of course we did not talk any more about it and I did not say a word about that business with the handkerchief.

May 29th. On June 10th or 12th, Mother and Dora are going to Frazensbad, because they both have to take mud baths. Besides, Father says that a change will give Dora new thoughts, so that she won't go about hanging her head like a sick chicken. To-day Dora told me something very interesting. Unmarried men have little books and with these they can go to visit women "of a certain kind" in Graben and in the Karntnerstrasse. There, Dora says, they have to pay 10 florins or 10 crowns. In Dora's class there is a girl whose father is police surgeon, and they have all to be examined every month to see if they are healthy, and if not they can't visit these "ladies," and that's why the Preusses can never keep a servant. In my bath yesterday I noticed that I had a certain line, so I must be fr—. But I shan't have more than 1 or 2 children at most for the line is very faint. When I'm studying I often think of such things, and then I read a whole page and turn over and have not the remotest idea what I've been reading. It's very tiresome, for soon the other school insp. for maths. and the other subjects is coming, and I should not like to make a fool of myself; especially not because perhaps the inspectors talk us over with one another about who is clever and who stupid.

May 30th. The concert was glorious. When I hear such grand music I always have to keep myself well in hand for I fear I should cry. It's very stupid, of course, but at such times I can only think of sad things, even if it's just a small piece. Dora can play Brahms' Hungarian Dances, too, but that never makes me want to cry. I only get annoyed because I can't play them myself. I could all right, but I have not got patience to practice long enough. I never tell anyone that I want to cry when I am listening to music, not even Hella, though I tell her everything, except of course about Mad. Yesterday I made a fool of myself; at least so Dora says. I don't know how it happened, we were talking about books at supper, and I said: "What's the use of books, one can't learn anything out of them; everything is quite different from what they say in books." Then Father got in a wax and said: "You little duffer, you can thank your stars there are books from which you can learn something. Anyone who can't understand a book always says it is no good." Dora gave me a look, but I didn't know what she meant, and I went on: "Yes, but there's an awful lot that the encyclopedia puts all wrong." "What have you been ferreting in the encyclopedia for; we shall have to keep the key of the bookcase in a safer place." Thank goodness Dora came to my help and said: "Gretel wanted to look up something about the age of elephants and mammoths, but it's quite different in the encyclopedia from what Prof. Rigl told her last year." I was saved. Dora can act splendidly; I've noticed it before. In the evening she rowed me, and said: "You little goose, will you never learn caution; first that stupidity about Viktor and to-day this new blunder! I've helped you out of a hole once but I shan't do it again." And then she spent all the time writing a letter, to him of course—! Hella and I have just been reading a lot of things in the encycl., about Birth and Pregnancy, and I on my own about abor—; we came across the words Embyro and Foetus, and I said nothing at the time but tied 2 knots in my handkerchief to remind me, and yesterday I looked them up. Mad. need not be anxious even if she really did get like that. But every doctor knows about it and one often dies of it. I wonder if Mad. knows anything about it. We were talking about the differences between men and women, and it came out that when Hella has her bath she is still washed by Anna who has been with them for 12 years. Nothing would induce me to allow that, I would not let anyone wash me, except Mother; certainly not Dora, for I

67

don't want her to know what I look like. The nurse in the hosp. told Hella that she is developed just like a little nymph, so lovely and symetrical. Hella says that is nothing unusual, that every girl looks like that, that the female body is Nature's Work of Art. Of course she's read that somewhere, for it does not really mean anything. Nature's work of art; it ought to be: a work of art made by husband and wife!!!

May 30th. Dora and Mother are going to Franzensbad on June 6th, directly after Whitsuntide. Dora has got another new coat and skirt, grey with blue stripes; yesterday our white straw hats came, it suits me very well says Hella and everyone, with white ribbons and wild roses. There might have been a fearful row about what's just happened. When I went to telephone I had my Christmas umbrella with the rose-quartz handle and I left it in the telephone box; the girl in the tobacco shop found it there, and as she knows me she brought it here and gave it to the porter who brought it upstairs. Thank goodness it occurred to me at once to say that I went into the tobacco shop to buy stamps and I must have left it in the shop. No one noticed anything.

May 31st. They wanted me to go and stay with Hella for the month when Mother and Dora are away. It would be awfully nice, but I'm not going to, for I want to stay with Father. What would he do all alone at meal times, and whom would he have to talk to in the evenings? Father was really quite touched when I said this and he stroked my hair as he can and no one else, not even Mother. So I'm going to stay at home whatever happens. Flowers are very cheap now, so I shall put different flowers on the table every day, I shall go to the Market every day to buy a little posy, so that they can always be fresh. It would be stupid for me to go to the Brs., why should I, Resi has been with us for such a long time, she knows how to do everything even if Mother is not there and everything else I can arrange. Father won't want for anything.

June 1st. We've had such an experience to-day! It's awful; it's quite true then that one takes off every stitch when one is madly fond of anyone. I never really believed it, and I'm sure Dora did not, although Mad. hinted it to her; but it's true. We've seen it with our own eyes. I was just sitting and reading Storm's The Rider of the Grey Horse and Dora was arranging some writing paper to take to Franzensbad when Resi came and said: Fraulein Dora, please come here a moment, I want you to look at something! From the tone of her voice I saw there was something up so I went too. At first Resi would not say what it was but Dora was generous and said: "It's all right, you can say everything before her." Then we went into Resi's room and from behind the curtain peeped into the mezzanin. A

68

young married couple live there!!! At least Resi says people say they are not really married, but simply live together!!!! And what we saw was awful. She was absolutely naked lying in bed without any of the clothes on, and he was kneeling by the bedside quite n— too, and he kissed her all over, everywhere!!! Dora said afterwards it made her feel quite sick. And then he stood up—no, I can't write it, it's too awful, I shall never forget it. So that's the way of it, it's simply frightful. I could never have believed it. Dora went as white as a sheet and trembled so that Resi was terribly frightened. I nearly cried with horror, and yet I could not help laughing too. I was really afraid he would stifle her because he's so big and she's so small. And Resi says he is certainly much too big for her, and that he nearly tears her. I don't know why he should tear her but certainly he might have crushed her. Dora was so terrified she had to sit down and Resi hurried to get her a glass of water, because she believed she was going to faint. I had not imagined it was anything like that, and Dora certainly had not either. Or she would never have trembled so. Still I really don't see why she should tremble like that. There is no reason to be frightened, one simply need not marry, and then one need never strip off every stitch, and oh dear, poor Mademoiselle who is so small and the lieutenant is very tall. But just think if anyone is as fat as Herr Richter or our landlord. Of course Herr Richter is at least 50, but last January the landlord had another little girl, so something must have happened. No, I'm sure it's best not to marry, for it is really too awful. We did not look any more for then came the worst, suddenly Dora began to be actually sick, so that she could hardly get back to our room. If she had not been able to, everything would have come out. Mother sent for the doctor directly and he said that Dora was very much overworked; that it was a good thing she was going away from Vienna in a few days. No girl ought to study, it does not pay. Then he said to me: "You don't look up to much either. What are you so hollow-eyed for?" "I'm so frightened about Dora," I said. "Fiddlededee," said the doctor, "that does not give anyone black rings round the eyes." So it must be true that one gets to look ill when one always has to think about such things. But how can one help it, and Hella says: It's awfully interesting to have black rings under the eyes and men like it.

We were going to make an excursion to-morrow to Kahlenberg and Hermannskogel, but probably it won't come off. Its 11 already and I'm fearfully tired from writing so much; I must go to bed. I do hope I Shall be able to sleep, but — — — —

June 3rd. Father took Hella and me to Kahlenberg; we enjoyed ourselves tremendously. After dinner, when Father was

69

reading the paper in the hotel, we went to pick flowers, and I told Hella all about what we'd seen on Friday. She was simply speechless, all the more since she had never heard what Mad. told us about taking off everything. She won't marry either, for it's too disagreeable, indeed too horrid.—The doctor said too: This perpetual learning is poisonous for young girls in the years of development. If he only knew what we had seen. Hella is frightfully annoyed that she was not there. She can be jolly glad, I don't want to see it a second time, and I shall never forget it all my life long; what I saw at the front door was nothing to this. Then Hella went on making jokes and said: "I say, just think if it had been Viktor." "Oh, do shut up," I screamed, and Father thought we were quarrelling and called out: "You two seem to be having a dispute in the grand style." If he'd only known what we were talking about!!! Oswald has been home since Friday evening; he did not arrive till half past 10. But he did not come on the excursion with us yesterday, although Father would have liked him to; he said he would find it much too dull to spend the day with two "flappers;" that means that we're not grown up enough for him and is a piece of infernal cheek especially as regards Hella. She says she will simply ignore him in future. Since I am his sister I can't very well do that, but I shan't fetch and carry for him as he would like me to. He's no right to insult even his sister.

Dora has just said to me: It's horrible that one has to endure that (you know what!!! — — — —) when one is married. Resi had told her about those two before, and that only the Jews do it just like that. She said that other people did not strip quite naked and that perhaps it's different in some other ways!! — — — But Mad. implied that it was just that way, only she did not say anything about the crushing; but I suppose that's because of the cruelty of the Jews — — —. I'm afraid every night that I'm going to dream about it, and Dora has dreamed about it already. She says that whenever she closes her eyes she sees it all as if it were actually before her.

June 4th. We understand now what Father meant the other day when he was speaking about Dr. Diller and his wife and said: "But they don't suit one another at all." I thought at the time he only meant that it looks so absurd for so tiny a woman to go about with a big strong man. But that's only a minor thing; the main point is something quite different!!!! Hella and I look at all couples now who go by arm in arm, thinking about them from that point of view, and it amuses us so much as we are going home that we can hardly keep from laughing. But really it's no laughing matter, especially for the woman.

June 5th. This morning Mother took Dora with her to pay a

farewell call at the Richter's. But there was no one at home, that is Frau R. was certainly at home, but said she was not because they are very much offended with Father. In the afternoon Dora and I had a lot of things to get, and we met Viktor, by arrangement of course. Dora cried a lot; they went into the Minorite church while I went for a walk in Kohlmarkt and Herrengasse. He is going to America in the beginning of July, before Dora comes home. He has given her some exquisite notepaper stamped with his regimental arms, specially for her to write to him on, and a locket with his portrait. To-morrow she is going to send him her photo, through me, I shall be awfully glad to take it. Dora has been much nicer to me lately.

June 6th. Mother and Dora left early this morning. Mother has never gone away from us before for long at a time, so I cried a lot and so did she. Dora cried too, but I know on whose account. Father and I are alone now. At dinner he said to me: "My little housewife." It was so lovely. But it's frightfully quiet in the house, for 2 people don't talk so much as 4. It made me feel quite uncomfortable. To-day I talked several things over with Resi. What I think worst of all is that one saw the whole of his behind, it was really disgusting. Dora said the other day she thought it was positively infamous. Resi said they might at least have pulled down the blind so that nobody could see in, that's what respectable people would do. But respectable people simply would not strip, or at least they'd cover themselves respectably with the bedclothes. Then Resi told me some more about the bank clerk and his wife, that is not-wife. She does not know if her parents know about it, and what excuse she makes for not living at home. She is not a Jewess, though he is a Jew. Resi absolutely curled up with laughing because I said: "Ah, that is why he insists that they shall both strip though ordinarily only the wife has to strip." But she herself said a little while ago that only Jews do it that way, and to-day she laughed as if I were talking utter nonsense. Really she does not know exactly herself, and she cloaks it with laughter because she's annoyed, first because she does not know, and then also I'm sure because she really began to talk about the matter. One thing that puzzles me is that I never dream about it. I should like to know whether perhaps Dora never really dreamed of it, though she pretended she did. As for Hella saying she dreamed of it the day before yesterday, I'm sure that was pure invention, for she was not there at all. She says it's a good thing she was not for if she had been she would have burst out laughing. But I fancy if she'd seen what we saw she would have found there was nothing to laugh at.

June 7th. It's frightfully dull after dinner and in the evening before bed time, especially because this year, since the affair at the front door, Dora and I have always had plenty to talk about. I miss it. I wish Hella would come and stay with us for the 4 weeks. But she does not want to. Father had work to do to-day, so I'm quite alone and feel as if I'd like to cry.

June 9th. Yesterday, when I was feeling so melancholy, Resi came to make my bed, and we talked about the married couple opposite, and then she told me awful things about a young married couple where she was once. She left because they always went into the bath together; she says she's certain that something happened there. And then she told me about an old gentleman who made advances to her; but of course she would not have anything to do with him; besides he was married, and anyhow he would never have married a servant for he was a privy councillor. Yesterday Father said: Poor little witch, it's very lonely for you now; but look here, Resi is no fit company for you; when your little tongue wants to wag, come to my room. And I was awfully stupid, I began to cry like anything and said. "Father, please don't be angry, I'll never think and never talk of such things any more." Father did not know at first what I meant, but afterwards it must have struck him, for he was so kind and gentle, and said: "No, no, Gretel, don't corrupt your youth with such matters, and when there's anything that bothers you, ask Mother, but not the servants. A girl of good family must not be too familiar with servants. Promise me." And then, though I'm so big he took me on his knee like a child and petted me because I was crying so. "It's all right, little Mouse, don't worry, you must not get so nervous as Dora. Give me a nice kiss, and then I'll come with you to your room and stay with you till you go to sleep." Of course I stayed awake on purpose as long as I could, till a quarter to 11.

And then I dreamed that Father was lying in Dora's bed so that when I woke up early in the morning I really looked across to see if he had not gone to bed there. But of course I'd only dreamed it.

June 12th. To-morrow there's a great school excursion; I am so glad, a whole day with Frau Doktor M. and without any lessons. We are going up Eisernes Tor. Last year there was no outing, because the Fourth did not want to go to the Anninger, but to the Hochschneeberg, and the Head did not want to go there.

June 13th. We had a lovely outing. Hella and I spent the whole day with Frau Doktor M.; in the afternoon Franke said: "I say, why do you stick to Frau Doktor like that? One can't get a word with you." So then we went for a good walk through the forest with Franke and she told us about a student who is in the Eighth now and who is madly in love with her. For all students are in love with her, so she says. We were not much interested in that, but then she

72

told us that Frau Doktor M. is secretly engaged to a professor in Leipzig or some other town in Germany. Her cousin is Frau Doktor's dressmaker, and she is quite certain of it. Her parents are opposed to it because he is a Jew but they are frantically in love with one another and they intend to marry. And then we asked Franke, since she is a Jewess too whether it was all true what Mali, who was here when Resi was in hospital, had told us about the Jews. And Franke said: "Oh yes, it is true I can confirm it in every point. But it's not so bad about the cruelty, every man is cruel, especially in this matter." No doubt she's right, but it's horrible to think that our lovely and refined Frau Doktor M is going to have a cruel husband. Hella says that if she is satisfied, I don't need to get excited about it. But perhaps she does not know that − − −. When we came out of the wood the Herr Religionsprofessor who is awfully fond of Frau Doktor M. called out: "Frau Doktor, you have lost your two satellites!" And everybody laughed because we'd come back. Father came to fetch Hella and me, and since it was nearly 11 o'clock Hella stayed the night with us. It was awfully nice, but at the same time I was sorry because I could not have any more talk with Father. When we were getting up in the morning we splashed one another and played the fool generally, so that we were nearly late for school. The staff was still in high spirits, including Professor Wilke, about whom we had not bothered ourselves all day; that is he did not come until the afternoon when he came to meet us on our way. We believe he is in love with Frau Doktor M. too, for he went about with her all the time, and it was probably on her account that he came. None of the other professors were there, for they were all taking their classes in the different Gymnasiums.

June 14th. I am so excited. We were going to school to-day at 9 and suddenly we heard a tremendous rattling with a sword; that is Hella heard it, for she always notices that sort of thing before I do, and she said: "Hullo, that's an o— in a frightful hurry," and looked round; "I say, there's Viktor behind us" and he really was, he was saluting us and he said: Fraulein Rita, can you give me a moment; you'll excuse me won't you, Fraulein Hella? He always calls me Rita, and it shows what a nice refined kind of a man he is that he should know my friend's name. Hella said directly: "Don't mention it, Herr Oberleutenant, don't let me be in your way if it's anything important," and she went over to the other side of the street. He looked after her and said: "What a lovely, well-mannered young lady your friend is." Then he came back to the main point He has already had 2 letters from Dora, but not an answer to his letter, because she can't fetch it from the post office, poste restante. Then he implored me to enclose a letter from him in mine to Dora. But since Mother naturally reads my letters, I told him it was not so simple as all that; but I knew of a splendid way out of the difficulty; I would write to Mother and Dora at the same time, so that Dora could get hold of his letter while Mother was not noticing. Viktor was awfully pleased and said: "You're a genius and a first-class little schemer," and kissed my hand. Still, he might have left out the "little." If one's is so little, one can't very well be a schemer. From the other side of the street Hella saw him kiss my hand. She says I did not try to draw it away, but held it out to him like a grand lady and even dropped it at the wrist. She says we girls of good family do that sort of thing by instinct. It may be so, for I certainly did not do it intentionally. In the afternoon I wrote the two letters, just the ordinary one to Mother and a short one to Dora with the enclosure, and took it to the post myself.

June 16th. I've already got so used to being alone with Father that I take it as a matter of course. We often drive in the Prater, or go in the evening to have supper in one of the parks, and of course Hella comes with us. I am frightfully excited to know what Dora will write. I forgot to write in my diary the other day that I asked Viktor if he was really going to New York. He said he had no idea of doing anything of the kind, that had only been a false alarm on the part of the Old Man. That's what he calls his father. I don't think it's very nice of him, a little vulgar, and perhaps that is why Father can't stand him. In fact Father does not like any officers very much, except Hella's father, but then he's fairly old already. I say, Hella mustn't read that, it would put her in an awful wax; but her father really is at least 4 or 5 years older than Father.

June 17th. Frau Doktor M. is ill, but we don't know what's the matter with her. We were all frightfuly dull at school. The head took her classes and we were left to ourselves in the interval. I do hope she has not got appendicitis, that would be awful.

June 18th. She isn't back yet. Frau Doktor Steiner says she has very bad tonsillitis and won't be able to come for at least a week.

June 19th. There was a letter from Dora to-day. I'm furious. Not a word about my sisterly affection, but only: "Many thanks for your trouble." It's really too bad; he is quite different!! I shan't forget this in a hurry. Hella says that she only hinted at it like that to be on the safe side. But it's not true, for she knows perfectly well that Father never reads our letters. She simply takes it as a matter of course. Yesterday was the first time I stayed away from school since I went to the High School. Early in the morning I had such a bad sore throat and a headache, so Father would not let me go. I got better as the day went on, but this morning I was worse again. Most

74

likely I shall have to stay at home for 2 or 3 days. Father wanted to send for the doctor, but it really was not necessary.

June 20th. When Resi was doing our room to day she wanted to begin talking once more about various things, but I said I did not particularly care to hear about such matters, and then she implored me never to tell Mother and Father anything about what she had said to us about the young married couple; she said she would lose her place and she would be awfully sorry to do that.

June 21st. My knees are still trembling; there might have been a frightful row; luckily Father was out. At half past 6, when Hella and I were having a talk, the telephone bell rang. Luckily Resi had gone out too to fetch something so I answered the telephone, and it was Viktor! "I must see you to-morrow morning early or at 1 o'clock; I waited for you in vain at 1 to-day." Of course, for I was still ill, that is still am ill. But well or ill I must go to school to-morrow. If Father had been at home; or even Resi, she might have noticed something. It would have been very disagreeable if I had had to ask her not to give me away. Hella was frightfully cheeky, she took the receiver out of my hand and said: "Please don't do this again, it's frightfully risky for my friend." I was rather annoyed with her, but Hella said he certainly deserved a lecture.

To-morrow we are going to a concert and I shall wear my new white dress. It does look rather nice after all for sisters to be dressed alike. I've taken to wearing snails,[3] Father calls them "cow-pats;" but everyone else says it's exceedingly becoming.

June 22nd. He was awfully charming when he came up to us and said: "Can a repentant sinner be received back into grace?" And he gave each of us a lovely rose. Then he handed me a letter and said: "I don't think we need make any secret before your energetic friend." Really I did not want to forward any more letters but I did not know how to say so without offending him, for Dora's cheek is not his fault, and I did not want to say anything to-day, 1 because of the roses, and 2 because Hella was there. There can't be more than 2 or 3 times more, so I shan't bother. But Dora doesn't deserve it, really. Franke is a vulgar girl. She saw us together the other day, and the next day she asked: Where did you pick up that handsome son of Mars? Hella retorted: "Don't use such common expressions when you are speaking of Rita's cousin." "Oh, a cousin, that's why he kisses her hand I suppose?" Since then we only speak to Franke when we are positively obliged. Not to speak to her at all would be too dangerous, you never can tell; but if we speak only a little, she can't take offence.

---

[3] Flat rolls of hair-plait covering the ears.—Translators' Note.

June 23rd. The school insp. came yesterday, the old one who always comes for Maths. He is so kind and gentle that all the girls can answer everything; we like him better than the one who comes for languages. Verbenowitsch was awfully puffed up because he praised her. Good Lord, I've been praised often enough, but that does not make me conceited. Anyhow he did not call on me yesterday because I'd been absent 4 days. Frau Doktor M. came back to-day. She looks awfully pale and wretched, I don't know why; it's such a pity that she does not let us walk home with her, except last year when there was all that fuss about Fraulein St.'s bead bag. She bows to us all very politely when we salute her, but she won't walk with any of the pupils, though Verbenowitsch is horribly pushing and is always hanging about on the chance.

June 26th. It's really stupid how anxious I am now at Communion lest the host should drop out of my mouth. I was so anxious I was very nearly sick. Hella says there must be some reason for it, but I don't know of any, except that the accident which that girl Lutter in the Third had made me even more anxious that I was before. Hella says I'd better turn Protestant, but nothing would induce me to do that; for after Com. one feels so pure and so much better than one was before. But I'm sorry to say it does not last so long as it ought to.

June 27th. Mother is really ill. Father told me about it. He was awfully nice and said: If only your Mother is spared to us. She is far from well. Then I asked: Father, what is really wrong with Mother? And Father said: "Well, dear, it's a hidden trouble, which has really been going on for a long time and has now suddenly broken out." "Will she have to have an operation?" "We hope we shall be able to avoid that. But it's a terrible thing that Mother should be so ill." Father looked so miserable when he said this that I did my best to console him and said: "But surely the mud baths will make her all right, or why should she take them?" And Father said: "Well, darling, we'll hope for the best." We went on talking for a long time, saying that Mother must take all possible care of herself, and that perhaps in the autumn Aunt Dora would come here to keep house. I asked Father, "Is it true that you don't like Aunt Dora?" Father said: "Not a bit of it, what put that idea into your head?" So I said: "But you do like Mother much better, don't you?" Father laughed and said: "You little goose, of course I do, or I should have married Aunt Dora and not Mother." I should have liked awfully to ask Father a lot more, but I did not dare. I really do miss Dora, especially in the evenings.

July 2nd. I was in a tremendous rage at school to-day. Professor W., the traitor, did not come because he had confession and communion in the Gymnasium, and the matron did not know anything about the subject so there was no one to take his class. Then the Herr Religionsprofessor took it, he had come earlier than usual to write up the reports. But since the Jewish girls were there too, of course there was no religion lesson. But the H. Rel. Prof. had a chat with us. He asked each of us where we were going to spend the summer, and when I said I was going to Rodaun, Weinberger said: I say, only to Rodaun! and several of the other girls chimed in: Only to Rodaun; why that's only a drive on the steam tram. I was frightfully annoyed, for we generally go to Tyrol or Styria; I said so directly, and then Franke said: Last year too, I think, you went somewhere quite close to Vienna, where was it, Hain—, and then she stopped and made as if she had never heard of Hainfeld. Of course that was all put on, but she's very angry because we won't speak to her since that business about the cousin! But now I was to learn what true friendship is. While I was getting still more angry, Hella said: Rita's Mother is now in Franzensbad, the world-famous health resort; she is ill, and Prof. Sch. has to go and see her at least once a week. The Herr Rel. Prof. was awfully nice and said: Rodaun is a lovely place. The air there is very fine and will certainly do your Mother a lot of good. That's the chief thing, isn't it children? I hope that God will spare all your parents for many years. When the Herr Rel. Prof. said that, Lampel, whose Mother died last winter, burst out crying, and I cried too, for I thought of my talk with Father. Weinberger and Franke thought I was crying because I was annoyed because we were only going to Rodaun. In the interval Franke said: After all, there's no harm in going to Rodaun, that's no reason for crying. But Hella said: "Excuse me, the Lainers can go anywhere they please, they are so well off that many people might envy them. Besides, her Mother and her sister are in Franzensbad now, where everything is frightfully expensive, and in Rodaun they have rented a house all for themselves. Rita is crying because she is anxious about her Mother, not because of anything you said." Of course we don't speak a word to Franke now. Mother does not want us to anyhow, she did not like her at all when she met her last year. Mother has a fine instinct in such matters.

July 6th. We broke up to-day. I have nothing but Very Goods, except of course in —— Natural History! That was to be expected. What — — (I can't bring myself to write the name) said was perfectly right. Nearly all the girls who were still there brought Frau Doktor M. and Frau Doktor St. flowers as farewell tokens. This time, Hella and I were allowed to go with Frau Doktor M. to the metropolitan. When we kiss her hand she always blushes, and we love doing it. This summer holidays she is going to — — — Germany, of course; really Hella need not have asked; it's obvious!!!

July 8th. Mother and Dora are coming home today. We are going to meet them at the station. By the way, I'd quite forgotten. The other day Father hid a new 5 crown piece in my table napkin, and when I lifted up my table napkin it fell out, and Father said: In part payment of your outlay on flowers for the table. Father is such a darling, the flowers did not cost anything like 5 crowns, 3 at most, for though they were lovely ones, I only bought fresh ones every other day. Now I shall be able to buy Mother lots of roses, and I shall either take them to the station or put them on her table. On the one hand I'm awfully glad Mother is coming home, but on the other hand I did like being alone with Father for he always talked to me about everything just as he does to Mother; that will come to an end now.

July 10th. Mother and Dora look splendid; I'm especially glad about Mother; for one can see that she is quite well again. If we had not taken the house in Rodaun, we might just as well go to Tyrol, for one can't deny it would be much nicer. Dora looks quite a stranger. It's absurd, for one can't alter in 1 month, still, she really looks quite different; she does her hair differently, parted over the ears. I have had no chance yet to say anything about the "trouble," and she has not alluded to it. In the autumn she will have to have a special exam. for the Sixth because she went away a month before the end of term. Father says that is only pro forma and that she must not take any lesson books to the country. Hella went away yesterday, she and her Mother and Lizzi are going first to Gastein and then to stay with their uncle in Hungary. Life is dull without Hella, much worse than without Dora; without her I was simply bored sometimes in the evening, at bedtime. Dora gives it out that in Franzensbad people treated her as a grown-up lady. I'm sure that's not true for anyone can see that she's a long way from being a grown-up lady yet.

July 11th. I can't think what's happened to Dora. When she goes out she goes alone. She doesn't tell me when she is going or where, and she hasn't said a word about Viktor. But he must know that she is back. To-morrow we are going to Rodaun, by train of course, not by the steam tram. The day after to-morrow, the 13th, Oswald has the viva voce exam for his matriculation. He says that in every class there are at least 1 or several swotters, like Verbenowitsch in ours, he says they spoil the pitch for the others, for, because of the swotters, the professors expect so much more of the others and sit upon them. This may be so in the Gymnasium, but certainly not at the High School. For though Verb. is always sucking up to the staff, they can't stand her; they give her good reports, but none of them really like her. Mother says the 13th is an unlucky day, and it makes her anxious about Oswald. Because of that she went to High Mass yesterday instead of the 9 o'clock Mass as usual. I never thought of praying for Oswald, and anyhow I think he'll get through all right.

July 13th. Thank goodness Oswald has wired he is through, that is he has wired his favourite phrase: Finis with Jubilation. At any rate that did not worry Mother as he did over the written exam., when he made silly jokes all the time. He won't be home until the 17th, for the matriculation dinner is on the 15th. Father is awfully pleased too. It's lovely here; of course we have not really got a whole house to ourselves, as Hella pretended at school, but a flat on the first story; in the mezzanin a young married woman lives, that is to say a newly married couple!! Whenever I hear that phrase it makes me shake with horror and laughter combined. Resi must have thought of it too, for she looked hard at Dora and me when she told us. But they have a baby already, so they are not really a newly married couple any more. The landlord, who lives on the same floor as us, is having a swing put up for me in the garden for it is horrid not to have a swing in the country.

July 16th. At last Dora has said something to me about Viktor, but she spoke very coldly; there must be something up; she might just as well tell me; she really ought to seeing all that I've done. I have not seen him since that last letter of June 27th; that time something must have hap— no that word means something quite different, there must be something up, but I do wonder what. Hella is delighted with Gastein, she writes that the only thing wanting is me. I can quite understand that, for what I want here is her. Before the end of term Ada wrote to ask whether we were not coming to H. this year; she said she had such a frightful lot to tell me, and she wants my advice. I shall be very glad to advise her, but I don't know what it is about.

July 18th. Something splendid, we are − − − But no, I must write it all out in proper order. Oswald came home yesterday, he is in great form and said jokingly to Dora that she is so pretty he thinks he would fall in love with her if she were not his sister. Just before it was time to go to supper, Mother called us in, and I was rather annoyed when I saw that it was only a quarter to 8. Then Father came in with a paper in his hand as he often does when he comes back from the office, and said: "Dear Oswald and you two girls, I wanted to give you and especially Oswald a little treat because of the matriculation." Aha, I thought, the great prize after all! Then Father opened the paper and said: "You have often wondered as children why we have no title of nobility like the other

Lainers. My grandfather dropped it, but I have got it back again for you Oswald, and also for you two girls. Henceforward we shall call ourselves Lanier von Lainsheim like Aunt Anna and your uncles." Oswald was simply speechless and I was the first to pull myself together and give Father a great hug. But first of all he said: "Do credit to the name." Oswald went on clearing his throat for a frightfully long time, and then he said: Thank you, Father, I shall always hold the name in trust, and then they kissed one another. We were on our best behaviour all through the evening, although Mother had ordered roast chicken and Father had provided a bottle of champagne. I am frightfully happy; it's so splendid and noble. Think of what the girls will say, and the staff! I'm frantically delighted. To-morrow I must write and tell Hella all about it.

July 19th. I've managed it beautifully. I did not want to write just: We are now noble, so I put it all in the signature, simply writing Always your loving friend Rita Lainer von Lainsheim. I told Resi about it first thing this morning, but Father scolded me about that at dinner time and said it was quite unnecessary; it seems the nobility has gone to your head. Nothing of the sort, but it's natural that I should be frightfully glad and Dora too has covered a whole sheet of paper writing her new name. Father says it does not really make us any different from what we were before, but that is not true, for if it were he would not have bothered to revive the title. He says it will make it easier for Oswald to get on, but I'm sure there's more in it than that. Resi told the landlord about it and in the afternoon he and his wife called to congratulate us.

July 20th. Oswald says he won't stay here, it's much too dull, he is going for a walking tour through the Alps, to Grossglockner, and then to the Karawanken. He will talk of Father as the "Old Man," and I do think it is so vulgar. Dora says it is absolutely flippant.

July 24th. Hella's answer came to-day; she congratulates me most heartily, and then goes on to write that at first she was struck dumb and thought I'd gone crazy or was trying to take her in. But her mother had already heard of it from her father for it had been published in the Official Gazette. Now we are both noble, and that is awfully nice. For I have often been annoyed that she was noble when I was not.

July 25th. Oswald left to-day. Father gave him 300 crowns for his walking tour, because of the matriculation. I said: "In that case I shall matriculate as soon as I can" and Oswald said: "For that one wants rather more brains in one's head than you girls have." What cheek, Frau Doktor M. passed the Gymnasium matriculation and Frau Doktor Steiner passed it too as an extra. Dora said quietly:

Maybe I shall show you that your sister can matriculate too; anyhow you have always said yourself that the chief thing you need to get through the matriculation is cheek. Then I had a splendid idea and said: "But we girls have not got cheek, we study when we have to pass an examination!" Mother wanted us to make it up with him, but we would not. In the evening Dora said to me: Oswald is frantically arrogant, though he has had such a lot of Satisfactories and has only just scraped through his exam. By the way here's another sample of Oswald's stupidity; directly after the wire: "Finis with Jubilation" came another which ought to have arrived first, for it had been handed in 4 hours earlier, with nothing but the word "Through" [Durch]. Mother was frightfully upset by it for she was afraid it really meant failed [durchgefallen], and that the other telegram had been only an idiotic joke. Dora and I would never condescend to such horseplay. Father always says Oswald will sow all his wild oats at the university, but he said to-day that he was not going to the university, but would study mining, and then perhaps law.

July 29th. It's sickeningly dull here, I simply don't know what to do; I really can't read and swing the whole day long, and Dora has become as dull as she used to be; that is, even duller, for not only does she not quarrel, but she won't talk, that is she won't talk about certain things. She is perfectly crazy about the baby of the young couple in the mezzanin; he's 10 months old, and I can't see what she sees to please her in such a little pig; she's always carrying him about and yesterday he made her all wet, I wished her joy of it. It made her pretty sick, and I hope it will cure her infatuation.

Thank goodness to-morrow is my birthday, that will be a bit of a change. To-morrow we are going to the Parapluie Berg, but I hope we shan't want our umbrellas. Father is coming back at 1 so that we can get away at 2 or half past. Hella has sent me to-day a lock-up box for letters, etc.!!! of course filled with sweets and a tremendously long letter to tell me how she is getting on in Gastein. But they are only going to stay a month because it is frantically expensive, a roll 5 krenzer and a bottle of beer 1 crown. And the rolls are so small that one simply has to eat 3 for breakfast and for afternoon tea. But it's awfully smart in the hotel, several grooms; then there are masses of Americans and English and even a consul's family from Sydney in Australia.—I spend most of the day playing with two dachshund puppies. They are called Max and Moritz, though of course one of them is a bitch. That is really a word which one ought not to write, for it means something, at least in its other meaning.

THIRD YEAR, AGE THIRTEEN TO FOURTEEN

THIRD YEAR

July 31st. Yesterday was my birthday, the thirteenth. Mother gave me a clock with a luminous dial which I wanted for my night-table. Of course that is chiefly of use during the long winter nights; embroidered collars; from Father, A Bad Boy's Diary, which one of the nurses lent Hella when she was in hospital; it's such a delightfully funny book, but Father says it's stupid because no boy could have written all that, a new racquet with a leather case, an awfully fine one, a Sirk, and tennis balls from Dora. Correspondence cards, blue-grey with silver edge. Grandfather and Grandmother sent a basket of cherries, red ones, and a basket of currants and strawberries; the strawberries are only for me for my birthday. Aunt Dora sent three neckties from Berlin for winter blouses. In the afternoon we went to the Par.-Berg. It would have been awfully jolly if only Mother could have gone too or if Hella had been there.

August 1st. I got a letter from Ada to-day. She sends me many happy returns, for she thinks it is on the 1st of August, and then comes the chief thing. She is frightfully unhappy. She writes that she wants to escape from the cramping environment of her family, she simply can't endure the stifling atmosphere of home. She has been to St. P. to see the actor for whom she has such an admiration, he heard her recite something and said she had real dramatic talent; he would be willing to train her for the stage, but only with her parents' consent. But of course they will never give it. She writes that this has made her so nervous she feels like crying or raving all day long, in fact she can't stand so dismal a life any longer. I am her last hope. She would like me to come to stay with them, or still better if she could come and stay with us for two or 3 weeks, then she would tell Mother about everything, and perhaps it might be possible to arrange for her to live with us in Vienna for a year; in the autumn Herr G., the actor, is coming to the Raimund Theatre and she could begin her training there. At the end of her letter she says that it rests with my discretion and my tact to make her the happiest creature in the world! I don't really know what I shall be able to do. Still, I've made a beginning; I said I found it so frightfully dull—if only Hella were here, or at least Ada, or even Marina. Then Mother said: But Marina is away in the country, in Carinthia, and it's not

82

likely that Ada will be able to come. Father, too, is awfully sorry that I find it so dull, and so at supper he said: Would you really like Ada to come here? Certainly her age makes her a better companion for you than Dora. You seemed to get on better together last year. And then he said to Mother: Do you think it would bother you, Berta, to have Ada here? and Mother said, "Not a bit; if Gretel would like it; it's really her turn now, Dora came with me to Franzensbad, Oswald is having his walking tour, and only our little pet has not had anything for herself; would you like it Gretel?" "Oh yes, Mother, I should like it awfully, I'll write directly; it's no fun to me to carry about that little brat the way Dora does, and jolly as the Bad Boy's Diary is I can't read it all day." So I am writing to Ada directly, just as if I had thought of it and wanted her to come. I shall be so frightfully happy if it all comes off and if Ada really becomes a great actress, like Wolter whom Mother is always talking of, then I shall have done something towards helping Vienna to have a great actress and towards making Ada the happiest creature in the world instead of the unhappiest.

August 2nd. In my letter I did not say anything to Ada about our having been ennobled, or as Dora says re-ennobled, since the family has been noble for generations; she will find out about it soon enough when she comes here. Mother keeps on saying: Don't put on such airs, especially about a thing which we have not done anything particular to deserve. But that's not quite fair, for unless Father had done such splendid service in connection with the laws or the constitution or something two years ago, sometimes sitting up writing all night, perhaps he would never have been re-ennobled. Besides, I really can't see why Father and Mother should have made such a secret about it last winter. They might just as well have let us know. But I suppose Father wanted to give us a real surprise. And he did too; Dora's face and the way Oswald cleared his throat!! As far as I can make out no one seems to have noticed what sort of a face I was making.

August 3rd. I've found out now why Dora is so different, that is why she is again just as she was some time ago, before last winter. During the 4 weeks in Fr. she has found a real friend in Mother! To-day I turned the conversation to Viktor, and all she said at first was: Oh, I don't correspond with him any more. And when I asked: "Have you had a quarrel, and whose fault was it?" she said: "Oh, no, I just bade him farewell." "What do you mean, bade him farewell; but he's not really going to America, is he?" And then she said: "My dear Rita, we had better clear this matter up; I parted from him upon the well-justified wish of our dear Mother." I must say that though I'm awfully, awfully fond of Mother, I really can't imagine having her as a friend. How can one have a true friendship with one's own mother? Dora really can't have the least idea what a true friendship means. There are some things it's impossible for a girl to speak about to her mother, I could not possibly ask her: Do you know what, something has happened, really means? Besides, I'm not quite sure if she does know, for when she was 13 or 15 or 16, people may have used quite different expressions, and the modern phrases very likely did not then mean what they mean now. And what sort of a friendship is it when Mother says to Dora: You must not go out now, the storm may break at any moment, and just the other evening: Dora you must take your shawl with you. Friendship between mother and daughter is just as impossible as friendship between father and son. For between friends there can be no orders and forbiddings, and what's even more important is that one really can't talk about all the things that one would like to talk of. All I said last night was: "Of course Mother has forbidden you to talk to me about certain things; do you call that a friendship?" Then she said very gently: "No, Rita, Mother has not forbidden me, but I recognise now that it was thoughtless of me to talk to you about those things; one learns the seriousness of life quite soon enough." I burst out laughing and said: "Is that what you call the seriousness of life? Have you really forgotten how screamingly funny we found it all? It seemed to me that your memory has been affected by the mud baths." She did not answer that. I do hope Ada will come. For I need her now just as much as she needs me.

August 4th. Glory be to God, Ada's coming, but not directly because they begin their family washing on the 5th and no one can be spared to come over with her till the 8th. I am so glad, the only thing I'm sorry about is that she will sleep in the dressing-room and not Dora. But Mother says that Dora and I must stay together and that Ada can leave the door into the dining-room open so that she won't feel lonely.

August 7th. The days are so frightfully long. Dora is as mild and gentle as a nun, but she talks to me just as little as a nun, and she's eternally with Mother. The two dachshunds have been sold to some one in Neulengbach and so it is so horribly dull. Thank goodness Ada is coming to-morrow. Father and I are going to meet her at the station at 6.

August 8th. Only time for a word or two. Ada is more than a head taller than I am; Father said: "Hullo you longshanks, how you have shot up. I suppose I must treat you as a grown-up young lady now? And Ada said: Please, Herr Oberlandesgerichtsrat; please treat me just as you used to; I am so happy to have come to stay with you." And her mother said: "Yes, unfortunately she is happy anywhere but at home; that is the way with young people to-day." Father helped Ada out and said: "Frau Haslinger, the sap of life was rising in us once, but it's so long ago that we have forgotten." And then Frau Dr. H. heaved a tremendous sigh as if she were suffocating, and Ada took me by the arm and said under her breath: "Can you imagine what my life is like now? Her mother is staying the night here, and she spent the whole evening lamenting about everything under the sun" (that's what Ada told me just before we went to bed); but I did not pay much attention to what Frau H. was doing, for I'm positively burning with curiosity as to what Ada is going to talk to me about. To-morrow morning, directly after breakfast!

August 12th. For 3 days I've had no time to write, Ada and I have had such a lot to say to one another. She can't and won't live any longer without art, she would rather die than give up her plans. She still has to spend a year at a continuation school and must then either take the French course for the state examination or else the needlecraft course. But she wants to do all this in Vienna, so that in her spare time she can study for the stage under Herr G. She says she is not in love with him any longer, that he is only a means to an end. She would sacrifice anything to reach her goal. At first I did not understand what she meant by anything, but she explained to me. She has read Bartsch's novel Elisabeth Kott, the book Mother has too, and a lot of other novels about artistic life, and they all say the same thing, that a woman cannot become a true artist until she has experienced a great love. There may be something in it. For certainly a great love does make one different; I saw that clearly in Dora; when she was madly in love with Viktor, and the way she's relapsed now!! She is learning Latin again, to make up for lost time! Ada does not speak to her about her plans because Dora lacks true insight! Only to-day she mentioned before Dora that whatever happened she wanted to come to Vienna in the autumn so that she could often go to the theatre. And Dora said: You are making a mistake, even people who live in Vienna don't go to the theatre often; for first of all one has very little time to spare, and secondly one often can't get a seat; people who live in the country often fancy that everything is much nicer in Vienna than it really is.

August 14th. Just a word, quickly. To-day when Ada was having a bath Mother said to us two: "Girls, I've something to tell you; I don't want you to get a fright in the night. Ada's mother told me that Ada is very nervous, and often walks in her sleep." "I say," said I, "that's frightfully interesting, she must be moonstruck; I suppose it always happens when the moon is full." Then Mother said: "Tell me, Gretel, how do you know about all these things? Has Ada talked to you about them?" "No," said I, "but the Frankes had a maid who walked in her sleep and Berta Franke told Hella and me about it." It has just struck me that Mother said: how do you know about all these things? So it must have something to do with that. I wonder whether I dare ask Ada, or whether she would be offended. I'm frightfully curious to see whether she will walk in her sleep while she is staying here.

August 15th. Hella's answer came to-day to what I had written her about the friendship between Mother and Dora. Of course she does not believe either that that is why Dora bade farewell to Viktor, for it is no reason at all. Lizzi has never had any particular friendship with her mother, and Hella could never dream of anything of the sort; she thinks I'm perfectly right, one may be awfully fond of one's parents, but there simply can't be any question of a friendship. She would not stand it if I were so changeable in my friendships. She thinks Dora can never have had a true friendship, and that is why she has taken up with Mother now. The Bruckners are coming back on the 19th because everything is so frightfully expensive in Gastein. After that most likely they will go to stay with their uncle in Hungary, or else to Fieberbrunn in Tyrol. For Hella's name day I have sent her A Bad Boy's Diary because she wanted to read it again. Now we have both got it, and can write to one another which are the best bits so that we can read them at the same time.

August 20th. Last night Ada really did walk in her sleep, probably we should never have noticed it, but she began to recite Joan of Arc's speech from The Maid of Orleans, and Dora recognised it at once and said: "I say, Rita, Ada really is walking in her sleep." We did not stir, and she went into the dining-room, but the dining-room door was locked and the key taken away, for it opens directly into the passage, and then she knocked up against Mother's sofa and that woke her up. It was horrible. And then she lost her way and came into our room instead of going into her own; but she was already awake and begged our pardon and said she'd been looking for the W. Then she went back to her own room. Dora said we had better pretend that we had not noticed it, for otherwise we should upset Ada. Not a bit of it, after breakfast she said: "I suppose I gave you an awful fright last night; don't be vexed with me, I often get up and walk about at night, I simply can't stay in bed. Mother says I always recite when I am walking like that; do I? Did I say anything?" "Yes," I said, "you recited Joan of Arc's speech." "Did I really," said she, "that is because they won't let me go on the stage; I'm certain I shall go off my head; if I do, you will know the real reason at any rate." This sleep-walking is certainly very interesting, but it makes me feel a little creepy towards Ada, and it's perfectly true what Dora has always said: One never knows what Ada is really looking at. It would be awful if she were really to go off her head. I've just remembered that her mother was once in an asylum. I do hope she won't go mad while she is staying here.

August 21st. Mother heard it too the night before last. She is so glad that she had warned us, and Dora says that if she had not known it beforehand she would probably have had an attack of palpitation. Father said: "Ada is thoroughly histerical, she has inherited it from her mother." In the autumn Lizzi is going to England to finish her education and will stay there a whole year. Fond as I am of Ada and sorry as I am for her, she makes me feel uneasy now, and I'm really glad that she's going home again on Tuesday. She told me something terrible to-day: Alexander, he is the actor, has venereal disease, because he was once an officer in the army; she says that all officers have venereal disease, as a matter of course. At first I did not want to show that I did not understand exactly what she meant, but then I asked her and Ada told me that what was really amiss was that that part of the body either gets continually smaller and smaller and is quite eaten away, or else gets continually larger because it is so frightfully swollen; the last kind is much better than the other, for then an operation can help; a retired colonel who lives in H. was operated upon in Vienna for this; but it did not cure him. There is only one real cure for a man with a venereal disease, that a young girl should give herself to a man suffering from it! (Mad. often said that too), then she gets the disease and he is cured. That made Ada understand that she did not really love A., but only wanted him to train her; for she could never have done that for him, and she did not know how she could propose that to him even if she had been willing to. Besides, it is generally the man concerned who asks it of the girl. And when I said: "But just imagine, what would you do if you got a baby that way," and she said: "That does not come into the question, for when a man has venereal disease it is impossible to have a child by him. But after all, only a woman who has had a baby can become a true artist." Franke, who has a cousin on the stage said something of the same sort to Hella and me; but we thought, Franke's cousin is only in the Wiener Theatre, and that might be true there; but it may be quite different in the Burg Theatre and in the Opera and even in the People's Theatre. I told Ada about this, and she said: Oh, well, I'm only a girl from the provinces, but I have known for ages that every actress has a child.

23rd. Ada really is a born artist, to-day she read us a passage from a splendid novel, but oh, how wonderfully, even Dora said: "Ada, you are really phenomenal!" Then she flung the book away and wept and sobbed frightfully and said: "My parents are sinning against their own flesh and blood; but they will rue it. Do you remember what the old gypsy woman foretold of me last year: 'A great but short career after many difficult struggles; and my line of life is broken!' That will all happen as predicted, and my mother can recite that lovely poem of Freiligrath's or Anastasius Grun's, or whosoever it is 'Love as long as thou canst, love as long as thou mayst. The hour draws on, the hour draws on, when thou shalt stand beside the grave and make thy moan.'" Then Ada recited the whole poem, and when I went to bed I kept on thinking of it and could not go to sleep.

August 24th. To-day I ventured to ask Ada about the sleep-walking, and she said that it was really so, when she walked in her sleep it was always at that time and when the moon is full. The first time, it was last year, she did it on purpose in order to frighten her mother, when her mother had first told her she would not be allowed to go on the stage. It does not seem to me a very clever idea, or that she is likely to gain anything by it. The day after to-morrow someone is coming to fetch her home, and for that reason she was crying all the morning.

August 25th. Hella was here to-day with her mother and Lizzi. Hella had a splendid time in Gastein. She wanted to have a private talk with me, to tell me something important. That made it rather inconvenient that Ada was still there. Hella never gets on with Ada, and she says too that one never really knows what she is looking at, she always looks right through one. We could not get a single minute alone together for a talk. I do hope Hella will be able to come over once more before she goes to Hungary. Last week they went to Fieberbrunn in Tyrol because an old friend of her mother's from Berlin is staying there.

August 26th. Ada went home to-day, her father came to fetch her. He says she has a screw loose, because she wants to go on the stage.

August 28th. Hella came over to-day; she was alone and I met her at the steam tram. At first she did not want to tell me what the important thing was because it was not flattering to me, but at last she got it out. The Warths were in Gastein, and since Hella knows Lisel because they used to go to gym. together, they had a talk, and that cheeky Robert said: Is your friend still such a baby as she was

88

that time in er . . . er . . ., and then he pretended he could not remember where it was; and he spoke of that time as if it had been 10 years ago. But the most impudent thing of all was this; he said that I had not wanted to call him Bob, because that always made me think of a certain part of the body; I never said anything of the kind, but only that I thought Bob silly and vulgar, and then he said (it was before we got intimate): "Indeed, Fraulein Grete, I really prefer that you should use my full name." I remember it as well as if it had happened this morning, and I know exactly where he said it, on the way to the Red Cross. Hella took him up sharply: That may be all quite true, we have never discussed such trifles, and, at that time we were "all, every one of us, still nothing but children." Of course she meant to include ——. I won't even write his name. Another thing that made me frightfully angry is that he said: I dare say your friend is more like you now, but at that time she was still quite undeveloped. Hella answered him curtly: "That's not the sort of phrase that it's seemly to use to a young lady," and she would not speak to him any more. I never heard of such a thing, what business is it of his whether I am developed or not! Hella thinks that I was not quite particular enough in my choice of companions. She says that Bob is still nothing but a Bub [young cub]. That suits him perfectly, Bob—Bub; now we shall never call him anything but Bub; that is if we ever speak of him at all. When we don't like some one we shall call him simply Bob, or better still B., for we really find it disagreeable to say Bob.

August 31st. The holidays are so dull this year, Hella has gone to Hungary, and I hardly ever talk to Dora, at least about anything interesting. Ada's letters are full of nothing but my promises about Vienna. It's really too absurd, I never promised anything, I merely said I would speak to Mother about it when I had a chance. I have done so already, but Mother said: There can be no question of anything of the kind.

September 1st. Hullo, Hurrah! To-morrow Hella's father is going to take me to K— M—in Hungary to stay with Hella. I am so awfully delighted. Hella is an angel. When she was ill last Christmas her father said: She can ask for anything she likes. But she did not think of anything in particular, and had her Christmas wishes anyhow, so she saved up this wish. And after she had been here she wrote to her father in Cracow, where he is at manoeuvres, saying that if he would like to grant her her chief wish, then, when he came back to Vienna, he was to take me with him to K— M—; this was really the greatest wish she had ever had in her life! So Colonel Bruckner called at Father's office to-day and showed him Hella's letter. To-morrow at 3 I must be at the State Railway terminus.

Unfortunately that's a horrid railway. The Western Railway is much nicer, and I like the Southern Railway better still.

September 2nd. I am awfully excited; I'm going to Vienna alone and I have to change at Liesing, I do hope I shall get into the right train. I got a letter from Hella first thing this morning, in which she wrote: "Perhaps we shall be together again in a few days." That's all she said about that; I suppose she did not know yet whether I was really coming. Mother will have to send my white blouses after me, because all but one are dirty. I'm going to wear my coat and skirt and the pink blouse. I'm going to take twenty pages for my diary, that will be enough; for I'm going to write whatever happens, in the mornings I expect, because in the holidays I'm sure Hella will never get up before 9; on Sundays in Vienna she would always like to lie in bed late, but her father won't let her.

But whatever happens I won't learn to ride, for it must be awful to tumble off before a strange man. It was different for Hella, for Jeno, Lajos, and Erno are her cousins, and one of them always rode close beside her with his arm round her waist: but that would not quite do in my case.

September 6th. Oh it is so glorious here. I like Jeno best, he goes about with me everywhere and shows me everything; Hella is fondest of Lajos and of Erno next. But Erno has still a great deal to learn, for he was nearly flunked in his exam. Next year Lajos will be a lieutenant, and this autumn Jeno is going to the military academy, Erno has a slight limp, nothing bad, but he can't go into the army; he is going to be a civil engineer, not here, he is to go to America some day.

I have time to write to-day, for all 4 of them have gone to S. on their cycles and I have never learned.

It was lovely on the journey! It's so splendid to travel with an officer, and still more when he is a colonel. All the stationmasters saluted him and the guards could not do enough to show their respect. Of course everyone thought I was his daughter, for he has always said "Du" to me since I was quite a little girl. But to Ada Father always says "Sie." We left the train at Forgacs or Farkas, or whatever it is called, and Hella's father hired a carriage and it took us 2 hours to drive to K— M—. He was awfully jolly. We had our supper in F., though it was only half past 6. It was a joke to see all the waiters tumbling over each other to serve him. It s just the same with Father, except that the stationmasters don't all salute. Father looks frightfully distinguished too, but he is not in uniform.

Here is something awfully interesting: Herr von Kraics came yesterday from Radufalva, his best friend left him the Radufalva estate out of gratitude, because 8 years ago he gave up his fiancee with whom the friend was in love. It's true, Colonel Bruckner says that K. is a wretched milksop; but I don't think so at all; he has such fiery eyes, and looks a real Hungarian nobleman. Hella says that he used to run himself frantically into debt, because every six months he had an intimacy with some new woman; and all the presents he gave reduced him almost to beggary. Still, it's difficult to believe that, for however fond a woman may be of flowers and sweets, one does not quite see why that should reduce anyone to beggary. Before we went to sleep last night Hella told me that Lajos had already been "infected" more or less; she says there is not an officer who has not got venereal disease and that is really what makes them so frightfully interesting. Then I told her what Ada had told me about the actor in St. P. But Hella said: I doubt if that's all true; of course it is more likely since he was an actor, and especially since he was in the army at one time, but generally speaking civilians are wonderfully healthy!!! And she could not stand that in her husband. Every officer has lived frantically; that's a polite phrase for having had venereal disease, and she would never marry a man who had not lived. Most girls, especially when they get a little older; want the very opposite! and then it suddenly occurred to me that that was probably the real reason why Dora bade farewell to Lieutenant R., and not the friendship with Mother; it is really awfully funny, and no one would have thought it of her. Hella's father thinks me charming; he is really awfully nice. Hella's uncle hardly ever says anything, and when he does speak he is difficult to understand; Hella's father says that his sister-in-law wears the breeches. That would never do for me; the man must be the master. "But not too much so" says Hella. She always gets cross when her father says that about wearing breeches. I got an awful start yesterday; we went out on the veranda because we heard the boys talking, and found Hella's great uncle lying there on an invalid couch. She told me about him once, that he's quite off his head, not really paralysed but only pretends to be. Hella is terribly afraid of him, because long ago, when she was only 9 or 10 years old, he wanted to give her a thrashing. But her uncle came in, and then he let her go. She says he was only humbugging, but she is awfully afraid of him all the same. He keeps his room, and he has a male attendant, because no nurse can manage him. He ought really to be in an asylum but there is no high class asylum in Hungary.

September 9th. There was a frightful rumpus this morning; the great uncle, the people here call him "kutya mog" or however they spell it, and it means mad dog, well, the great uncle spied in on us. He can walk with a stick, our room is on the ground floor, and he came and planted himself in front of the window when Hella was washing and I was just getting out of bed. Then Hella's father came and made a tremendous row and the uncle swore horribly in Hungarian. Before dinner we overheard Hella's father say to Aunt Olga: "They would be dainty morsels for that old swine, those innocent children." We did laugh so, we and innocent children!!! What our fathers really think of us; we innocent!!! At dinner we did not dare look at one another or we should have exploded. Afterwards Hella said to me: "I say, do you know that we have the same name day?" And when I said: "What do you mean, it seems to me you must have gone dotty this morning," she laughed like anything and said: "Don't you see, December 27th, Holy Innocents' Day!" Oh it did tickle me. She knew that date although she's a Protestant because December 27th is Marina's birthday, and in our letters we used to speak of that deceitful cat as "The Innocent."

The three boys and I have begun to use "Du" to one another, at supper yesterday Hella's father said to Erno: "You seem frightfully ceremonious still, can't you make up your minds to drop the 'Sie?'" So we clinked glasses, and afterwards when Jeno and I were standing at the window admiring the moon, he said: "You Margot, that was not a real pledge of good-fellowship, we must kiss one another for that; hurry up, before anyone comes," and before I could say No he had given me a kiss. After all it was all right as it was Jeno, but it would not have done with Lajos, for it would have been horrid because of Hella, or Ilonka as they call her here.

Hella has just told me that they saw us kissing one another, and Lajos said: "Look Ilonka, they are setting us a good example." We are so awfully happy here. It's such a pity that on the 16th Jeno and Lajos have got to leave for the Academy, where Jeno is to enter and Lajos is in his third year: Erno, the least interesting of the three, is staying till October. But that is always the way of life, beautiful things pass and the dull ones remain. We go out boating every day, yesterday and to-day by moonlight. The boys make the boat rock so frightfully that we are always terrified that it will upset. And then they say: "You have your fate in your own hands; buy your freedom and you will be as safe as in Abraham's bosom."

September 12th. The great uncle hates us since what happened the other day; whenever he sees us he threatens us with his stick, and though we are not really afraid, because he can't do anything to us, still it's rather creepy. One thinks of all sorts of things, stories and sagas one has read. That is the only thing I don't quite like here. But we are leaving on the 18th. Of course Lajos and Jeno will often come to see the Bruckners; I'm awfully glad. I don't know why, I always fancied that they could only speak Magyar; but that is not so at all, though they always speak it at home when they are alone. Hella told me to-day for the first time that all the flowers on the table by her bed one Sunday in hospital had been sent by Lajos; and she did not wish to tell me at that time because he wished her to keep it a secret. This has made me rather angry, for I see that I have been much franker with her than she has been with me.

September 16th. The boys left to-day, and we stayed up till midnight last night. We had been to N— K—, I don't know how to spell these Hungarian names, and we did not get back till half past 11. It was lovely. But it seems all the sadder to-day, especially as it is raining as well. It's the first time it's rained since I came. Partings are horrid, especially for the ones left behind; the others are going to new scenes anyhow. But for the people left behind everything is hatefully dull and quiet. In the afternoon Hella and I went into Jeno's and Lajos' room, it had not been tidied up yet and was in a frightful mess. Then Hella suddenly began sobbing violently, and she flung herself on Lajos' bed and kissed the pillow. That is how she loves him! I'm sure that is the way Mad. loves the lieutenant, but Dora is simply incapable of such love, and then she can talk of her true and intimate friendship with Mother. Hella says she has always been in love with Lajos, but that her eyes were first opened when she saw Jeno and me going about together and talking to one another. Now she will love Lajos for evermore. Next year they will probably get engaged, she can't be engaged till she is 14 for her parents would not allow it. It is for her sake that he is going into the Hussars because she likes the Hussars best. They all live frightfully hard, and are tremendously smart.

September 21st. Since Saturday we have been back In Vienna, and Father, Mother, and Dora came back from Rodaun on Thursday. Dora really is too funny; since Ada stayed with us and walked in her sleep Dora is afraid she has been infected. She does not seem to know what the word really means! And while I was away she slept with Mother, and Father slept in our room, because she was afraid to sleep alone. Of course no one takes to walking in their sleep simply from sleeping alone, but that was only a pretext; Dora has never been very courageous, in fact she is rather a coward, and she was simply afraid to sleep alone. If Father had been afraid too, I suppose I should have had to come back post-haste, and if I had been afraid to travel alone, and there had been no one to come with me, that would have been a pretty state of affairs. I told them so. Father laughed like anything at my "combinations," and Dora got in a frightful wax. She is just as stupid and conceited as she was before she fell in love. So Hella is right when she says: Love enobles [veredelt]. Erno made a rotten joke about that when he heard Hella

93

say it once. He said: "You've made a slip of the tongue, you meant to say: Love makes fools of people [vereselt]." Of course that's because he's not in love with anyone.

September 22nd. School began again to-day. Frau Doktor M. is perfectly fascinating, she looks splendid and she said the same to both of us. Thank goodness she's the head of our class again. In French we have a new mistress Frau Doktor Dunker, she is perfectly hideous, covered with pimples, a thing I simply can't stand in any one; Hella says we must be careful never to let her handle our books; if she does we might catch them. In Maths and Physics we have another new mistress, she is a Doktor too, and she speaks so fast that none of us can understand her; but she looks frightfully clever, although she is very small. We call her "Nutling" because she has such a tiny little head and such lovely light-brown eyes. Otherwise the staff is the same as last year, and there are a few new girls and some have left, but only ones we did not know intimately. This is Franke's last year at the Lyz., she will be 16 in April and has a splendid figure. Her worst enemy must admit that. Dora is having English lessons from the matron, and she is awfully pleased about it, for she is one of her favourites and it will help her too in her matriculation.

September 25th. Yesterday and the day before Mother was so ill that the doctor had to be sent for at half past 10 at night. Thank goodness she is better now. But on such days I simply can't write a word in my diary; I feel as if I oughtn't to. And the days seem everlasting, for nobody talks much, and it's awful at mealtimes. Mother was up again to-day, lying on the sofa.

September 29th. I've had such an awful toothache since the day before yesterday. Dora says it's only an ache for a gold filling like Frau Doktor M.'s. Of course that's absurd; for first of all, surely I ought to know whether my own tooth hurts or not, and secondly the dentist says that the tooth really is decayed. I have to go every other day and I can't say I enjoy it. At the same time, this year we have such a frightful lot to learn at school. The Nutling is really very nice, if one could only understand better what she says, but she talks at such a rate that in the Fifth, where she teaches too, they call her Waterfall. Nobody has ever given Frau Doktor M. a nickname, not even an endearing one. The only one that could possibly be given to her is Angel, and that could not be a real name, it's quite unmeaning. In the drawing class we are going to draw from still life, and, best of all, animal studies too, I am so delighted.

October 4th. Goodness, to-day when we were coming home from the Imperial Festival, we met Viktor in M. Street, but unfortunately he did not see us. He was in full-dress uniform and was walking with 3 other officers whom neither I nor Hella know. We were frightfully angry because he did not recognise us; Hella thinks it can only be because we were both wearing our big new autumn hats, which shade our faces very much.

October 11th. There was a frightful row in the drawing lesson to-day. Borovsky had written a note to one of her friends: "The little Jewess, F. (that means the Nutling) is newly imported from Scandalavia with her horsehair pate with or without inhabitants." Something of that sort was what she had written and as she was throwing it across to Fellner, Fraulein Scholl turned round at that very moment and seized the note. "Who is F.?", she asked, but no one answered. That made her furious and she put the note in her pocket. At 1 o'clock, when the lesson was over, Borovsky went up to her and asked her for the note. Then she asked once more: "Who is F.?" And Fellner, thinking I suppose that she would help Borovsky out, said: "She forgot to write Frau Doktor Fuchs." Then the row began. I can't write it all down, it would take too long; of course Borovsky will be expelled. She cried like anything and begged and prayed, and said she did not mean it, but Fraulein Scholl says she is going to give the letter to the head.

October 12th. Continuation; the head is laid up with a chill, so Frl. Scholl gave the note to Frau Doktor M.; that was both good and bad. Good because Borovsky will perhaps be able to stay after all, and bad because Frau Doktor M. was frightfully angry. She gave us a fine lecture about True Good Manners, simply splendid. I was so glad that I was not mixed up in the business, for she did give Borovsky and Fellner a rating. It's probably true, then, that her own fiance is a Jew. Its horrible that she above all should be going to have a cruel husband; at least if all that Resi told us is true; and I expect there is some truth in it. We are frightfully curious to know whether the Nutling has heard anything about it and if so what she will do.

October 13th. I don't think the Nutling can have heard anything for she seemed just as usual; but Hella thinks and so do I that she would not show anything even if Frl. Scholl had told her; anyhow it was horridly vulgar; one is not likely to pass it on to the person concerned. Why we think she does not know anything is that neither Borovsky nor Fellner were called up.

October 14th. To-day the needlewoman brought Dora's handkerchiefs with her monogram and the coronet, lovely; I want some like them for Christmas. And for Mother she has embroidered six pillow-cases, these have a coronet too; by degrees we shall have the coronet upon everything. By the way, here is something I'd forgotten to write: In one of the first days of term Father gave each of us one of his new visiting cards with the new title, I was to give mine to Frau Doktor M. and Dora hers to Frau Prof. Kreidl, to have the names properly entered in the class lists. Frau Prof. Kreidl did not say anything, but Frau Doktor M. was awfully sweet. She said: "Well, Lainer, I suppose you are greatly pleased at this rise in rank?" And I said: "Oh yes, I'm awfully delighted, but only inside," then she said: That's right; "Religion, name, and money do not make the man." Was not that charming! I write the v before my name awfully small; but anyone who knows can see it. What a shame that she is not noble! She would be worthy of it!!

October 15th. Oswald has gone to Leoben to-day, he is to study mining, but against Father's will. But Father says that no one must be forced into a profession, for if he is he will always say throughout life that he only became this or that on compulsion. The other evening Dora said that Oswald had only chosen mining in order to get away from home; if he were to study law or agricultural chemistry he could not get away from Vienna, and that is the chief thing to him. Besides, he is a bit of a humbug; for when he came home from Graz after matriculation he said in so many words: "How delightful to have one's legs under one's own table again and to breathe the family atmosphere." Dora promptly said to him: "Hm, you don't seem to care so very much about home, for always when you come home for the holidays the first thing you do is to make plans for getting away." For she is annoyed too that Oswald can travel about wherever he likes. And yet he goes on talking about being "subjected to intolerable supervision"!! What about us? He can stay out until 10 at night and never comes to afternoon tea, and in fact does just what he likes. If I go to supper with Hella and am just ever so little late, there's a fine row. As for the lectures poor Dora had to endure when Viktor was waiting for her, I shall never forget them. Of course she denies it all now, but I was present at some of them so I know; otherwise he would not have called me "the Guardian Angel." She behaves now as if she had forgotten all about that, so I often remind her of it on purpose when we are alone together. The other day she said: "I do beg you, Grete (not Rita), don't speak any more of that matter; I have buried the affair for ever." And when I said: "Buried, what do you mean? A true love can't simply be buried like that," she said: "It was not a true love, and that's all there is to say about it."

October 16th. I had a frantically anxious time in the arithmetic lesson to-day. All of a sudden Hella flushed dark red and I thought to myself: Aha, that's it! And I wrote to her on my black-line paper: Has it begun??? for we had agreed that she would tell me directly, she will be 14 in February and it will certainly begin soon.

Frau Doktor F. said: Lainer, what was that you pushed over to Br.? and she came up to the desk and took the black-line paper. "What does that mean: Has it begun???" Perhaps she really did not know what I meant, but several of the girls who knew about it too laughed, and I was in a terrible fright. But Hella was simply splendid. "Excuse me, Frau Doktor, Rita asked whether the frost had begun yet." "And that's the way you spend your time in the mathematics lesson?" But thank goodness that made things all right. Only in the interval Hella said that really I am inconceivably stupid sometimes. What on earth did I want to write a thing like that for? When it begins, of course she will let me know directly. As a matter of fact it has not begun yet. We have agreed now that it will be better to say "Endt," a sort of portmanteau word of developed [entwickelt] and at last [endlich] . That will really be splendid and Hella says that I happened upon it in a lucid interval. It's really rather cheeky of her, but after all one can forgive anything to one's friend. She absolutely insists that I must never again put her in such a fix in class. Of course it happened because I am always thinking: Now then, this is the day.

November 8th. On Father's and Dora's birthday Mother was so ill that we did not keep it at all. I was in a terrible fright that Mother was seriously ill, or even that − − − − − No, I won't even think it; one simply must not write it down even if one is not superstitious. Aunt Dora came last week to keep house for Mother. We are not going skating, for we are always afraid that Mother might get worse just when we are away. As soon as she is able to get up for long enough Father is going to take her to see a specialist in the diseases of women; so it must be true that Mother's illness comes from that.

November 16th. Oh it's horrible, Mother has to have an operation; I'm so miserable that I can't write.

November 19th. Mother is so good and dear; she wants us to go skating to take our thoughts off the operation. But Dora says too that it would be brutal to go skating when Mother is going to have an operation in a few days. Father said to us yesterday evening: "Pull yourselves together children, set your teeth and don't make things harder for your poor Mother." But I can't help it, I cry whenever I look at Mother.

November 23rd. It is so dismal at home since Mother went away; we had to go to school and we believed she would not leave until the afternoon, but the carriage came in the morning. Dora says that Father had arranged all that because I could not control myself. Well, who could? Dora cries all day; and at school I cried a lot and so did Hella.

November 28th. Thank goodness, it's all safely over, Mother will be home again in a fortnight. I'm so happy and only now can I realise how horribly anxious I have been. We go every day to see Mother at the hospital; I wish I could go alone, but we always go all together, that is either with Father or with Aunt Dora. But I suspect that Dora does go to see Mother quite alone, she gave herself away to-day about the flowers, she behaves as if Mother were only her mother. On Thursday, the first time we saw Mother, we all whispered, and Mother cried, although the operation had made her quite well again. Unfortunately yesterday, Aunt Alma was there when we were, and Father said that seeing so many people at once was too exciting for Mother, and we must go away. Of course he really meant that Aunt Alma and Marina had better go away, but Aunt did not understand or would not. Why on earth did Aunt come? We hardly ever meet since the trouble about Marina and that jackanapes Erwin; only when there is a family party; Oswald says it's not a family gathering but a family dispersal because nearly always some one takes offence.

November 30th. To-day I managed to be alone with Mother. At school I said I had an awfully bad headache and asked if I might go home before the French lesson; I really had. What I told Mother was that Frau Doktor Dunker was ill, so we had no lesson. Really one ought not to tell lies to an invalid, but this was a pious fraud as Hella's mother always calls anything of the sort, and no one will find out, because Frau Doktor Dunker has nothing to do with the Fourth, so Dora won't hear anything about it. Mother said she was awfully pleased to be able to see me alone for once. That absolutely proves that Dora does go alone. Mother was so sweet, and Sister Klara said she was a perfect angel in goodness and patience. Then I burst out crying and Mother had to soothe me. At first, after I got home, I did not want to say anything about it, but when we were putting on our things after dinner to go and see Mother I said en passant as it were: "This is the second time I shall be seeing Mother to-day." And when Dora said: What do you mean? I said quite curtly: "One of our lessons did not come off, and so I took the chance too of being able to see Mother alone." Then she said: Did the porter let you in without any trouble? It surprises me very much that such very young girls, who are almost children still, are allowed to go in alone. Luckily Aunt came in at that moment and said: "Oh well, nobody thinks Gretl quite a child now, and both of you can go alone to the hospital all right." On the way we did not speak to one another.

December 5th. For St. Nicholas day we took Mother a big flower pot, and tied to the stick was a label on which Father had written; "Being ill is punishable as an unpermissible offence in the

98

sense of Section 7 the Mothers' and Housewives' Act." Mother was frightfully amused. The doctor says she is going on nicely, and that she will be able to come home in a few days.

December 6th. It was awful to-day. In the evening when we were leaving the dining-room Father said: "Gretl you have forgotten something." And when I came back he took me by the hand and said: "Why didn't you tell me that you want so much to see Mother alone? You need not make such a secret of it." And then I burst out crying and said: "Yes, I need not keep it secret from you, but I don't like Dora to know all about it. Did she tell you what happened the other day?" But Father does not know anything about my pretended headache, but only that I wanted so much to see Mother alone. He was awfully kind and kissed and petted me, saying: "You are a dear little thing, little witch, I hope you always will be." But I got away as quick as I could, for I felt so ashamed because of my fibbing. If it were not for Dora I'm sure I should never tell any lies.

December 6th. Father is an angel. He and I went to see Mother in the morning, and Aunt and Dora went in the afternoon. And since Father had to go into the Cafe where he had an appointment with a friend, I went on alone to see Mother and he came in afterwards. Mother asked me about my Christmas wishes; but I told her I had only one wish, that she should get well and live for ever. I was awfully glad that Dora was not there, for I could never have got that out before her. Still, she made me tell her my wishes after all, so I said I wanted handerkerchiefs with "monogram and coronet," visiting cards with von, a satchel like that which most of the girls in the higher classes have, and the novel Elizabeth Kott. But I am not to have the novel, for Mother was horrified and said: My darling child, that's not the sort of book for you; who on earth put that into your head; Ada, I suppose? From what I know of your tastes, it really would not suit you at all. So I had to give that up, but I'm certain I should not find the book stupid.

December 11th. Mother came home again to-day; we did not know what time she was coming, but only that it was to be to-day. And because I was so glad that Mother is quite well again, I sang two or three songs, and Mother said: That is a good omen when one is greeted with a song. Then Dora was annoyed because she had not thought of singing. We had decorated the whole house with flowers.

December 15th. I am embroidering a cushion for Mother and Dora is making her a footstool so that she can sit quite comfortably when she is reading. For Father we have bought a new brief bag because his own is so shabby that it makes us quite ashamed; but he always says: "It will do for a good while yet." For a long time I did not know what to get for Aunt Dora, and at length we have decided upon a lace fichu; for she is awfully fond of lace. I am giving Hella a sketch book and a pencil case; she draws beautifully and will perhaps become an artist, for Dora I am getting a vanity bag and for Oswald a cigarette case with a horse's head on it, for he is frightfully taken up with racing and the turf.

December 16th. Owing to Mother's illness I've had simply no time to write anything about the school, although there has been a great deal to write about, for example that Prof. W. is very friendly again, although he no longer gives us lessons, and that most of the girls can't bear the Nutling because she makes such favourites of the Jewish girls. It's quite true that she does, for example Franke, who is never any good, will probably get a Praiseworthy in Maths and Physics; and she lets Weinberger do anything she likes. I always get Excellent both for school work and prep.; so it really does not matter to me, but Berbenowitsch is frightfully put out because she is no longer the favourite as she was with Frau Doktor St. The other day it was quite unpleasant in the Maths lesson. In the answer to a sum there happened to be 1-3, and then the Nutling asked what 1-3 would be as a decimal fraction; so we went on talking about recurring [periodic] decimals and every time she used the word period, some of the girls giggled, but luckily some of them were Jews, and she got perfectly savage and simply screamed at us. In Frau Doktor St's lesson in the First, some of the girls giggled at the same thing and she went on just as if she had not noticed it, but afterwards she always spoke of periodic places, and then one does not think of the real meaning so much. Frau Doktor F. said she should complain to Frau Doktor M. about our unseemly behaviour. But really all the girls had not giggled, for ex. Hella and I simply exchanged glances and understood one another at once. I can't endure that idiotic giggling.

December 20th. Oswald came home to-day; he's fine. It's quite true that he has really had a moustache for a long time, but was not allowed to grow it at the Gymnasium; in boarding schools the barber comes every Saturday, and they have to be shaved. He always says that at the Gymnasium everything manly is simply suppressed. I am so glad I am not a man and need not go to Gymnasium. Anyhow he has a splendid moustache now. Hella did not recognise him at first and drew back in alarm, she only knew him after a moment by his voice. We have reckoned it up, and find that she has not seen him since the Easter before last. At first he called her Fraulein, but her mother said: Don't be silly. It did not seem silly to me, but most polite!!!

December 23rd. Mother is so delighted that Oswald is home again and he really is awfully nice; he is giving her a wonderful flowers-of-iron group representing a mountain scene with a forest, and in the foreground some roe deer as if in a pasture.

December 25th. Only time for a few words. Mother was very well yesterday, and it has not done her any harm to stay up so long. I am so happy. We both got a tie pin with a sapphire and 3 little diamonds, they have been made out of some earrings which Mother never wears now. But the nice thing about it is that they are made from her earrings. The satchel and Stifter's Tales are awfully nice and so are the handkerchiefs with the coronet and everything else. Hella gave me a reticule with my monogram and the coronet as well. Oswald has given Dora and me small paperweights and Father a big one, bronze groups. We really need two writing tables, but there is no room for two. So I am going to arrange the little corner table as my writing table and have all my things there.

December 27th. At the Bruckners yesterday it was really awful. Hella's mother is perfectly right; when anyone looks like that she ought not to pay visits when she knows that other people may be there. Hella told me the day before yesterday how frightfully noticeable it is in her cousin that she is in an i— c—! Her mother was very much put out on her account and she wanted to prevent Emmy's standing up. We were simply disgusted and horrified. But her husband is awfully gentle with her; She is certainly not pretty and especially the puffiness under her eyes is horrid. They say that many women look like that when they are pr. She was wearing a maternity dress, and that gives the whole show away! Hella says that some women look awfully pretty when they are in an i— c—, but that some look hideous. I do hope I shall be one of the first kind, if I ever . . . No, it is really horrible, even if it makes one pretty; when I think of Frau von Baldner and what she looked like last summer, yet Father has always said she is a a perfect beauty. Really no one is pretty in an i— c—. Soon after tea Hella and I went up to her room, and she said it had really been too much for her and that she could not have stood it much longer. And we went on talking about it for such a long time, that it really made both of us nearly ill. On Sunday Emmy and her husband are coming to dine with the Brs., and Hella begged me to ask her to dinner with us, or she would be quite upset. So of course she is coming here and thank goodness that will save her from feeling ill. And then she said that I must not think she wanted to come to us because of Oswald, but only for that other reason. I understand that perfectly well, and she does not need to make any excuses to me.

29th. Hella came to dinner to-day, she was wearing a new dress, a light strawberry colour, and it suited her admirably. In the evening Oswald said: "two or three years more, and Hella will look

101

ripping." It does annoy me so this continual will. Hella's father simply said of me that I was charming,, and not that idiotic: I was going to become charming. I do hate the way people always talk out into the future. However, Oswald paid Hella a great deal of attention. In the afternoon, when Hella and I were talking about him, I wanted to turn the conversation to Lajos, but she flushed up and said he was utterly false, for since October he had only been to see them once, on a Sunday, just when they were going to the theatre. Of course he says he does not care a jot about the visits unless he can see her alone. She can't realise that that shows the greatness of his love. I understand it perfectly. But it is really monstrous that Jeno has asked after me only once, quite casually. And he really might have sent me a card at Christmas. But that's what young men are like. The proverb really applies to them: Out of sight out of mind.

December 30th. Frau Richter called to-day, but only in the morning for a quarter of an hour. Not a word was said about Viktor, though I stayed in the drawing-room on purpose. Dora did not put in an appearance, though I'm sure she was at home. He is extraordinarily like his mother, he has the same lovely straight nose, and the small mouth and well-cut lips; but he is very tall and she is quite small half a head shorter than Mother. We owe them a call, but I don't much think that we shall go.

December 31st. I really have no time, since this is New Year's Eve, but I simply must write. Dora and I went skating this morning, and we met Viktor on the ice; he went frightfully pale, saluted, and spoke to us; Dora wished to pass on, but he detained her and said that she must allow him to have a talk, so he came skating with us since she would not go to a confectioner's with him. She was certainly quite right not to go to a confectioner's. Of course I don't know what they talked about, but in the afternoon Dora cried frightfully, and Viktor never said good-bye to me; it's impossible that he can have forgotten, so either I must have been too far away at the time, or else Dora did not want him to; most likely the latter. I'm frantically sorry for him, for he is passionately in love with her. But she won't come to her senses until it is too late. I don't think she has said a word to Mother either. But all the afternoon she was playing melancholy music, and that shows how much she had felt it.

January 2nd. Yesterday I had no time to write because we had callers, pretty dull for the most part, the Listes and the Trobisches; Julie Tr. is such a stupid creature, and I don't believe she knows the first thing about those matters; Annie is not quite all there, Lotte is the only tolerable one. Still, since we played round games for prizes, it was not as dull as it might have been, and Fritz and Rudl are quite nice boys. In the evening Mother was so tired out that Father said he really must put a stop to all this calling; I can't say I care much myself for that sort of visits, especially since Dora always will talk about books. People always talk about such frightfully dull books whenever they have nothing else to say. School began again to-day, with a German lesson thank goodness. Though I'm not superstitious in general, I must say I do like a good beginning. Besides, first thing in the morning we met two chimneysweeps, and without our having tried to arrange it in any way they passed us on our left. That ought to bring good luck.

January 5th. Most important, Hella since yesterday evening — — — —! She did not come to school yesterday, for the day before she felt frightfully bad, and her mother really began to think she was going to have another attack of appendicitis. Instead of that!!! She looks so ill and interesting, I spent the whole afternoon and evening with her; and at first she did not want to tell me what was the matter. But when I said I should go away if she did not tell me, she said: "All right, but you must not make such idiotic faces, and above all you must not look at me." "Very well," I said, "I won't look, but tell me everything about it." So then she told me that she had felt frantically bad, as if she was being cut in two, much worse than after the appendicitis operation, and then she had frantically high fever and shivered at the same time, all Friday, and yesterday — — — tableau!! And then her mother told her the chief things, though she knew them already. Earlier on Friday the doctor had said: "Don't let us be in a hurry to think about a relapse, there may be other!! causes." And then he whispered to her mother, but Hella caught the word enlighten. Then she knew directly what time of day it was. She acted the innocent to her mother, as if she knew nothing at all, and her mother kissed her and said, now you are not a child any more, now you belong among the grown-ups. How absurd, so I am still a child! After all, on July 30th I shall be 14 too, and at least one month before I shall have it too, so I shan't be a child for more than six months more. Hella and I laughed frightfully, but she is really a little puffed up about it; she won't admit that she is, but I noticed it quite clearly. The only girl I know who did not put on airs when that happened was Ada. Because of the school Hella is awfully shy, and before her father too. But her mother has promised her not to tell him. If only one can trust her!!!

January 7th. Hella came to school to-day in spite of everything. I kept on looking at her, and in the interval she said: "I have told you already that you must not stare at me in that idiotic way, and this is the second time I've had to speak to you about it. One must not make a joke about such things." I was not going to stand that. One must not look at her; very well, in the third lesson I sat turning away from her; then suddenly she hooked one of my feet with hers so that I nearly burst out laughing, and she said: "Do look round, for that way is even stupider." Of course Dunker promptly called us to order, that is, she told Hella to go on reading, but Hella said promptly that she felt very unwell, and that what she had said to me was, she would have to go home at 12. All the girls looked at one another, for they all know what unwell means, and Frau Doktor Dunker said Hella had better leave directly, but she answered in French—that pleases Dunker awfully—that she would rather stay till the end of the lesson. It was simply splendid!

January 12th. We went to the People's Theatre to-day to the matinee of The Fourth Commandment. The parting from the grandmother was lovely; almost everyone was in tears. I managed to keep from crying because Dora was only two places from me, and so did Hella, probably for the same reason. Anyway she was not paying much attention to the play for in the main interval Lajos, who had been in the stalls, came up and said how d'you do to Hella and her mother. He wanted to go home with them after the performance. Jeno has mumps, it is a horrid sort of illness and if I had it I should never admit it. Those illnesses in which one is swelled up are the nastiest of all. The Sunday after next Lajos and Jeno have been invited to the Brs. and of course they asked me too, I am so glad.

January 18th. I have not written for a whole week, we have such a frantic lot of work, especially in French in which we are very backward, at least Dunker says so!! She can't stand Madame Arnau, that's obvious. For my part I liked Mad. Arnau a great deal better, if only because she had no pimples. And Prof. Jordan's History class is awfully difficult, because he always makes one find out the causes for oneself; one has to learn intelligently!, but that is very difficult in History. No one ever gets an Excellent from him, except Verbenowitsch sometimes, but she learns out of a book, not our class book, but the one on which Herr Prof. J. bases his lectures. And because she reads it all up beforehand, naturally she always knows all the causes of the war and the consequences. Really consequences means something quite different, and so Hella and I never dare look at one another when he is examining us and asks: What were the consequences of this event? Of course the Herr Prof. imagined that Franke was laughing at him when she was only laughing at consequences; and it was impossible for her to explain, especially to a gentleman!!!!

January 20th. When Dora and I were coming home from skating to-day we met Mademoiselle, and I said how d'you do to her at once, and I was asking her how she (much emphasised) was getting on, when suddenly I noticed that Dora had gone on, and Mademoiselle said: "Your sister seems in a great hurry, I don't want to detain her." When I caught Dora up and asked her: "Why did you run away?" she tossed her head and said: "That sort of company does not suit me." "What on earth do you mean, you were so awfully fond of Mad., and besides she is really lovely." That's true enough, she said; but it was awfully tactless of her to tell me of all that—you know what. Such an intimacy behind her parents' backs cannot possibly lead to happiness. Then I got in such a fearful temper and said: "Oh do shut up. Father and Mother did not know anything about Viktor either, and you were happy enough then. It is just the secrecy that makes one so happy." Then she said very softly: "Dear Grete, you too will change your views," and then we did not say another word. But I was awfully angry over her meanness; for first of all she wanted to hear the whole story, although Mad. never offered to tell her, and now she pretends that she did not wish it. If I only knew where to find Mad. I would warn her. Anyhow, this day week at 7 I shall take care to be in W. Street, and perhaps I may meet her, for she probably has a private lesson somewhere in that neighborhood.

January 24th. Mother is very ill again to-day, in spite of the operation. I have decided that I won't go on Sunday to the Brs. although Jeno will be there, and that I won't wait about for Mademoiselle on Monday. I have not told Hella anything about this for she would probably say it was very stupid of me, but I would rather not; not because Dora has twice spoken to me pointedly about a clear conscience, but because I don't enjoy anything when Mother is ill.

January 26th. Mother is an angel. Yesterday she asked Aunt Dora: "By the way, Dora, has Grete put a fresh lace tucker in her blue frock, ready for the Brs. to-morrow?" Then I said: "I'm not going Mother," and Mother asked: "But why not, surely not on my account?" Then I rushed up to her and said: "I can't enjoy anything when you are ill." And then Mother was so awfully sweet, and she wept and said: "Such moments make one forget all pains and troubles. But really you must go, besides I'm a good deal better to-day, and to-morrow I shall be quite well again." So I answered: "All right, I'll go, but only if you are really well. But you must tell me honestly." But in any case I shan't go to meet Mademoiselle on Monday.

January 28th. It was Mathematics to-day at school, so I could not write yesterday. We had a heavenly time on Sunday. We laughed till our sides ached and Hella was nearly suffocated with laughing. Lajos is enough to give one fits; it was absolutely ripping the way he imitated the wife of Major Zoltan in the Academy and Captain Riffl. I can hardly write about it, for my hand shakes so with laughing when I think of it. And then, while Hella and Lajos were singing songs together, Jeno told me that every student in the Neustadt has an inamorata, a real one. Mostly in Vienna, but some in Wiener Neustadt though that is dangerous because of being caught. All the officers know about it, but no one must be found out. Then I told him about Oswald's affair and he said: "Oswald was a great donkey, you'll excuse me for saying so since he's your brother; but really he made a fool of himself. He was only a civilian; it's quite different in the army." Then I got cross and said: "That's all very well, Jeno, but you are not an officer yourself, so I don't see how you can know anything about it." Then he said to Hella: "I say, Ilonka, you must keep your friend in better order, she is rather inclined to be insubordinate." She is to make a written note of every act of insubordination, and then he will administer exemplary punishment. All very fine, but it will take two to that.

January 30th. I wish I knew whether Mademoiselle really passed through W. Street again at 7 o'clock on Monday, for she certainly said very distinctly: "Au revoir, ma cherie!" She is so pretty and so pale; perhaps she is really ill, and she must be awfully nervous about — — — That would be terrible. We wonder whether she knows about certain means, but one simply can't tell her.

February 2nd. I've had a wonderful idea and Hella thinks it a positive inspiration. We are going to write anonymously to Mademoiselle about those means, and Hella will write, so that no one can recognise my writing. We think something of that sort must have happened to Mademoiselle, for the other day I heard Mother say to Aunt Dora: "If we had known that, we should never have engaged her for the children; it will be a terrible thing for her parents." And Aunt Dora said: "Yes, those are the sort of people who hide their disgrace under the water." It seems quite clear, for disgrace means an illegitimate child. And the worst of it is, that they know that she has done that. We must help the poor thing. And that is why Dora is so indignant all of a sudden. But how can she know? there is nothing to notice yet in Mademoiselle; if there had been I should certainly have seen it, for Hella often says I've a keen eye for it. That is quite true, I was the first person to notice it in the maid at Prof. Hofer's, when even Father had not noticed it.

February 4th. Well, we have written to her, at least Hella has, saying there are such means, and that she will find all the details in the encyclopedia. We have addressed it to F. M. and signed it "Someone who understands you." Unfortunately we shall never be able to find out whether she got the letter, but the main thing is that she should.

February 7th. What a frightful lot of anxiety a letter can give one! In the interval to-day the school servant came up to me and said: Please are you Fraulein Lainer of the Third. "There is a letter for you." I blushed furiously, for I thought, it must be from Mademoiselle, but my blushing made Frau Berger think it must be from a young man: "Really I ought to give it to the head mistress; I am not allowed to deliver any letters to the pupils, but in your case I will make an exception. But please remember if it happens again I shall have to hand it in to the office." Then I said: "Frau Berger, I am quite certain it is not from a gentleman, but from a young lady," and when she gave it to me I saw directly that it really was not from a gentleman but only from Ada! It really is too stupid of her! At the New Year she reproached me for having broken my word, and now she begs me to enquire at the Raimund Theatre or at the People's Theatre whether Herr G. is there; she says she can't live without him in St. P. But in the holidays she told me that she was not in love with him, that for her he was only a means to an end. I'm absolutely certain she said that. Nothing will induce me to go to enquire at a theatre office, and Hella says too that to make such a suggestion is a piece of impudence. I shall just write her an ordinary letter, telling her what a row she might have got me into at school. I really think Ada has a bee in her bonnet, as Father always says.

February 10th. I never heard of such a thing! I was sent for to the office to-day because the school servant had complained that on two occasions I had thrown down some orange peel at the entrance. It's quite true that I did drop one piece there yesterday, but I pushed it out of the way with my foot into the corner, and as for any other time I know nothing about it. But I see which way the wind is blowing. Frau Berger thought I would give her some money for that letter; just fancy, how absurd, money for a letter like that, I wouldn't give 20 kreuzer for such a letter. But since then she's been in a frightfully bad temper, I noticed it on Wednesday when we were wiping our shoes at the door. What I said to the head was: "It happened only once, and I kicked the peel into the corner where no one could tread on it, but I certainly did not do it twice, and Bruckner can confirm what I say." Then the head said: "Oh well, we need not make a state affair of it, but the next time you drop something, please pick it up." Frau Berger is furious, and all we girls in our class have decided that while we won't make more mess than we need, still, we shan't be too particular. If any one of us happens to drop a piece of paper she will just let it lie. Such cheek, one really can't stand it!

February 12th. We got our reports to-day. I have not got any Satisfactories, only Praiseworthy and Excellent. Father and Mother are awfully pleased and they have given each of us 2 crowns. Indeed Dora has practically nothing but Excellents, only three Praiseworthies; but she studies frantically hard, and she is learning Latin again with Frau Doktor M. If she is still teaching the lower classes next year, I shall go too, for that way we shall have her for 3 hours longer each week. By the way, Franke has actually got Praiseworthy in Maths. and Physics, though she's hardly any good. The Nutling seems to give extraordinarily good reports, for twice in the Maths. schoolwork Hella has had an Unsatisfactory, and yet now in her report she has Praiseworthy. With Frau Doktor M. one has really to deserve one's report, and it was just the same last year with Fr. Dr. St. The worst of all is with Herr Prof. Jordan. Not a single one of us has got an Excellent except that deceitful cat Verbenowitsch. To-morrow the Brs. are giving a great birthday party because of Hella's 14th birthday. Lajos and Jeno are coming and the two Ehrenfelds, because Hella is very fond of them, especially Trude, the elder, that is she is 2 days older than Kitty, for they are twins!! How awful!!! They only came to the Lyz this year, and Hella meets them skating every day, I don't because we have no season tickets this year but only take day tickets when we can go, because of Mother's illness. I am giving Hella an electric torch with a very powerful reflector, so that it really lights up the whole room, and an amber necklace.

February 14th. It's a good thing that we have the half-term holiday to-day and to-morrow for that gives me time to write all about yesterday. It was simply phenomenal! I went to wish Hella many happy returns quite early, and I stayed to dinner and Lajos and Jeno had been invited to dinner too in the afternoon the 2 Ehrenfelds came and brought a box of sweets, and 3 of Hella's girl cousins and two boys, one of whom is frightfully stupid and never speaks a word, and several aunts and other ladies, for the grown-ups had their friends too. But we did not bother about them, for the dining-room, Lizzi's room, and Hella's room had been arranged for us. Hella had been sent such a lot of flowers that they nearly gave us a headache. At dinner Lajos proposed a toast to Hella and another at tea. Hella was splendid, and in the evening she said to me: "At 14 one really does become a different being." For in proposing his toast Lajos had said that every 7 years a human being is completely changed, and Hella thinks that is perfectly true. Thank goodness, in 6 1/2 months I shall change my whole being too. There really did seem to be something different about her, and when we all had to blow to extinguish the candles on her birthday cake, all except the life-light in the middle, as a sign that the other years have passed, she really got quite pale, for she was afraid that in joke or through awkwardness some one would blow out her life-light. Thank goodness it was all right. I don't much care for such things myself, for I'm always afraid that something might happen. Of course I know that it's only a superstition, but it would have been horribly unpleasant if anyone had blown out the life-light. Openly!! Lajos gave Hella an enormous square box of sweets, and secretly!! a silver ring with a heart pendant. He wanted her to wear this until it is replaced by a gold one—the wedding ring. But she can't because of her parents, so she begged me to allow her to say that I had given it her, but that would not do either because of Father and Mother. These things are such a nuisance, and that is why no young man will ever go on living at home where one is continually being questioned about everything one has, and does, and wears. After tea we sang: "Had I but stayed on my lonely Hearth" and other sad songs, because they are the prettiest, and in the evening we danced while Hella's Father played for us; and then Elwira, the tall cousin, danced the czardas with Lajos, it was wonderful. I've never known such a birthday party as yesterday's. It's only possible in winter; you can never have anything like it on my birthday, July 30th, for the people one is fondest of are never all together at that time. Really no one ought to have a birthday in the holiday months, but always sometime between the end of September and June. I do wish I were 14, I simply can't wait. Hella's mother said to Hella, You are not a child any longer, but a grown-up; I do wish I were too!!!

February 16th. We have a new schoolfellow. All the girls and all the staff are delighted with her. She is so small she might be only 10, but awfully pretty. She has brown curls (Hella says foxy red, but I don't agree) hanging down to her shoulders, large brown eyes, a lovely mouth, and a complexion like milk and roses. She is the daughter of a bank manager in Hamburg; he shot himself, I don't know why. Of course she is in mourning and it suits her wonderfully. She has a strong North German accent. Frau Doktor Fuchs is simply infatuated with her and the head is awfully fond of her too.

February 19th. Hella and I walked home to-day with Anneliese. She is called Anneliese von Zerkwitz. Her mother has been so frightfully upset by her father's death that she'll probably have to be sent to a sanatorium; that is why Anneliese has come to Vienna to stay with her uncle. He is a professor and they live in Wiedner Hauptstrasse. Dora thinks her charming too, the whole school is in love with her, she is going to gym. with us; I am so glad. Of course she won't stand near Hella and me because she's so small;

but we can always keep an eye on her, show her everything, and help her with the apparatus. Hella is a trifle jealous and says: "It seems to me that Anneliese has quite taken my place in your affections." I said that was not a bit true, but did she not think Anneliese awfully loveable? "Yes," said Hella, "but one must not neglect old friends on that account." "I certainly shan't do anything of the kind; but Anneliese really needs some one who will show her everything and explain everything." Besides, the head mistress and Frau Doktor M. placed her in front of me and said to us: "Give her a helping hand."

February 20th. It's such a pity that I can't ask Anneliese here, for Mother has been in bed for the last week. But she is going to Hella's on Sunday, and since I am going too of course I am frightfully glad. Naturally I would much rather have her here; but unfortunately it's impossible because of Mother. Dora thinks that Mother will have to have another operation, but I don't believe it, for such an operation can only be done once. What I can't understand is why there should be anything wrong with Mother if the operation was successful. Dora is afraid that Mother has cancer, that would be horrible; but I don't believe she has, because if one has cancer one can't recover.

February 23rd. It was heavenly at the Bruckners! Anneliese did not come until 4, for they don't have dinner until 3. She wore a white embroidered frock with black silk ribbons. Hella's mother kissed her with tears in her eyes. For her mother really is in a sanatorium because is suffering from nervous disease. Anneliese is living with her uncle and aunt. But she often cries because of her father and mother. Still, she enjoyed herself immensely in the round games, winning all the best prizes, a pocket comb and mirror, a box of sweets, a toy elephant, a negro with a vase, and other things as well. I won a pen-wiper, a double vase, a pencil holder, a lot of sweets, and a note book, Hella won a lot of things too, and so did her two cousins and Jenny.

Then we had some music and Anneliese sang the Wacht am Rhein and a lot of folk songs; her voice is as sweet as herself. She was fetched at 7, I stayed till 8.

March 1st. To-morrow Hella and I have been in vised to Anneliese's. I am so awfully glad. I shall ask Mother to let me wear my new theatre blouse and the green spring coat and skirt. The temperature went up to 54 degrees to-day.

March 3rd. Yesterday we went to Anneliese's. She shares a room with her cousin; she is only 11 and goes to the middle school, but she is a nice girl I expected to find everything frightfully smart at Professor Arndt's, but it was not so at all. They have only 3 rooms not particularly well furnished. He has retired on a pension, Emmy is their granddaughter, she lives with them because her father is in Galicia, a captain or major I think. It was not so amusing as at Hella's. We played games without prizes, and that is dull; it is not that one plays for the sake of the prizes, but what's the use of playing if one does not win anything? Then they read aloud to us out of a story book. But what Hella and I found exasperating was that Anneliese's uncle said "Du" to us both. For Hella is 14, and I shall be 14 in a few months. But Hella was quite right; in conversation she said: "At the High School only the mistresses say Du to us, the professors have to say Sie." Unfortunately he went away soon after, so we don't know whether he took the hint. Hella says too that it was not particularly entertaining.

March 9th. Oh dear, Mother really has got cancer; of course Father has not told us so, but she has to have another operation. Dora has cried her eyes out and my knees are trembling. She's going to hospital on Friday. Aunt Dora is coming back on Thursday and will stay here till Mother is well again. I do so dread the operation, and still more Mother's going away. It's horrible, but still lots of people have cancer and don't die of it.

March 22nd. Mother is coming home again tomorrow. Oh I am so glad! Everything is so quiet in the hospital and one hardly dares speak in the passages. Mother said: "I don't want to stay here any longer, let me go back to my children." We went to see Mother in hospital every day and took her violets and other flowers, for she was not allowed to eat anything during the first few days after the operation. But it's quite different now that she's home again. I should have liked to stay away from school to-day, but Mother said: "No, children, go to school, do it to please me." So of course we went, but I simply could not attend to my lessons.

March 24th. Mother is asleep now. She looks frightfully ill and still has a lot of pain. I'm sure the doctors can't really understand her case; for if they had operated properly she would not still have pain after the second operation. I should like to know what Mother has been talking to Dora about, for they both cried. Although Dora and I are on good terms now, she would not tell me, but said she had promised Mother not to speak about it. I can't believe that Mother has told Dora a secret, but perhaps it was something about marrying. For Dora only said: "Besides, Mother did not need to say that to me, for my mind was quite made up in any case." I do hate such hints, it's better to say nothing at all. As soon as Mother can get up she is going to Abbazia for a change, and most likely Dora will go with her.

March 26th. Mother and Dora are going to Abbazzia next

week. Dora thinks I envy her the journey, and she said: "I would willingly renounce the journey and the seaside if only Mother would get well. And this year when I have to matriculate, I certainly should not go for pleasure." I'm so awfully miserable that I simply can't wear a red ribbon in my hair, though red suits me best. I generally wear a black one now, but since yesterday a brown one, for Mother said: "Oh, Gretel, do give up that black ribbon; it looks so gloomy and does not suit you at all." Of course I could not tell Mother how I was feeling, so I took the brown one and said the red ribbon was quite worn out.

April 12th. I never get my diary written. It's so gloomy at home for Mother is very bad. Oswald is coming home to-morrow for the Easter holidays and Mother is looking forward so to seeing him. I was to have gone with Hella and her father to Maria-Zell, for this year they are probably going to take a house for the summer in Mitterbach or Mitterberg near Maria-Zell. But I am not going after all, for I don't feel inclined, and I think Mother is better pleased that I should not; for she said: "So I shall have all my three darlings together here at Easter." When she said that I wanted to cry, and I ran quickly out of the room so that she might not see me. But she must have seen, for after dinner she said: "Gretel, if you really want to go with the Bruckners, I should like you to; I should be so glad for you to have a little pleasure, you have not had much enjoyment all the winter." And then I could not stop myself, and I burst out crying and said: "No, Mother, I won't go on any account. All I want is that you should get quite well again." And then Mother cried too and said: "Darling, I'm afraid I shall never be quite well again, but I should like to stay until you are all grown up; after that you won't need me so much." Then Dora came in and when she saw that Mother was crying she said that Father had sent for me. He hadn't really but in the evening she told me that Mother's illness was hopeless, but that I must not do anything to upset her or let her see what I was feeling. And then we both cried a lot and promised one another that we would always stay with Father.

May 16th. Mother died on April 24th, the Sunday after Easter. We are all so awfully unhappy. Hardly anyone says a word at mealtimes, only Father speaks to us so lovingly. Most likely Aunt Dora will stay here for good. It's not three weeks yet since Mother was buried, but in one way we feel as if she had already been dead three years, and in another way one is always suddenly wanting to go into her room, to ask her something or tell her something. And when we go to bed we talk about her for such a long time, and then I dream about her all night. Why should people die? Or at least only quite old people, who no longer have anyone to care about it. But a mother and a father ought never to die. The night after Mother died Hella wanted me to come and stay with them, but I preferred to stay at home; but late in the evening I did not dare to go into the hall alone, so Dora went with me. Father had locked the door into the drawing-room, where Mother was laid out, but all the same it was awfully creepy. They did not call me on the 24th until after Mother was dead; I should have so liked to see her once more. Good God, why should one die? If only I had been called Berta after her; but she did not wish that either of us should be called after her, nor did Father wish it in Oswald's case.

May 19th. When Mother was buried, one thing made me frightfully angry with Dora, at least not really angry but hurt, that she should have gone into church and come out of church with Father. For I have always gone with Father and Dora has always gone with Mother. And while poor Mother was in hospital, Dora went with Aunt. But at the funeral Father went with her, and I had to go with Aunt Dora. A few days later I spoke to her about it, and she said it was quite natural because she is the elder. She said that Oswald ought to have gone with me, that that would have been the proper thing. But he went alone. Another thing that annoys me is this; when Aunt Dora came here in the autumn, Dora and I sat on the same side of the table at dinner and supper, and Aunt sat opposite Mother, and when Mother took to her bed her place was left vacant. After she died Oswald sat on the fourth side, and now for about a week Dora has been sitting in Mother's place. I can't understand how Father can allow it!

May 19th. At dinner to-day no one could eat anything. For we had breast of veal, and we had had the same thing on the day of poor Mother's funeral, and when the joint was brought in I happened to look at Dora and saw that she was quite red and was sobbing frightfully. Then I could not contain myself any more and said: "I can't eat any breast of veal, for on Mother's burial day — — —," then I could not say any more, and Father stood up and came round to me, and Dora and Aunt Dora burst out crying too. And after dinner Aunt promised us that we should never have breast of veal again. For tea, Aunt Dora ordered an Ulm cake because we had eaten hardly anything at dinner.

May 26th. To-day is the first day of Dora's written matriculation. Father wanted her to withdraw because she looks so ill, but she would not for she said it would be a distraction for her and that she would like to finish with the High School. Next year she is to go to a preparatory school for the Gymnasium. She ought really to go to a dancing class, for she is nearly 17, but since she is in mourning it is quite impossible and of course she does not want to

113

go anyhow. The head thought too that Dora would withdraw from the examination because she is so overwrought, but she did not want to withdraw. The staff were so awfully sweet to us after Mother's death, at least the women teachers were. The professors don't bother themselves about our private concerns, for they only see us for 1 or 2 hours a week. Frau Doktor Steiner, from whom we don't have any lessons this year, was awfully sympathetic; I saw plainly that she had tears in her eyes, and Frau Doktor M. was an angel as she always is! We did not go to the spring festival on May 20th, though Father said we could go if we liked. Hella and Anneliese were awfully anxious that I should go; but I would not, and indeed I shall never go to any more amusements. No doubt the others enjoyed themselves immensely, but for Dora and me it would have been horrible. In the evenings I often fancy to myself that it is not really true, that Mother has simply gone to Franzensbad and will be back soon. And then I cry until my head aches or until Dora says: "Oh Gretel, I do wish you'd stop, it's awful." She often cries herself, I can hear her quite well, but I never say anything.

June 4th. So Dora looks upon Mother's death as a sign of God's displeasure against Father! But what could we have done to prevent it? She said, Oh, yes, we did a lot of things we ought not to have done, and above all we had secrets from Mother. That is why God has punished us. It's horrible, and now that she is always speaking of the eye of God and the finger of God it makes me so terribly afraid to go into a dark room, because I always feel there is some one there who is eying me and wants to seize me.

June 8th. Father is in a frightful rage with Dora; yesterday evening, when I opened the drawing-room door and there was Father coming out, quite unintentionally I gave a yell, and when Father asked what was the matter I told him about God's displeasure; only I did not tell him it was against him, but only against Dora and me. And then Father was frightfully angry for the first time since Mother's death, and he told Dora she was not to upset me with her ill-conditioned fancies, and Dora nearly had an attack of palpitation so that the doctor had to be sent for. Aunt came to sleep in our room and we both had to take bromide. To-day Father was awfully kind to us and said: "Girls, you've no reason to reproach yourselves, you have always been good children, and I hope you always will be good." Yes, I will be, for Mother's eye watches over us. Hella thinks I look very poorly, and she asked me to-day whether perhaps . . . . ?? But I told her that I would not talk about such things any more, that it would be an offence to my Mother's memory. She wanted to say something more, but I said:

"No, Hella, I simply won't talk about that any more. You can't understand, because your mother is still alive."

June 12th. It is awful; just when I did not want to think any more about such things, there comes an affair of that very sort! I'm in a frightful mess through no fault of my own. Just after 9 to-day a girl from the Second came in to our Mathematic lesson and said: "The head mistress wishes to see Lainer, Bruckner, and Franke in the office directly." All the girls looked at us, but we did not know why. When we came into the office, the door of the head's room was shut and Fraulein N. told us to wait. Then the head came out and called me in. Inside a lady was sitting, and she looked at me through a lorgnon. "Do you spend much time with Zerkwitz?" asked the head. "Yes, said I," and I had a foreboding. "This lady is Zerkwitz's mother, she complains that you talk about very improper things with her daughter; is it so?" "Hella and I never wanted to tell her anything; but she begged us to again and again, and besides we thought she really knew it anyhow and only pretended she didn't." "What did you think she knew, and what did you talk to her about?" broke in Anneliese's mother. "Excuse me," said the head, "I will examine the girls; so Bruckner was concerned in the matter too?" "Very seldom," said I; "Yes, the chief offender is Lainer, the girl whose mother died recently." Then I choked down my tears, and said: "We should never have said a word about these matters unless Anneliese had kept on at us." After that I would not answer any more questions. Then Hella was called in. She told me afterwards that she knew what was up directly she saw my face. "What have you been talking about to Zerkwitz?" Hella would not say at first, but then she said in as few words as possible: "About getting babies, and about being married!" "Gracious goodness, such little brats, and to talk about such things," said Anneliese's mother. "Such corrupt minds." "We did not believe that Anneliese did not really know, or we should never have told her anything," said Hella just as I had; she was simply splendid. "As regards Alfred, we have nothing to do with that, and we have often advised her not to allow him to meet her coming home from school; but she would not listen to us." "I am talking about your conversations with which you have corrupted the poor innocent child," said Frau von Zerkwitz. "She certainly must have known something about it before, or she would not have gone with Alfred or wanted to talk about it with us," said Hella. "Heavenly Father, that is worse still; such corruptness of mind!" Then we were sent out of the room. Outside, Hella cried frightfully, and so did I, for we were afraid there would be a row at home. We could not go back into the Mathematic lesson because we had been crying such a lot. In the interval Hella walked past Anneliese and said out loud: "Traitress!!" and spat at her. For that she was ordered out of the ranks. I stepped out of the ranks too, and when Frau Professor Kreindl said: "Not you, Lainer, you go on," I said: "Excuse me, I spat at her too," and went and stood beside Hella. All the girls looked at us. It was plain that Frau Prof. Kreindl knew all about it already for she did not say any more. In the German lesson from 11 to 12 Frau Doktor M. said: "Girls, why can't you keep the peace together? This continual misconduct is really too bad, and serves only to make trouble for you and for your parents and for us." Just before 12 Hella and I were summoned to the head's room again. "Girls," she said, "it's a horrible business this. Even if your own imaginations have been prematurely poisoned, why should you try to corrupt others? As for you, Lainer, you ought to be especially ashamed of yourself that such complaints should be made of you when your mother has been buried only a few weeks." "Excuse me," said Hella, "all this happened in the spring, and even earlier, in the winter, for we were still skating at the time. Rita's mother was pretty well then. Besides, Zerkwitz was continually pestering us to tell her. I often warned Rita, and said: 'Don't trust her,' but she was quite infatuated with Zerkwitz. Please, Frau Direktorin, don't say anything about it to Rita's father, for he would be frightfully upset."

Hella was simply splendid, I shall never forget. She does not want me to write that; we are writing together. Hella thinks we must write it all down word for word, for one never can tell what use it may be. No one ever had a friend like Hella, and she is so brave and clever. "You are just as clever," she says, "but you get so easily overawed, and besides you are still quite nervous because of your mother's death. I only hope your father won't hear anything about it." That stupid idiot dug up the old story about the two students on the ice, a thing that was over and done with ages ago. "You should never trust anyone," says Hella, and she's perfectly right. I never could have believed Anneliese would be such a sneak. We don't know yet what was up with Franke. As she came in she put her finger to her lips, meaning of course "Betray nothing!"

June 15th. The school inspector came to-day. I was at the blackboard in the Maths lesson, when there was a knock at the door and the head came in with the Herr Insp. For a moment I thought he had come about that matter, and I went as white as a sheet (at least the girls say I did; Hella says I looked like Niobe mourning for her children). Thank goodness, the sum was an easy one, and besides I can always do sums; in Maths and French I am the best in the class. But the Herr Insp. saw that I had tears in my eyes and said something to the head; then the head said: "She has recently lost her mother." Then the Herr Insp. praised me, and like a stupid idiot

I must needs begin to howl. The head said: "It's all right L., sit down," and stroked my hair. She is so awfully sweet, and I do hope that she and Frau Doktor M. will say a word for me at the Staff Meeting. And I do hope that Father won't hear anything of it, for of course he would reproach me dreadfully because it all comes so soon after Mother's death. But really it all happened long before that. The way it all happened was that Hella's mother went away to see Emmy, her married niece, who was having her first baby. And then it was that we told the "innocent child" (that's what we call the deceitful cat) everything. Hella still thinks that the "innocent child" was a humbug. That is quite likely, for after all she is nearly fourteen; and at 14 one must surely know a great deal already; it's impossible that at that age a girl can continue to believe in the stork story, as Anneliese is said!!! to have done. Hella thinks that I shall soon be "developed" too, because I always have such black rings under my eyes. I overheard Frau von Zerkwitz say, "Little brats;" but Hella says that the head hemmed loudly to drown it. Afterwards Hella was in fits of laughter over the expression "little brats" for her mother always says about such things; Little brats like you have no concern with such matters. Good Lord, when is one to learn all about it if one does not know when one is nearly 14! As a matter of fact both Hella and I learned these things very early, and it has not done us any harm. Hella's mother always says that if one learns such things too early one gets to look old; but of course that's nonsense. But why do mothers not want us to know? I suppose they're just ashamed.

June 16th. Yesterday evening after we had gone to bed, Dora said: "What were you really talking about to Z., or whatever her name is? The head called me into the office to-day and told me that you had been talking of improper matters. She said I must watch over you in Mother's place!" Well that would be a fine thing! Besides, it all happened when Mother was still alive. A mother never knows what children are talking of together. Dora thinks that I shall have a written Reprimand from the Staff Meeting. I should hate that because of Father; that would mean another fearful row; although Father is really awfully sweet now; I have not had a single rowing since Mother first got ill. It's quite true that death makes people gentle, but why? Really one would have thought people would get disagreeable, because they've been so much distressed. Last week the tombstone was put up and we all went to see it. I should like to go alone to the cemetery once at least, for one does not like to weep before the others.

June 18th. The "innocent child" does not come to gym. any longer, at least she has not been since that affair. We think she's afraid, although we should not say anything to her. We punish her with silent contempt, she'll feel that more than anything. And thank goodness she does not come to play tennis. I do hate people who are deceitful, for one never knows where to have them. When a girl tells an outright cram, then I can at least say to her: Oh, clear out, don't tell such a frightful whacker; I was not born yesterday. But one has no safeguard against deceitfulness. That's why I don't like cats. We have another name for the "innocent child," we call her the "red cat." I think she knows. Day after tomorrow is the school outing to Carnuntum. I am so excited.We have to be at the quay at half past 7.

June 21st. The outing was lovely. Hella was to come and fetch me. But she overslept herself, so her mother took a taxi; and luckily I had waited for her. I should like to be always driving in a taxi. Dora would not wait, and went away at a quarter to 7 by electric car. At a quarter to 8 Hella came in the taxi, and just before the ship weighed anchor (I believe one ought only to say that of a sailing ship at sea, but it does not matter, I'm not Marina who knows everything about the navy), that is just at the right moment, we arrived. They all stared at us when we came rushing up in the taxi. I tumbled down as I got out of the car, it was stupid; but I don't think they all noticed it. Aunt Dora said that for this one day we had better put off our mourning, and Father said so too, so we wore our white embroidered frocks and Aunt Dora was awfully good and had made us black sashes; it looked frightfully smart, and they say that people wear mourning like that in America. I do love America, the land of liberty. Boys (that is young students) and girls go to school together there!! — — — But about the outing. In the boat we sat next Frau Doktor M., she was awfully nice; Hella was on the right and I was on the left, and we sat so close that she said: "Girls, you're squashing me, or at least you're crushing my dress!" She was wearing a white frock and had a coral necklace which suited her simply splendidly. When we were near Hainburg Hella's hat fell into the Danube, and all the girls screamed because they thought a child had fallen overboard. But thank goodness it was only the hat. We went up the Schlossberg and had a lovely view, that is, I did not look at anything except Frau Doktor M. because she was so lovely; Professor Wilke was with us, and he went about with her all the time. The girls say he will probably marry her, perhaps in the holidays. Oh dear, that would be horrid. Hella thinks that is quite out of the question because of the German professor; at any rate it would be better for her to marry Professor W. than the other, because he is said to be a Jew. "Still, with regard to all the things that hang upon marriage, it's the same with every man," said I. "That's just the chief point, you little goose," said Hella. And Frau Doktor M. said: "Do you

118

allow your chum to talk to you like that? What is the chief point?" I was just going to say: "We can't tell you that," when Hella interrupted me and said: "Just because I'm her chum I can talk to her like that; she would not let anyone else do it." Then we went to dinner. Unfortunately we did not sit next "her." We had veal cutlets and four pieces of chocolate cake, and as the Herr Religionsprof. went by he said: "How many weeks have you been fasting?" Before dinner we went to the museum to see the things they had dug up in the Roman camp. The head mistress and Fraulein V. explained everything. It was most instructive. In the afternoon we went to Deutsch-Altenburg. It was great fun at tea. Then we had games and all the staff joined in, the Fifth had got up a comedy by one of the girls. We were all in fits of laughter. Then suddenly there came along a whole troop of officers of the flying corps, frightfully smart, and one of them sat down at the piano and began to play dance music. Another came up to the head and begged her to allow the "young ladies" to dance. The head did not want to at first, but all the girls of the Fifth and Sixth begged her to, and the Herr Rel. Prof. said: "Oh, Frau Direktorin, let them have the innocent pleasure," and so they really were allowed to dance. The rest of us either danced with one another or looked on. And then, when Hella and I were standing right in front, up came a splendid lieutenant and said: "May I venture to separate the two friends for a little dance?" "If you please," said I, and sailed off with him. To dance with a lieutenant is glorious. Then the same lieutenant danced with Hella and in the evening on the way home she said that the lieutenant had really wanted to dance with her first, but I had been so prompt with my "If you please" and had placed my hand on his shoulder. Of course that's not true, but it is not a thing one would quarrel about with one's best friend, and anyhow he danced with both of us. Unfortunately we were not able to dance very long because we got so hot. Oh, and I had almost forgotten, a captain with a black moustache saluted Frau Doktor M., for they know one another. She blushed furiously; so he is probably the man she will marry, and not Herr Prof. Wilke and not the Jewish professor. He would please me a great deal better. They were all so awfully smart! Before we left a lieutenant brought in a huge bunch of roses, and the officers gave a rose to each member of the staff, the ladies I mean. Then something awfully funny happened. There is a girl in the Sixth who looks quite old, as if she might be 24, and "our" lieutenant offered her a rose too. And then she said: "No thank you, I am not one of the staff, I'm in the Sixth." Everyone burst out laughing, and she was quite abashed because the lieutenant had taken her for one of the staff. And the Herr Rel. Prof. said to her: "Tschapperl, you might just as

119

well have taken it." But really she was quite right to refuse. I think there must have been 20 officers at least. Of course Hella told the lieutenant that she was a colonel's daughter. I wonder if we shall ever see him again.

I am writing this four days after the outing. Dora told me yesterday that when I was dancing with the lieutenant the Herr Rel. Prof. said to the Frau Direktorin: "Do just look at that young Lainer; little rogue, see what eyes she's making." Making eyes, forsooth! I did not make eyes, besides, what does it mean anyhow to make eyes!! Of course I did not shut my eyes; if I had I should probably have fallen down, and then everyone would have laughed. And I don't like being laughed at. I hardly saw Dora all through the outing, and she did not dance. She said very cuttingly: "Of course not, for after all we are in mourning, even if we did wear white dresses; you are only a child, for whom that sort of thing does not matter." That sort of thing, as if I had done something dreadful! I don't love Mother any the less, and I don't forget her. Father was quite different; the day before yesterday evening he said: "So my little witch has made a conquest; you're beginning early. But it's no good taking up with an officer, little witch, they're too expensive." But I would like to have the lieutenant, I would go up with him in an aeroplane, up, up, till we both got quite giddy. In the religion lesson yesterday, when the Herr Prof. came in he laughed like anything and said: "Hullo, Lainer, is the world still spinning round you? The Herr Leutnant has not been able to sleep since." So I suppose he knows him. Still, I'm quite sure that he has not lost his sleep on my account, though very likely he said so. If I only knew what his name is, perhaps Leo or Romeo; yes, Romeo, that would suit him admirably!

June 26th. When I was writing hard yesterday Aunt Alma came with Marina and that jackanapes Erwin who was really responsible for all the row that time. Since Mother died we have been meeting again. I don't think Mother liked Aunt Alma much, nor she her. Just as Father and Aunt Dora are not particularly fond of one another. It is so in most families, the father does not care much for the mother's brothers and sisters and vice versa. I wonder why? I wonder whether He has a fiancee, probably he has, and what she looks like. I wish I knew whether He likes brown hair or fair hair or black hair best. But about the visit! Of course Marina and I were very standoffish. She is so frightfully conceited because she goes to the Training College. As if that were something magnificent! The High School is much more important, for from the High School one goes on to the university, but not from the Training College; and they don't learn English, nor French properly, for it is only optional.

Aunt Alma knows that it annoys Father when anyone says we don't look well, so she said: "Why, Dora looks quite overworked; thank goodness it's nearly over, and she won't get much out of it after all, it's really better for a girl to become a teacher." Erwin lounged in his chair and said to me: "Do you dare me to spit on the carpet?" "You are ill-bred enough to do it; I can't think why Marina, the future schoolmistress, does not give you a good smacking," said I. Then Aunt Alma chimed in: "What's the matter children? What game are you playing?" "It's not a game at all; Erwin wants to spit on the carpet and he seems to think that would be all right." Then Aunt said something to him in Italian, and he pulled a long nose at me behind Father's back, but I simply ignored it; little pig, and yet he's my cousin! Kamillo is supposed to have been just as impudent as Bub. But we have never seen him, for he has been in Japan as an ensign for the last two years. Mourning does not suit Marina at all; there's a provincial look about her and she can't shake it off. Her clothes are too long and she has not got a trace of b—, although she was 17 last September; she is disgustingly thin.

June 27th. The Herr Insp. came to our class to-day, in French this time. Frau Doktor Dunker is always frightfully excited by his visits, and at the beginning of the lesson she said: "Girls, the Inspector is coming to-day; pull yourselves together; please don't leave me in the lurch." So it must be true what Oswald always says that the inspectors come to inspect the teachers and not the pupils. "At the inspection," Oswald often says, "every pupil has the professor in his hands." Being first, of course I was called upon, and I simply could not think what "trotteur" meant. I would not say "Trottel" [idiot], and so I said nothing at all. Then Anneliese turned round and whispered it to me, but of course I was not going to say it after her, but remained speechless as an owl. At length the Herr Inspektor said: "Translate the sentence right to the end, and then you'll grasp its meaning." But I can't see the sense of that; for if I don't know one of the words the sentence has no meaning, or at least not the meaning it ought to have. If Hella had not been absent to-day because of − −, she might have been able to whisper it to me. Afterwards Frau Doktor Dunker reproached me, saying that no one could ever trust anyone, and that I really did not deserve a One. "And the stupidest thing of all was that you laughed when you did not know a simple word like that." Of course I could not tell her that my first thought had been to translate it "Trottel." Unseen translation is really too difficult for us.

June 28th. The Staff Meeting is to-day. I'm on tenter hooks to know whether I shall have a Reprimand, or a bad conduct mark in my report. That would be awful. It does not matter so much to

Hella, for her father has just gone away to manoeuvres in Hungary or in Bosnia, and by the time he is back the holidays will have begun and no one will be bothering about reports any more. So I shall know to-morrow. Oh bother, to-morrow is a holiday and next day is Sunday. So for another 2 1/2 days I shall have "to linger in suspense," but a different sort of suspense from what Goethe wrote about.

June 30th. We were at home yesterday and this afternoon because of Dora's matriculation. The Bruckners went to Breitenstein to visit an aunt, who is in a convalescent home, and so I could not go with them. In the evening we went to Turkenschanz Park to supper, but there was nothing on. By the way, I have not written anything yet about the "innocent child" at the outing. On the boat she began fussing round Hella and me and wanted to push into the conversation, indirectly of course! But she did not succeed; Hella is extraordinarily clever in such matters; she simply seemed to look through her Really I'm a little sorry for her, for she hasn't any close friends beyond ourselves; but Hella said: "Haven't you had enough of it yet? Do you want to be cooked once more with the same sauce?" And when Hella's hat fell into the water and we were still looking after it in fits of laughter, all of a sudden we found Anneliese standing behind us offering Hella a fine lace shawl which she had brought with her for the evening because she so readily gets earache. "Wouldn't you like to use this shawl, so that you won't have to go back to Vienna without a hat?" "Please don't trouble yourself, I'm quite used to going about bare-headed." But the way she said it, like a queen! I must learn it from her. She is really shorter than I am, but at such moments she looks just like a grownup lady. I told her as much, and she rejoined: "Darling Rita, you can't learn a thing like that; it's inborn." She rather annoyed me, for she always seems to think that an officer's daughter is a thing apart.

July 1st. Thank goodness, everything has passed off without a public scandal. Frau Doktor M. spoke to me in the corridor, saying: "Lainer, you've had a narrow escape. If certain voices had not been raised on your behalf, I really don't know — — —." Then I said: "I'm quite certain, Frau Doktor, that you alone have saved me from a Bad Conduct Mark." And I kissed her hand. "Get along, you little baggage, for the one part simply a child, and for the other with your head full of thoughts which grown-ups would do well to dispense with."

After all, one can't help one's thoughts, and we shall be more careful in future as to the persons to whom we talk about that sort of thing. Here's another thing I forgot to mention about the outing: When we got back into Vienna by rail, most of the parents came to

122

meet us at the station; Father was there too, and so was the "innocent child's" mother. Thank goodness Father did not know her. When we got out of the train there was a great scrimmage, because we were all trying to sort ourselves to our parents, and suddenly I heard Hella's voice: "No, Madam, your child is not in our bad company." I turned round sharply, and there was Hella standing in front of Frau von Zerkwitz who had just asked her: "Hullo, you, what has become of my little Anneliese?" The answer was splendid; I should never have been able to hit upon it; I always think of good repartees after the event. It was just the same that time when the old gentleman in the theatre asked Hella if she was alone there, and she snapped at him. He said: Impudent as a Jewess, or an impudent Jewess! It was too absurd, for first of all it's not impudent to make a clever repartee, and secondly it does not follow because one can do it that one is a Jewess. So Hella finished up by saying to him: "No, you've made a mistake, you are not speaking to one of your own sort."

We break up on the 6th; but because of Dora's matriculation we are staying here until the 11th. Then we are going to Fieberbrunn in Tyrol, and this year we shall stay in a hotel, so I am awfully pleased. Hella had a splendid time there last year.

July 2nd. My goodness, to-day I have . . . ., no, I can't write it plain out. In the middle of the Physics lesson, during revision, when I was not thinking of anything in particular, Fraulein N. came in with a paper to be signed. As we all stood up I thought to myself: Hullo, what's that? And then it suddenly occurred to me: Aha!! In the interval Hella asked me why I had got so fiery red in the Physics lesson, if I'd had some sweets with me. I did not want to tell her the real reason directly, and so I said: "Oh no, I had nearly fallen asleep from boredom, and when Fraulein N. came in it gave me a start." On the way home I was very silent, and I walked so slowly (for of course one must not walk fast when . . .) that Hella said: "Look here, what's up to-day, that you are so frightfully solemn? Have you fallen in love without my knowing it, or is it at long last . . . .?" Then I said "Or is it at long last!" And she said: "Ah, then now we're equals once more," and there in the middle of the street she gave me a kiss. Just at that moment two students went by and one of them said: "Give me one too." And Hella said: "Yes, I'll give you one on the cheek which will burn." So they hurried away. We really had no use for them: to-day!! Hella wanted me to tell her everything about it; but really I hadn't anything to tell, and yet she believed that I wouldn't tell. It is really very unpleasant, and this evening I shall have to take frightful care because of Dora. But I must tell Aunt because I want a San— T—. It will be frightfully awkward. It was different in Hella's case, first of all because she had such frightful cramps before it began so that her mother knew all about it without being told, and secondly because it was her mother. I certainly shan't tell Dora whatever happens, for that would make me feel still more ashamed. As for a San— T—, I shall never be able to buy one for myself even if I live to be 80. And it would be awful for Father to know about it. I wonder whether men really do know; I suppose they must know about their wives, but at any rate they can't know anything about their daughters.

July 3rd. Dora does know after all. For I switched off the light before I undressed, and then Dora snapped at me: "What on earth are you up to, switch it on again directly." "No I won't." Then she came over and wanted to switch it on herself; "Oh do please wait until I've got into bed." "O-o-h, is that it," said Dora, "why didn't you say so before? I've always hidden my things from you, and you haven't got any yet." And then we talked for quite a long time, and she told me that Mother had commissioned her to tell me everything when — — — Mother had told her all about it, but she said it was better for one girl to tell it to another, because that was least awkward. Mother knew too that in January Hella had . . . But how? I never let on! It was midnight before we switched off the light.

July 6th. Oh, I am so unhappy, when we went to get our reports to-day and said good-bye to Frau Doktor M., she was awfully sweet, and at the end she said: "I hope that you won't give too much trouble to my successor." At first we did not understand, for we thought she only meant that it is always uncertain whether the same member of the staff will keep the same class from year to year, but then she said: "I am leaving the school because I am going to be married." It gave me such a pang, and I said: "Oh, is it true?" "Yes, Lainer, it's quite true." And all the girls thronged round her and wanted to kiss her hand. No one spoke for a moment, and then Hella said: "Frau Doktor, may I ask you something? But you mustn't be angry!" "All right, ask away!" "Is it the captain we met in Carnuntum?" She was quite puzzled for a minute, and then she laughed like anything and said, "No, Bruckner, it is not he, for he has a wife already." And Gilly, who is not so frightfully fond of her as Hella and I are, said: "Frau Doktor, please tell us whom you are going to marry." "There's no secret about it, I am going to marry a professor in Heidelberg." That is why she has to leave the High School. It's simply ruined my holidays. Hella has such lovely ideas. The girls would not leave Frau Doktor alone, and they all wanted to

124

walk home with her. Then she said: "My darling girls, that's impossible, for I am going to Purkersdorf to see my parents." And then Hella had her splendid idea. The others said: "Please may we come with you as far as the metropolitan?" and at length she said they might. But Hella said, "Come along," and we hurried off to the metropolitan before them and took tickets to Hutteldorf so that we should be able to get back in plenty of time, and there we were waiting on the platform when she came and when all the girls came with her as far as the entrance. Then we rushed up to her and got into the train which came in at that moment. Of course we had second class tickets, for Hella, being an officer's daughter, mayn't travel third, and Frau Doktor M. always travels second too. And we all three sat together on a seat for two, though it was frightfully hot. She was so nice to us; I begged her to give us her photograph and she promised to send us one. Then, alas, we got to Hutteldorf. "Now, girls, you must get out." Then we both burst out crying, and she kissed us! Never shall I forget that blessed moment and that heavenly ride! As long as the train was still in sight we both waved our handkerchiefs to her and she waved back! When we wanted to give up our tickets Hella looked everywhere for her purse and could not find it; she must have left it in the ticket office. Luckily I still had all my July pocket money and so I was able to pay the excess fare, and then for once in a way I was the sharp-witted one; I said we had travelled third and had only passed out through the second, so we had not to pay so much; and no one knew anything about it, there's no harm in that sort of cheating. Of course we really did go back third, although Hella said it would spoil the memory for her. That sort of thing does not matter to me. We did not get home until a quarter past 1, and Aunt Dora gave me a tremendous scolding. I said I had been arranging books in the library for Frau Doktor, but Dora had enquired at the High School at 12, and there had been no one there. We had already gone away then, I said, and had gone part of the way with Frau Doktor M., for she was leaving because of her marriage. Then Dora was quite astonished and said: "Ah, now I understand." The other day when she had to go into the room while the staff meeting was on, the staff was talking about an engagement, and Fraulein Thim was saying: "Not everyone has the luck to get a university professor." That must have been about her. Certainly Thim won't get one, not even a school porter. To-day, (I've been writing this up for two days), I had such a delightful surprise; she sent me her photo, simply heavenly!! Father says the portrait is better looking than the reality. Nothing of the sort, she is perfectly beautiful, with her lovely eyes and her spiritual expression! Of course she has sent Hella a photo too. We are going to have pocket leather cases made for the photographs, so that we can take them with us wherever we go. But we shall have to wait until after the holidays because Hella has lost her money, and nearly all mine was used up in paying the excess fares. And such a leather case will cost 3 crowns. Father has some untearable transparent envelopes, and I shall ask him for two of them. They will do as a makeshift.

Dora's matriculation is to-morrow, she's quite nervous about it although she is very well up in all the subjects. But she says it's so easy to make mistakes. But Father is quite unconcerned, though last year he was very much bothered about Oswald, and poor dear Mother was frightfully anxious: "Pooh," said Oswald, "I shall soon show them that there's no need to bother; all one wants at the metric is cheek, that's the whole secret!" And then all he telegraphed was "durch" [through] and poor Mother was still very anxious, and thought that it might mean durchgefallen [failed]. But of course it really meant durchgekommen [passed], for meanwhile the second telegram had come. And father had brought two bottles of champagne to Rodaun, ready to celebrate Oswald's return. There won't be anything of the sort after Dora's matriculation because Mother is not with us any more; oh it does make me so miserable when I think that 2 1/2 months ago she was still alive, and now ——.

July 9th. This morning, while Dora was having her exam (she passed with Distinction), I went to the cemetery quite alone. I told Aunt Dora I was going shopping with Hella and her mother, and I told Hella I was going with Aunt, and so I took the tram to Potzleinsdorf and then walked to the cemetery. People always ought to go to the cemetery alone. There was no one in the place but me. I did not dare to stay long, for I was afraid I should be home late. It's a frightfully long way to Potzleinsdorf, and it always seems so much further when one is alone. And when I came away from the cemetery I took a wrong turning and found myself in a quite deserted street near the Turkenschanze. That sort of thing is very awkward, and for a long time there was simply no one of whom I could ask the way. Then by good luck an old lady came along, and she told me I had only to take the next turning to get back to the tram line. And just as I did get there a Potzleinsdorf car came along, so I got in and reached home long before Dora. But in the afternoon Hella nearly gave me away, quite unintentionally. But since they were all talking about the matriculation I was able to smooth it over. Now that Dora has finished her matriculation she will have to tell me a great deal more about certain things; she promised she would. Before the matriculation she was always so tired because of the frightful grind, but that is over now, and I never do any work in the

126

holidays. What are holidays for? Frau Doktor Dunker has really given me only a Satisfactory, it's awfully mean of her; and I shall have to learn from her for three years more! Nothing will induce me to bother myself about French now, for she has a down on me, and when one's teacher has a down on one, one can work as hard as one likes and it's no good. It was so different with Frau Doktor M.!! I have just been looking at her photo so long that my eyes are positively burning; but I had to write up about to-day: even when one had been stupid once or twice, she never cast it up against one, never, never, never — — the sweet angel!

July 10th. We are going to F. to-morrow; I am so glad. It is frightfully dull to-day, for Hella went away yesterday to Berchtesgaden where she is to stay for 6 weeks, and on the way back she is going to Salzburg and perhaps Aunt Dora will take me to Salzburg for 2 days so that we can see one another again before Hella goes to Hungary. She is lucky! I can't go to K— M— this year, for we are going to stay in F. till the middle of September. I got my name day presents to-day because they are things for the journey: a black travelling satchel with a black leather belt, and half a dozen mourning handkerchiefs with a narrow black border, and an outfit for pokerwork, and a huge bag of sweets for the journey from Hella. The world is a wretched place without Hella. I do hope we shall marry on the same day, for Mother always used to say: "The most ardent girl friendships are always broken up when one of the two marries." I suppose because the other one is annoyed because she has not married. I wonder what it will be like at Frau Doktor M.'s wedding! and I wonder whether she knows about everything; very likely not, but if not I suppose her mother will tell her all about it before she is married. Dora told me yesterday that Mother had once said to her: "A girl always gets all sorts of false ideas into her head; the reality is quite different." But that is not so in our case, for we really know everything quite precisely, even to the fact that you have to take off every stitch; oh dear, I shall never forget it!—Oswald is coming to F. on the 20th, for first he is going to Munich for a few days.

July 12th. It's lovely here; mountains and mountains all round, and we're going to climb them all; oh, how I am enjoying myself! I simply can't keep a diary; it will have to be a weekary. For I must write to Hella at least every other day. We are staying in the Edelweiss boarding house; there are about 40 visitors, at least that's what we counted at dinner. There is a visitors' list hanging up in the hall, and I must study it thoroughly. The journey was rather dull, for Dora had a frightful headache so we could not talk all through the night. I stood in the corridor half the night. At one place in Salzburg there was a frightful fire; no one was putting it out, so I suppose no one knew anything about it. The boarding house is beautifully furnished, carpets everywhere; there are several groups of statuary in the hall. We are awfully pleased with everything. There are 4 courses at dinner and two at supper. Flowers on every table. Father says we must wait and see whether they change them often enough. Father has a new tweed suit which becomes him splendidly for he is so tall and aristocratic looking. We have coats and skirts made of thin black cotton material and black lace blouses, and we also have white coats and skirts and white blouses, and light grey tweed dresses as well. For Father is really quite right: "Mourning is in your heart, not in your dress." Still, for the present, we shall wear black, but we have the white things in case it gets frightfully hot. To-day, on a cliff quite near the house, we picked a great nosegay of Alpine roses. Dora has brought Mother's photo with her and has put the flowers in front of it; unluckily I forgot to bring mine. I should like to go to the top of the Wildeck or one of the other mountains. It would be lovely to pick Edelweiss for oneself. But Father says that mountaineering is not suited to our ages. The baths here always seem very cold, only about 54 or 60 degrees at most. Dr. Klein said we should only bathe when the water is quite warm. But apparently that won't be often. We have not made any acquaintances yet, but I like the look of the two girls wearing Bosnian blouses at the second table from ours. Perhaps we shall get to know them. One plan has come to nothing. I wanted to talk to Dora in the evenings about all sorts of important things, but it is impossible because Aunt Dora shares our room. Here's another tiresome thing; Father's room has a lovely veranda looking on to the promenade, while our room only looks into the garden. Of course the view is lovely, but I should have liked Father's room much better, only it is a great deal too small for three persons; there is only one bed and its furniture is of a very ancient order. I do hate that sort of furniture; the lady who keeps the boarding house calls it Empire!! I don't suppose she can ever have seen a room furnished in real Empire style.

July 15th. When Dora and I were out for a walk yesterday she told me a great deal about Aunt Dora. I never really knew before whether Uncle Richard was employed in the asylum or whether he was a patient there; but he is a patient. He has spinal disease and is quite off his head and often has attacks of raving madness. Once before he was sent to the asylum he tried to throttle Aunt Dora, and in another respect he did her a frightful lot of harm!!! I don't quite understand how, for Aunt Dora has never had any children. And why on earth do they make such a secret about Uncle Richard? But when I come to think of it, no one ever wanted to talk about

Mother's illness. There's no sense in this secrecy, for in the first place that always makes one think about things, and secondly one always finds out in the long run. At last Aunt Dora was so terribly afraid of Uncle that she always kept the door of her bedroom locked. It must be awful to have a husband who is a raging maniac. Father once said to Dora: your Aunt Dora is enough to drive one mad with her whims and fancies. Of course he didn't mean that literally, but I must watch carefully to find out what Aunt really does to annoy anyone so much. Most likely it is something connected with this matter. To my mind Aunt Alma has many more whims and fancies, and yet Uncle Franz has never gone raving mad. Dora says that Uncle Richard may go on living for another 20 years, and that she is frightfully sorry for Aunt Dora because she is tied to such a monster. Why tied? After all, he is in an asylum and can't do her any harm. Dora didn't know about all this before, Aunt only told her after Mother's death. Dora thinks it is better not to marry at all, unless one is madly in love with a man. And then only by a marriage contract!! In that case that would be excluded. But I always imagined a marriage contract was made because of a dowry and money affairs generally; and never thought of its having such a purpose. Frau Mayer, whom we met in the summer holidays two years ago, had married under such conditions. But it puzzles me, for if that is what men chiefly want when they marry, I don't see how any man can be satisfied with a marriage contract. There must be a mistake somewhere. Perhaps it is different among the Jews, for the Mayers were Jews.

July 21st. No, I never should have thought that Hella would prove to have been right in that matter. I got a letter 8 pages long from Anneliese to-day. That time when Hella had to stay at home for five days she believed that Anneliese would make fresh advances. But obviously she was afraid. So now she has written to me: My own dear Rita! You are the only friend of my life; wherever I go, all the girls and everybody likes me, and only you have turned away from me in anger. What harm did I do you — — —? After all, she did do me some harm; for there might have been a fine row if it had not been for Frau Doktor M., that angel in human form! She writes she is so lonely and so unhappy; she is with her mother at the Gratsch Hydropathic near Meran or Bozen, I forget which, I must look it up if I answer her. For I gave my word of honour to Hella that I would never forgive the "innocent child." But after all, to write an answer is mere ordinary politeness, and is far from meaning a reconciliation, and still less a friendship. She says that there are absolutely no girls in Gratsch, only grown-up ladies and old gentlemen, the youngest is 32! brr, I know I should find it deplorably dull myself. So I really will write to her, but I shall be exceedingly reserved. She finishes up with: Listen to the prayer of an unhappy girl and do not harden your heart against one who has always loved you truly. That is really very fine, and Anneliese always wrote the best compositions; Frau Doktor M. used often to praise them and to speak of her excellent style, but later she really did not like her at all. She often told her she ought not to be so affected, or she would lose the power of expression from sheer affectation. I shall not write to her immediately, but only after a few days, and, as I said, with great reserve.

July 23rd. I got to know the two girls to-day, their names are Olga and Nelly, one is 15 and the other 13; I don't know their surname yet, but only that they have a leather goods business in Mariahilferstr. Their mother's hair is quite grey already, their father is not coming until August 8th. We have arranged to go for a walk at 4 o'clock this afternoon, to Brennfelden.

July 26th. I have made up my mind to write every day before dinner, for after dinner we all go with our hammocks into the wood. After all I wrote to Anneliese three days ago, without waiting, so as not to keep her on tenterhooks. I have not written anything to Hella about it because I don't know how Anneliese will answer. Hella says she is having a royal time in Innichen; but the tiresome thing does not say just what she means by royal; she wrote only a bare 3 sides including the signature so of course I did not write to her as much as usual.

July 27th. Dora is not very much taken with the Weiners; she thinks they are frightfully stuck up. She says it's not the proper thing to wear gold bracelets and chains in the country, above all with peasant costume. Of course she is right, but still I like the two girls very much, and especially Olga, the younger one; Nelly puts on such airs; they go to a high school too, the Hietzinger High School; but Olga has only just got into the Second while Nelly is in the Fifth. Dora says they will never set the Danube on fire. No matter, leave it to others to do that. We enjoyed ourselves immensely on our walk. I'm going to spend the whole day with them to-day. Father says: "Don't see too much of them; you'll only get tired of them too soon." I don't believe that will happen with the Weiners.

July 29th. It's my birthday to-morrow. I wonder what my presents will be. I've already had one of them before we left Vienna, 3 pairs of openwork stockings, Aunt Dora gave them to me, exquisitely fine, and my feet look so elegant in them. But I must take frightful care of them and not wear them too often. Aunt says: "Perhaps now you will learn to give up pulling at your stockings when you are doing your lessons." As if I would do any lessons in the holidays.

LAST HALF-YEAR, AGE FOURTEEN AND A HALF

LAST HALF-YEAR

July 30th. Thank goodness this is my 14th!!! birthday; Olga thought that I was 16 or at least 15; but I said: No thank you; to look like 16 is quite agreeable to me, but I should not like to be 16, for after all how long is one young, only 2 or 3 years at most. But as to feeling different, as Hella said she did, I really can't notice anything of the kind; I am merely delighted that no one, not even Dora, can now call me a child. I do detest the word "child," except when Mother used to say: "My darling child," but then it meant something quite different. I like Mother's ring best of all my birthday presents; I shall wear it for always and always. When I was going to cry, Father said so sweetly: "Don't cry, Gretel, you must not cry on your 14th!! birthday, that would be a fine beginning of grown-upness!" Besides the ring, Father gave me a lovely black pearl necklace which suits me perfectly, and is at the same time so cool; then Theodor Storm's Immensee, from Aunt Dora the black openwork stockings and long black silk gloves, and from Dora a dark grey leather wristband for my watch. But I shan't wear that until we are back in Vienna and I am going to school again. Grandfather and Grandmother sent fruit as usual, but nothing has come from Oswald. He can't possibly have forgotten. I suppose his present will come later. Father also gave me a box of delicious sweets. At dinner Aunt Dora had ordered my favourite chocolate cream cake, and every one said: Hullo, why have we got a Sunday dish on a weekday? And then it came out that it was my birthday, and the Weiner girls, who knew it already, told most of the other guests and nearly everyone came to wish me many happy returns. Olga and Nelly had done so in the morning, and had given me a huge nosegay of wild flowers and another of cut flowers. This afternoon we are all going to Flagg; it is lovely there.

Evening: I must write some more. We could not have the expedition, because there was a frightful thunderstorm from 2 to 4 o'clock. But we enjoyed ourselves immensely. And I had another adventure: As I was leaving the dining-room in order to go to the . . . ., I heard a voice say: May I wish you a happy birthday, Fraulein? I turned round, and there behind me stood the enormously tall fair-haired student, whom I have been noticing for the last three days.

"Thank you very much, it's awfully kind of you," said I, and wanted to pass on, for I really had to go. But he began speaking again, and said: "I suppose that's only a joke about your being 14. Surely you are 16 to-day?" "I am both glad and sorry to say that I am not, said I, but after all everyone is as old as he seems. Please excuse me, I really must go to my room," said I hurriedly, and bolted, for otherwise − − − −!! I hope he did not suspect the truth. I must write about it to Hella, it will make her laugh. She sent me a lovely little jewel box with a view of Berchtesgaden packed with my favourite sweets, filled with brandy. In her letter she complains of the "shortness of my last letter." I must write her a long letter to-morrow. At supper I noticed for the first time where "Balder" sits; that's what I call him because of his lovely golden hair, and because I don't know his real name. He is with an old gentleman and an old lady and a younger lady whose hair is like his, but she can't possibly be his sister for she is much too old.

July 31st. The family is called Scharrer von Arneck, and the father is a retired member of the Board of Mines. The young lady is really his sister, and she is a teacher at the middle school in Brunn. I found all this out from the housemaid. But I went about it in a very cunning way, I did not want to ask straight out, and so I said: Can you tell me who that white-haired old gentleman is, he is so awfully like my Grandfather. (I have never see my Grandfather, for Father's Father has been dead 12 or 15 years, and Mother's Father does not live in Vienna but in Berlin.) Then Luise answered: "Ah, Fraulein, I expect you mean Herr Oberbergrat Sch., von Sch. But I expect Fraulein's Grandfather is not quite so grumpy." I said: "Is he so frightfully grumpy then?" And she answered: "I should think so; we must all jump at the word go or it's all up with us!" And then one word led to another, and she told me all she knew; the daughter is 32 already, her name is Hulda and her father won't let her marry, and the young gentleman has left home because his father pestered him so. He is a student in Prague, and only comes home for the holidays. It all sounds very melancholy, and yet they look perfectly happy except the daughter. By the way, it's horrid for the Weiners; Olga is 13 and Nelly actually 15, and their mother is once more − − − − I mean their mother is in an i− c−. They are both in a frightful rage, and Nelly said to me to-day: "It's a perfect scandal;" they find it so awkward going about with their mother. I can't say I'd noticed anything myself; but they say it has really been obvious for a long time; "the happy event!! will take place in October," said Olga. It really must be very disagreeable, and I took a dislike to Frau W. from the first. I simply can't understand how such a thing can happen when people are so old. I'm awfully sorry for the two Weiner girls. Something of the same sort must have happened in the case of the Schs., for Luise has told me that the young gentleman is 21 and his sister not 32 but 35, she had made a mistake; so she is 14 years older, appalling. I'm awfully sorry for her because her father won't let her marry, or rather would not let her marry. I'm sure Father would never refuse if either of us wanted to marry. I have written all this to Hella; I miss her dreadfully, for after all the Weiner girls are only strangers, and I could never tell my secrets to Dora, though we are quite on good terms now. Oswald is coming to-morrow.

August 1st. A young man has a fine time of it. He comes and goes when he likes and where he likes. A telegram arrived from Oswald to-day, saying he was not coming till the middle of August: Konigsee, Watzmann, glorious tramp. Letter follows. Father did not say much, but I fancy he's very much annoyed. Especially just now, after poor Mother's death, Oswald might just as well come home. Last year he was so long away after matriculation, quite alone, and now it's the same this year. One pleasure after another like that is really not the thing when one's Mother has been dead only three months. The day after we came here and before we had got to know anyone, I went out quite early, at half past 8, and went alone to the cemetery. It is on the slope of the mountain and some of the tombstones are frightfully old, in many cases one can't decipher the inscriptions; there was one of 1798 in Roman figures. I sat on a little bank thinking about poor Mother and all the unhappiness, and I cried so terribly that I had to bathe my eyes lest anyone should notice it. I was horribly annoyed to-day. A letter came from Aunt Alma, she wants to come here, we are to look for rooms for her, to see if we can find anything suitable, Aunt Alma always means by that very cheap, but above all it must be in a private house; of course, for a boarding house would be far too dear for them. I do hope we shan't find anything suitable, we really did not find anything to-day, for a storm was threatening and we did not go far. I do so hope we shall have no better success to-morrow; for I really could not stand having Marina here, she is such a spy. Thank goodness Aunt Dora and Dora are both very much against their coming. But Father said: That won't do girls, she's your aunt, and you must look for rooms for her. All right, we can look for them; but seeking and finding are two very different things.

August 2nd. This morning we went out early to look for the rooms, and since Dora always makes a point of finding what's wanted, she managed to hunt up 2 rooms and a kitchen, though they are only in a farm. The summer visitors who were staying there had to go back suddenly to Vienna because their grandmother died, and so the rooms are to let very cheap. Dora wrote to Aunt directly, and she said that we shall all be delighted to see them, which is a downright lie. However, I wrote a P.S. in which I sent love to them all, and said that the journey was scandalously expensive; perhaps that may choke them off a bit. Owing to this silly running about looking for rooms I saw nothing of the Weiners yesterday afternoon or this morning, and of course nothing of God Balder either. And at dinner we can't see the Scharrers' table because they have a table in the bay window, for they have come here every year for the last 9 years. I'm absolutely tired out, but there's something I must write. This afternoon the Weiners and we went up to Kreindl's, and Siegfried Sch. came with us, for he knows the Weiners, who have been here every year for the last 3 years. He talked chiefly to Dora, and that annoyed me frightfully. So I said not a word, but walked well behind the others. On the way home he came up to me and said: "I say, Fraulein Grete, are you always so reserved? Your eyes seem to contradict the idea." I said: "It all depends on my mood, and above all I hate forcing myself on any one." "Could you not change places at table with your mother?" "In the first place, she is not my Mother, who died on April 24th, but my Aunt, and in the second place, why do you say that to me, you had better say it to my sister!" "Don't be jealous! There's no reason for that. I can't help talking to your sister when we're in company; but I can assure you that you have no occasion whatever to be jealous." I wish I knew how I could manage that change of places, but I always sit next Father; anyhow I would not do it directly; next week at soonest. Farewell, my Hero Siegfried, sleep sweetly and dream of − −.

August 3rd, Anneliese wrote to me: "You heart of gold, so you are able to forgive my sins of youth? The world shines with a new light since I received your letter." I don't know that my letter was so forgiving as all that, for all I said was that I was very sorry she was so lonely in Gratsch, and that we could not alter the past, so we had better bury it. She sends me a belated birthday greeting (last winter we told one another when our birthdays were), and she sends me a great pressed forget-me-not. She waited to answer until it had been pressed. I don't know quite what I had better do. Big Siegfried could no doubt give me very good advice, but I can't very well tell him the whole story, for then I should have to tell him why we quarrelled, and that would be awful. I had better write to Hella before I answer. I must write to-day, for it will be quite three days before I can get an answer, and then 1 or two days more before Anneliese gets the letter, so that will be 5 days at least. It is raining in torrents, so it is very dull, for Father won't let us sit in the hall alone; I can't think why. Generally speaking Father's awfully kind, quite different from other fathers, but this is really disgusting of him. I shall lie down on the sofa after dinner and read Immensee, for I've not had a chance before.

August 6th. Well, the whole tribe arrived to-day; Marina in a dust-grey coat and skirt that fits her abominably, and Erwin and Ferdinand; Ferdinand is going through the artillery course in Vienna, at the Neustadt military academy; he's the most presentable of the lot. Uncle was in a frightful temper, growling about the journey and about the handbaggage, I think they must have had 8 or 10 packages, at least I had to carry a heavy travelling rug and Dora a handbag of which she said that it contained the accumulated rubbish of 10 years. Aunt Alma's appearance was enough to give one fits, a tweed dress kilted up so high that one saw her brown stockings as she walked, and a hat like a scarecrow's. When I think how awfully well dressed Mother always was, and how nice she always looked; of course Mother was at least 20 years younger than Aunt Alma, but even if Mother had lived to be 80 she would never have looked like that. Thank goodness, on the way from the station we did not meet any one, and above all we did not meet him. For once in a way they all came to dinner at our boarding house. We had two tables put together, and I seized the opportunity to change my place, for I offered Aunt Alma the place next Father and seated myself beside the lovely Marina, exactly opposite — — —! Anyway, Marina looked quite nice at dinner, for her white blouse suits her very well, and she has a lovely complexion, so white, with just a touch of pink in the cheeks. But that is her only beauty. The way she does her hair is hideous, parted and brushed quite smooth, with two pigtails. I've given them up long ago, though everyone said they suited me very well. But "snails" suit me a great deal better. He looked across at me the whole time, and Aunt Alma said: "Grete is blossoming out, I hope there's not a man in the case already." "Oh no," said Father, "country air does her such a lot of good, and when I take the children away for a change I don't forbid any innocent pleasures." My darling Father, I had to keep a tight hand on myself so as not to kiss him then and there. They were all so prim, with their eyes glued to their plates as if they had never eaten rum pudding before. It is true that Ferdinand winked at Marina, but of course she noticed nothing. They soon put away their first helps, and they all took a second, and then they went on talking. When we went to our rooms I knocked at Father's door and gave him the promised kiss and said: "You really are a jewel of a Father." "Well, will you, if you please, be a jewel of a daughter, and keep the peace with Marina and the others?" I said: "Oh dear, I simply can't stand her, she's such a humbug!" "Oh well," said Father, "it may be a pity, but you know one can't choose one's parents and one's relations." "I would not have chosen any different parents, for we could not have found another Father and another Mother like you." Then Father lifted me right up into the air as if I had still been a little girl, saying: "You are a little treasure," and we kissed one another heartily. I really do like Father better than anyone in the world; for the way I like Hella is quite different, she is my friend, and Dora is my sister; and I like Aunt Dora too, and Oswald if I ever see him again.

August 8th. Oh, I am so furious! To-day I got a postcard from Hella, with nothing on it but "Follow your own bent, with best wishes, your M." When we write postcards we always use a cipher which no one else can understand, so that M. means H. It's a good thing no one can understand it. Of course I wrote to Anneliese directly, and was most affectionate, and I sent a postcard to Hella, in our cipher, with nothing more than: Have done so, with best wishes, W. Not even your W. I do wonder what she will do. Hero Siegfried was lying with us to-day in the hayfield, and what he said was lovely. But I can't agree that all fathers without exception are tyrants. I said: "My Father isn't!" He rejoined: "Not yet, but you will find out in time. However, anyone with a character of his own won't allow himself to be suppressed. I simply broke with my Old Man and left home; there are other technical schools besides the one in Brunn. And since you say not all fathers; well just look at Hulda; whenever anyone fell in love with her the Old Man marred her chance, for no one can stand such tutelage." "Tutelage, what do you mean," said I, but just at that moment everyone got up to go away. To-morrow perhaps, poor persecuted man.

August 9th. Oh dear, it's horrible if it's all really true what Hella writes about being infected; an eruption all over the body, that is the most horrible thing in the world. I must tear up her letter directly, and since she could not write 8 whole pages in our cipher, I must absolutely destroy it, so that no one can get hold of a fragment of it. Above all now that Marina is here, for you never can tell — — —. But I know what I'll do; I'll copy the letter here, even if it takes 2 or 3 days. She writes:

Darling Rita, what did you say when you got yesterday's postcard. If you were angry, you must make it up with me. Consort with whom you please and write to whom you please; but all the consequences be on your own head. Father always says: Beware of red hair! And I insist that the "innocent child" has foxy red hair. But you can think what you like.

Now I've got something much more important to tell you. But you must promise me dirst that you will tear up my letter directly you have read it. Otherwise please send it back to me unread.

136

Just fancy. Here in B. there is a young married woman living with her mother and her cousin, a girl who is studying medicine; they are Poles and I have always had an enthusiastic admiration for the Poles. The young wife has got a divorce from her husband, for she was infected by him on the wedding night. Of course you remember what being infected is. But really it is something quite different from what we imagined. Because of that she got a frightful eruption all over her body and her face, and most likely all her hair will fall out; is it not frightful? Her cousin, the medical student, who is apparently very poor, is there to nurse her. Our servant Rosa told me about it, she heard of it from the housemaid where they have rooms. As you know, one can't talk to Lizzi about anything of that kind, and so I did not learn any more; but the other day, when I went to buy some picture postcards, I met the three ladies. The young wife was wearing a very thick veil, so that one could see nothing. They were sitting on a bench in the garden in front of their house, and I bowed in passing, on the way back. They bowed, and smiled in a friendly way. In the afternoon I had to lie down, for I was feeling very bad because of . . . .!! Then I suddenly heard some people talking on the veranda just outside my window—the veranda runs all round the house. At first I saw shadows passing, and then they sat down outside. I recognised the soft voice of the Polish student directly, and I heard her say to the wife of the mayor of J.: "Yes, my unfortunate cousin's experience has been a terrible one; that is because people sell girls like merchandise, without asking them, and without their having the least idea what they are in for." I got up at once and sat down close to the window behind the curtain so that I could hear everything. The mayor's wife said: "Yes, it's horrible what one has to go through when one is married. My husband is not one of that sort but − − −" And then I could not understand what she went on to say I overheard this conversation on Thursday. But that's not all I have to tell you. Of course my first thought was, if only I could have a talk with her; for she spoke about enlightenment and although we are both of us already very much enlightened, still, as a medical student, she must know a great deal more than we do, so that we can learn from her. And since she said that girls ought not to be allowed to run blindly into marriage, I thought she would probably tell me a little if I went cautiously to work. There was a word which she and the mayor's wife used more than once, segsual and I don't know what it means, and I'm sure you don't know either, darling Rita. She said something about segsual intimacies; of course when people talk about intimacies, one knows it has a meaning, but what on earth does segsual mean? It must mean something, since it is used with intimacy. Well, let me get on.

137

On Saturday there was a party, and the medical student came, and I left my Alpine Songs lying on the piano, and somebody picked it up and turned over the pages, and the word went round that the person to whom it belonged must sing something. At first I did not let on, but went out for a moment, and then came back saying: "I'm looking for my music book, I left it lying about somewhere." There was a general shout, and everyone said: "We've agreed that the person to whom that book belongs has got to sing." Now I knew that Fraulein Karwinska had accompanied the singing on such evenings before. So I said: "I shall be delighted to sing, provided Fraulein K. will accompany me, For you gentlemen play too loud for my voice." Great laughter, but I had got what I wanted. We were introduced, and I thought to myself: You will soon improve the acquaintance. On Sunday for once in a way I got up quite early, at half past 6, for Fraulein K. can only go out walking early in the morning since she spends the whole day with her cousin. She sits near the Luisenquelle, so I went there with a book, and as soon as she came I jumped up, said "good-morning," and went on: "I'm afraid I've taken possession of your bench." "Not at all," she said, "Do you study on Sundays?" "Oh no, this is only light reading," I answered, and I made haste to sit on the book, for in my hurry I had not noticed what it was. But luck was with me. She sat down beside me and said: "What is it you are reading that you hide so anxiously? I suppose it's something that your mother must not know about." "Oh no," said I, "we have not brought any such books to the country with us." "I take it that means that you do manage to get them when you are in town?" "Goodness me, one must try and learn a little about life; and since no one will ever tell one anything, one looks about for oneself to see if one can find anything in a book." "In the encyclopedia, I suppose?" "No, that's no good, for one can't always find the truth there." She burst out laughing and said: "What sort of truth do you want?" "I think you can imagine very well what sort of things I want to know." Of course one can speak more plainly to a medical student than one can to other girls, and she was not in the least disgusted or angry but said: "Yes, it's the same struggle everywhere." Then I made use of your favourite phrase and said: "Struggle, what do you mean? What I really want to know about is being infected." Then she flushed up and said: "Who's been talking to you about that? It seems to me that the whole town is chattering about my unhappy cousin. You must see that I can't tell you that." But I answered: "If you don't, who will? You study medicine, and are seeing and talking about such things all day." "No, no, my dear child (you can imagine how furious that made me), you are still much too young for that sort of thing." What do you think of that, we are too young at 14 1/2, it's utterly absurd. I expect that really her studies have not gone very far, and she would not admit it. Anyhow, I stood up, and said: "I must not disturb you any longer," and bowed and went away; but I thought to myself: "A fig for her and her studies; fine sort of a doctor she'll make!" What do you think about it all? We shall still have to trust to the encyclopedia, and after all a lot of what we can learn there is all right, and luckily we know most things except the word segsual. Next winter I expect we shall find it easier than we used to to get to the bookcase in your house. I don't bow to the silly idiot any more.

But darling Rita, with regard to the "innocent child," I don't want to influence you in any way, and I shan't be angry with you for preferring an unworthy person to me!!! Faithless though you are, I send you half a million kisses, your ever faithful friend, H. P.S. I have been 4 days writing this letter; tear it up, whatever you do!!!

Now that I have copied the letter, I really can't see why Hella wants me to tear it up. There's nothing so very dreadful in it. But there is one thing I shan't be able to do for Hella, to help her in looking up things in the encyclopedia. I think I should always feel that Mother would suddenly come in and stand behind us. No, I simply can't do it.

August 13th. Through that stupid copying I have been prevented writing about my own affairs, although they are far more important. Last Wednesday the Society for the Preservation of Natural Beauties had arranged a great excursion to Inner-Lahn in breaks. Dora did not want to go at first, but Father said that if it would give us pleasure, he would very much like to go with us, and Mother would be only too delighted to see that we were enjoying something once more. And two days before the excursion Dora finally decided that she would like to go; I knew why at once; she thought that by that time all the places would have been taken, and that we should have been told: Very sorry, no more room. But luckily she had made a great mistake. For the secretary said: With pleasure; how many places shall I reserve? and so we said: 7; namely, Father, Dora, and I, Aunt Alma (unfortunately), Marina (very unfortunately), and the two boys (no less unfortunately). "That will need an extra conveyance," replied the secretary, and we thought we should make a family party. But it was not so: Next Dora sat a gentleman whom I had seen once or twice before, and he paid her a tremendous amount of attention. Besides that there were 2 strange gentlemen, Frau Bang and her 2 daughters and her son, who is not quite all there; opposite was Hero Siegfried, a young lady who is I believe going on the stage, the two Weiner girls and their Mother (notwithstanding!!!), then I, and afterwards Marina, Father,

Aunt Alma, and the two boys opposite. I don't know who made up the other break-loads. At 6 in the morning we all met outside the school, for the schoolmaster acted as our guide. I did not know before that he has two daughters and a son who has matriculated this year. First of all they held a great review, and the gentlemen fortified themselves with a nip and so did some of the ladies; I did not, for I hate the way in which a liqueur burns one's throat so that every one, at any rate girls and ladies, make such faces when they are drinking, that is why I never drink liqueur. I did not care much about the drive out, for it was very cold and windy, most of us had red noses and blue lips; I kept on biting my lips to keep them red, for one looks simply hideous when one's lips are white or blue, I noticed that in Dora when we were skating last winter. Father went only on our account, and Aunt Dora stayed at home so that Aunt Alma could go. Marina wears "snails" now, the sight of her is enough to give one fits. Dora gets on with her quite well, which is more than I can say for myself. Only when we got out aid I notice that Siegfried's sister, Fraulein Hulda, had been sitting next the aspiring actress. She is awfully nice, and many, many years ago she must have been very pretty; she has such soft brown eyes, and her hair is the same colour as her brother's; but he has glorious blue eyes, which get quite black when he is angry, as he was when he was talking about his father. I should tremble before him in his wrath. He is so tall that I only come up to his shoulder. Father calls him the red tapeworm; but that's really not fair. He is very broad but so thin. In Unter-Toifen we stopped for breakfast, eating the food we had brought with us; about half an hour; then the schoolmaster hurried us all away, for we had quite 10 miles to walk. The two boys made a party with other boys, and we five girls, we 2, the 2 Weiners, and Marina, led the way. Aunt Alma walked with a clergyman's wife from Hildesheim, or whatever it was called, and with the schoolmaster's wife. It was awfully dull at first, so that I began to be sorry that I had begged Father to let us go. But after we had gone a few miles the schoolmaster's son and three bright young fellows came along and walked with us. Then we had such fun that we could hardly walk for laughing, and the elders had continually to drive us on. Marina was quite unrestrained, I could never have believed that she could be so jolly. One of the schoolmaster's daughters fell down, and some one pulled her out of the brook into which she had slid because she was laughing so much. I really don't know what time we got to Inner-Lahn, for we were enjoying ourselves so much. Dinner had been ordered ready for us, and we were all frantically hungry. We laughed without stopping, for we had all sat down just as we had come in, although Aunt Alma did not want us to at first. But she was outvoted. I was especially pleased to show Hero Siegfried that I could amuse myself very well without him, for he had frozen on to the aspiring actress, or she had frozen on to him—I don't know which, or at least I did not know then! Since we were sitting all mixed up everyone had to pay for himself, and Father said next day we had spent a perfect fortune; but that was not in the hotel, it happened later, when we were buying mementoes. And I think Dora gave Marina 3 crowns, so that she could buy some things too. But Dora never lets on about anything of that sort. I must say I like her character better and better; in those ways she is very like Mother. Well, our purchases were all packed into two or three rucksacks, and were kept for a raffle in Unter-Toifen on the way back. I must have spent at least 7 crowns, for Father had given each of us 5 crowns before we started, and I still had a lot of my August pocket money left, and now I've got only 40 hellers. After we had had dinner and bought the things we lay about in the forest or walked about in couples. I had curled myself up for a nap when some one came up behind me, and when I sat up this someone put his hands over my eyes and said: "The Mountain Spirit." And I recognised his hands instantly, and said: "Hero Siegfried!" Then he laughed like anything and sat down beside me and said: "You were enjoying yourself so much this morning that you had not even a glance to spare for me." "Contrariwise (I've got that from Dora), I never foist myself on anyone, and never hang around anyone's neck." Then he wanted to put his arm round my waist (and probably, most probably, he would have kissed me), but I sprang to my feet and called Dora or rather Thea, for before the gentlemen we pretend that we never call one another anything but Thea and Rita. Father says that that is awfully silly, and no longer suitable for Dora (but of course it was alright for me!), but we keep to our arrangement. Then he raised my hand to his lips and said: "Don't call!" But Dora came up, and with her the gentleman with the pincenez, who is a doctor of law belonging to the District Court of Innsbruck, and Marina and one of the young men, and I asked, "I say, when are we going to have tea?" "Just fancy, she is hungry again already," they all said, and laughed like anything. And Dora looked frightfully happy. She was wearing an edelweiss buttonhole which she had not been wearing before; in the evening she told me that Dr. P. had given it her. If possible he is even taller than Hero Siegfried, for Dora is taller than I am and her head only comes up to his ear. At 3 o'clock the last party came up to the belvedere, we had got there earlier. The view was lovely. But I must say I can enjoy a fine view much better when I am alone, that is with Father or quite a few persons; it is no good when there's such a crowd; each additional person seems to take something more away. In a lovely place and at the cemetery one must be alone. For a beautiful view usually makes one feel frightfully sad, and one ought not to have been laughing so much just before, or laugh directly afterwards. If I were alone in Inner-Lahn I'm sure I should become melancholy, for it is so gloriously beautiful there.

At 4 o'clock, after tea, we started back, for the schoolmaster thought the descent would not take more than two hours and a half, but we needed more than three. For we were all very tired, and a great many of them had sore feet, especially Aunt Alma! We had said before, that it would be too much for Aunt; but she had to come with us to take care of Marina, though Marina enjoyed herself extremely with a Herr Furtner, who is studying mining like Oswald, not in Leoben but in Germany. One does not really find out what a girl is like until one sees how she behaves with a man, or what she is like when one talks to her about certain things; as for the last, of course that's impossible with Marina since the experience we had. But anyhow she is nicer than one would have thought at first sight. It was lovely on the way home. Driving back from Unter-Toifen we sat quite differently.

In our break, instead of the Weiners, there were three students from Munich, they were awfully nice, and we sang all the songs we knew; especially "Hoch vom Dachstein, wo der Aar nur haust," and "Forelle" and "Wo mein Schatz ist," were lovely, and the people in two different breaks sang together. And then some of them sang some Alpine songs and yodelled till the hills echoed. Two or three of the men in the third break were rather tipsy and Hero Siegfried!! was one of them. Aunt Alma had a frightful headache; it was utterly idiotic for her to come, and we did not know yet what was still to happen. At every house from which a girl had come there was a serenade. And next evening there was to be a great raffle of the mementoes we had bought, but Father would not let us go to that.

August 14th. It is desperately dull. I don't know what on earth to do, so I am writing my diary. Besides, I have not written about the row yet. The next afternoon Aunt Alma came just as we were going out and said to Father: Ernst, please let me have a word with you. Now we all know Aunt Alma's let me have a word with you. In plain language it means: I'm going to make a scene. She began: "Ernst, you know I never like these big parties with a lot of strangers, for no good can come of them. Still, I made up my mind to go for the sake of the children, and chiefly for the sake of your motherless children. (Nobody asked her to; and Aunt Dora had to stay at home on her account.) Do you know what sort of people were in our company? That impudent young student whom Gretel is always running after (did you ever hear anything like it! I should like to know when I ran after him; I suppose in the wood I put my arm round his waist, and I suppose that it was I who began the acquaintance on my birthday) and that girl who's training for the stage did not come home after the excursion till the night was half over. God knows where they were! They were certainly no cleaner when they got home. (Naturally, for where could they have had a wash.) His father gave the young blackguard a fine talking to, but of course the girl's mother takes her side. It would positively kill me to think of my Marina doing anything of the kind." Father was able to get a word in at last: "But my dear Alma, what has all this to do with my girls? As far as I know these two people weren't in our break, isn't that so girls?" I was glad that Father turned to us, and I said: "Siegfried Sch. and the girl drove in the fourth break, I saw them getting in. And it was toute meme chause where he drove and with whom he was driving." (Of course that's not true, but I said it was because of Aunt.) "Such language and such a tone to your own Father!" Directly she said that Father was in such a passion as I have never seen him in before. "My dear Alma, I really must beg you not to interfere with my educational methods, any more than I ever attempt to interfere in your affairs." Father said this quite quietly, but he was simply white with rage, and Dora told me afterwards that I was quite white too, also from rage of course. Aunt Alma said: "I don't want to prophesy evil, but the future will show who is right Goodbye." As soon as she had gone Dora and I rushed to Father and said: "Please Father, don't be so frightfully angry; there's no reason why you should." And Father was awfully sweet and said: "I know quite well that I can trust you; you are my Berta's children." And then I simply could not contain myself, and I said: "No, Father, I really did flirt with Siegfried, and in the wood he put his arm round my waist; but I did not let him kiss me, I give you my word I did not. And if you want me to I'll promise never to speak to him again." And then Father said: "Really, Gretel, you have plenty of time yet for such affairs, and even if that red-haired rascal plays the gallant with you, he is only making himself a laughing-stock. And you don't want that, do you, little witch?" Then I threw my arms round Father and promised him on my word of honour that I would never speak to Siegfried again. For it really distresses me very much that he should make himself ridiculous; and that he should go out walking half the night with that girl; such shamelessness!

We were so much upset that we did not go for a walk, and of course did not go to the raffle. But I'm frightfully sorry about those things I paid 7 crowns for. I do hope he did not win any of them.

143

August 15th. Just a few words more. Early this morning, as I was going to breakfast, in the corridor I met S. (it's a good thing that is the initial both of his name and of Strick [rascal] as Father called him) and he said: "Good morning, Fraulein Gretchen. Why weren't you at the raffle? Hadn't you any share?"—"Oh yes, I had bought 7 crowns worth for it, but I had no fancy for the company I should meet." — — Why, what has taken you all of a sudden? They were the same people as at the excursion! — — — "Precisely for that reason," said I, and passed on. I think I gave him what for, for he simply must have understood. Father is really quite right, and it is not at all nice to abuse one's parents to strangers as he is always doing. I could not say a word against my parents to anyone, although I'm often frightfully angry with them; of course not about Mother, for she is dead. But not even about Father; I would rather choke down the greatest injustice. For when we had that trouble with Aunt Alma about Marina, I was really not in the least to blame, but he scolded me so, even while Aunt Alma was there, so that I can never forget it. But still, to a stranger, to some one whom I had only just got to know, I would never say a word against anyone in our family; though I used to get on so badly with Dora, I never said much against her even to Hella; at most that she was deceitful, and that really used to be so, though she seldom is now.

August 19th. It is so filthyly dull here; I can't bear the word filthy, but it's the only one that's strong enough. Oswald is coming this evening, at last. Thank goodness. S. has made several advances, but I have ignored them. Let him stick to his actress who can go out walking with him half the night. I really should like to know where they went. In the night, I never heard of such a thing! Dora says she took a dislike to S. from the first because he — — — — — it's an absolute lie! — — — has clammy! hands. It's simply not true, on the contrary he has such entrancingly cool hands, I'm sure I must know that better than Dora. But I've known for a long time that whenever anyone pays me attention Dora is unsympathetic, naturally enough. By the way, on Sunday I got a charming letter from Anneliese. I must answer it to-day.

August 22nd. Oswald is awfully nice. He did not forget my birthday, but he says that at that time he was stoney, in student's slang that means that he hadn't any money, and then he could not find anything suitable, but that he will repair the omission as soon as we get back to Vienna. But I don't know what I should like. Oswald is going to stay until we all go back to Vienna, and we are making a few excursions by ourselves. That is really the best way after all. I am not much with the Weiners now, for we had a little tiff on the big excursion. But Nelly is rather taken with Oswald, so she

144

came twice to our table to-day, once about a book we had lent her, and once to arrange for a walk.

August 24th. It is really absurd that one's own brother can think such a lot of one; but if he does, I suppose he knows. Oswald said to me to-day: "Gretl, you are so smart I could bite you. How you are developing." I said: "I don't want anyone to bite me," and he said: "Nor do I," but I was awfully delighted, though he is only my brother. He can't stand Marina, and as a man he finds Dora too stupid; I think he's right, really. And I simply can't understand Dr. P., that he can always find something to talk about to Dora. He has hardly said 10 words to me yet. Still, I don't care.

August 27th. We went up the Matscherkogel yesterday, and we had a lovely view. The two boys came, for they had begged their father to let them; but of course Aunt Alma and Marina did not come. Oswald calls Aunt Alma Angular Pincushion, but only when Father isn't there, for after all she is Father's sister. The Weiners wanted to come too, but I said that my brother was staying only a few days more, and that this was a "farewell excursion en famille." They were rather hurt, but they have made me very angry by the way in which they will go on talking about S. in front of me, on purpose, saying that he is engaged or is going to be engaged to the actress girl against his father's will. What does it matter to me? They keep on exchanging glances when they say that, especially Olga, who is really rather stupid. I am so sad now at times that I simply can't understand how I could have enjoyed myself so much on the big excursion. I'm always thinking of dear Mother, and I often wear my black frock. It suits my mood better.

August 30th. I believe the Schs. are leaving to-morrow. At least the old gentleman said to Father the day before yesterday: "Thank the Lord, we shall soon be able to enjoy the comforts of home once more." That is what Hella's grandmother used to say before they came back from the country. And to-day I saw two great trunks standing in the passage just outside Herr Scharrer's room. Oswald thinks the old gentleman charming; well, there's no accounting for tastes. I don't believe he's ever spoken to S., though he is a German Nationalist too, but of a different section; Oswald belongs to the Sudmark, and S. abused that section frightfully when I told him that Oswald belonged to the Sudmark.

August 31st. He has really gone to-day, that is, the whole family has gone. They came to bid us goodbye yesterday after supper, and they left this morning by the 9 o'clock train to Innsbruck. And his hands are not clammy, I paid particular attention to the point; it is pure imagination on Dora's part. He and

Oswald greeted one another with Hail! That's a splendid salutation, and I shall introduce it between Hella and me.

September 2nd. The Weiners left to-day too, because people are really beginning to stare at their mother too much. When Olga said goodbye to me she told me she hated having to travel with her mother and whenever possible she would lag behind a little so that people should not know they belonged together.

September 4th. I never heard of such a thing!! S. has come back, alone of course. Everyone is indignant, for he has only come back because of Fraulein A., the actress girl. But Oswald defends him like anything. This afternoon Frau Lunda said to Aunt Dora: "It's simply scandalous, and his parents certainly ought not to have allowed him to come, even if the girl's mother does not know any better." Then Oswald said: "Excuse me, Frau Lunda, Scharrer is no longer a schoolboy who must cling to his mother's apron-string; such tutelage would really be unworthy of a full-grown German." I was so pleased that he gave a piece of his mind to Frau L., for she is always glaring at one and is so frantically inquisitive. And tutelage is such an impressive word, S. used it once when he was speaking of his sister and why she had never married. Frau L. was furious. She turned to Aunt Dora and said: "Young men naturally take one another's part, until they are fathers themselves and then they hold other views."

September 8th. Thank goodness we are going home the day after to-morrow. It really has been rather dull here, certainly I can't join in the paean Hella sang about the place last year; of course they were not staying in the Edelweiss boarding house but in the Hotel Kaiser von Oesterreich. It makes a lot of difference where one is staying. By the way, it has just occurred to me. The young wife who had the eruption after infection can't have been divorced, as Hella wrote me the week before last; for her husband has been there on a visit, he is an actor at the Theatre Royal in Munich. So it would seem that actors really are all infected; and Hella always says it is only officers! She takes rather an exaggerated view.

September 14th. We have been back in Vienna since the 11th, but I have been absolutely unable to write, though there was plenty to write about. For the first person I met when I went out on the 11th to fetch some cocoa which Resi had forgotten, was Lieutenant R. Viktor, the Conqueror!! Of course he recognised me immediately, and was awfully friendly, and walked with me a little way. He asked casually after Dora, but it is obvious that he is not in love with her any more. And it was so funny that he should not know that Dora had matriculated this year and so would not be going to the High

146

School any more. I did not tell him that she intends to go on with her studies, for it is not absolutely settled yet.

September 16th. Hella came home yesterday; I am so glad; I greeted her with: Hail! but she said; "don't be silly," besides, it's unsuitable for an Austrian officer's daughter!!! Still, we won't quarrel about it after 2 months' separation, and Servus is very smart too though not so distinguished. She told me a tremendous lot more about that young married woman; some of the ladies in B. said that her cousin was in love with the husband. That would be awful, for then she would get infected too; but Hella says she did not notice anything, though she watched very closely during the fortnight he was there. He sang at two of the musical evenings, but she did not see any sign of it. Lizzi is engaged, but Hella could not write anything about it, for the engagement is only being officially announced now that they are back in Vienna; her fiance is Baron G. He is an attache in London, and she met him there. He is madly in love with her. In August he was on leave, and he came to B. to make an offer of marriage; that is why they stayed the whole summer in B. instead of going to Hungary. Those were the special circumstances, about which Hella said she could not write to me. I don t see why she could not have told me that, I should have kept it to myself; and after all, Lizzi is 19 1/2 now, and no one would have been surprised that she is engaged at last. They can't have a great betrothal party, for Baron G.'s father died in July. Hella is very much put out. Lizzi says it does not matter a bit.

September 18th. Lizzi's betrothal cards arrived to-day. It must be glorious to send out betrothal cards. Dora got quite red with annoyance, though she said when I asked her: "Why do you flush up so, surely there's no reason to be ashamed when anyone is engaged!" "Really, why should you think I am ashamed, I am merely extremely surprised." But one does not get so red as that from surprise.

September 19th. School began to-day; unfortunately, for she has gone. And what was the Third is now the Fourth, and that is detestable, to sit in the classroom without her. Luckily we have Frau Doktor St. as class mistress, and she is to teach us mathematics and physics once more; Frau Doktor F., whom we used to call Nutling and the Fifth used to call Waterfall has gone, for she has been appointed to the German High School in Lemberg. For the time being we are sitting in our old place, but Hella says we must ask Frau Doktor S. to let us have another seat, for the memory of the three years when we had Frau Doktor M. might make us inattentive. That is a splendid idea. In German we have a master, in French I am sorry to say it's still Frau Doktor Dunker, whose complexion has not

147

improved, and in English the head mistress. I am very pleased with that, for first of all I like her very much, and secondly I shall be in her good books from the start because Dora was her favourite. Of course I'm not learning Latin, for it would not interest me now that Frau Doktor M. has gone. Oh, and we have a new Religion teacher, for Herr Professor K. has retired, since he was 60 already.

September 21st. We have managed it. In the long interval, Hella said to Frau Doktor St., who was in charge. "Frau Doktor, may we venture to ask for something?" So she said: "What, in the very first week; well, what is it?" We said we should like to move from the third bench towards the window, for we found it very painful to go on sitting where we had sat when Frau Doktor M., was there. At first she refused, but after a while she said: "I'll see what I can do, if you are really not happy where you are." From 11 to 12 was the mathematic lesson, and as soon as Frau Doktor Steiner had taken her place she said: "This arrangement of your seats was only provisional. You had better sit more according to height." Then she rearranged us all, and Hella and I were moved to the 5th bench on the window side; the two twins, the Ehrenfelds got our places; in front of us is Lohr and a new girl called Friederike Hammer whose father is a confectioner in Mariahilferstrasse. We are awfully glad that we have got away from that hateful third bench where she used so often to stand near us and lay her hand on the desk.

September 29th. Professor Fritsch, the German professor, came to-day for the first time. He is always clearing his throat and he wears gold spectacles. Hella thinks him tolerably nice, but I don't. I'm quite sure that I shall never get an Excellent in German again. Yesterday the new Religion master came for the first time, and I sat alone, for Hella being a Protestant did not attend. He looks frightfully ill and his eyes are always lowered though he has burning black eyes. Next time I shall sit beside Hammer which will be company for us both.

October 2nd. We had confession and communion to-day, and since the staff will not allow us to choose our confessors, I had to go to Professor Ruppy. I did hate it. I whispered so low that he had to tell me to speak louder three times over. When I began about the sixth commandment he covered his eyes with his hand. But thank goodness he did not ask any questions about that. The only one of the staff who used to allow us to choose our confessors was Frau Doktor M. Really, she did not allow it directly but when one ran quickly to another confessional box, she pretended not to notice. The Herr Rel. Prof gives frightfully long penances; all the girls who went to him took a tremendous time to get through. I do hope he won't be so strict over his examinations or I shall get an

Unsatisfactory; that would be awful. October 3rd. Father was so splendid to-day! Aunt Dora must have told him that I asked her not long ago whether Father was likely to marry Frau Riedl, whose husband died almost exactly the same time as Mother, for Father is guardian to her three children. She was here to-day with Willi, because he has just begun going to school. Dora and I talked it over, and she said that if Father married Frau R., she would leave home. In the evening when we were at supper, I said: "If only Frau v. R. was not so ugly. Father, don't you think she's perfectly hideous? And Father laughed so lovingly and said: You need not be anxious, little witch, I'm not going to inflict a stepmother on you." I was so glad, and so was Dora and we kissed Father such a lot, and Dora said: "I felt sure that you would never break your oath to Mother," and she burst out crying. And Father said: "No, girls, I did not give any promise to your Mother, she would never have asked anything of the kind. But with grown girls like you it would never do to bring a stepmother into the house." And then I told Father that Dora would have gone away from home, and as for me, I should certainly have been frightfully upset. For if Father really wanted to marry again I should have to put up with it; and so would Dora. But Father said once more: "Don't worry, I certainly shan't marry again." And I said: "Not even Aunt Dora?" And he said: "Oh, as for her − −" And then he pulled himself up and said: "No, no, not even Aunt Dora." Dora has just told me that I am a perfect idiot, for surely I must know that Father is not particularly charmed by Aunt. And then she blamed me for having told Father that she would leave home if he were to marry again. I am a child to whom it is impossible to entrust any secrets!! Now we have been quarrelling for at least three quarters of an hour, so it is already half past 11. Luckily to-morrow is a holiday, because of the Emperor's birthday. But I am so glad to know for certain that Father is not going to marry Frau v. R I could never get on with a stepmother.

October 9th. It's horribly difficult in German this year. In composition we are not allowed to make any rough notes, we have to write it straight off and then hand it in. I simply can't. Professor Fritsch is very handsome, but the girls are terribly afraid of him for he is so strict. His wife is in an asylum and his children live with his mother. He has got a divorce from his wife, and since he has the luck to be a Protestant he can marry again if he wants to. Hella is perfectly fascinated by him, but I'm not in the least. For I always think of Prof. W. in the Second, and that's enough for me. I'm not going to fall in love with any more professors. In the Training College, where Marina is now, in her fourth year one of the professors last year married a former pupil. I would not do that at any price, marry a former professor, who knows all one's faults. Besides, he must be at least 12 or 20 years older than the girl; and that's perfectly horrible, one might as well marry one's father; he would be at least fond of her, and she would at least know the way he likes to have everything done; but to marry one's former professor, what an extraordinary thing to do!

October 15th. I'm frightfully anxious that Hella may have a relapse; she says that nothing would induce her to have a second operation, especially now that — — —; she says she would rather die. That would be awful! I did my best to persuade her to tell her mother that she has such pain; but she won't.

October 19th. In November, Hella's father will be made a general and will be stationed in Cracow. Thank goodness she is going to stay here with her grandmother until she leaves the Lyz. She will only go to Cracow at Christmas and Easter and in the summer holidays. She is frantically delighted. The good news has made her quite well again. Everyone at school is very proud that there will be a general's daughter in our class. It's true that there is a field-marshal's daughter in the Third, but he is retired. Father always says: Nobody makes any fuss over a retired officer.

October 22nd. We are so much excited that we've hardly any time to learn our lessons. At Christmas last year some one gave Hella's mother several of Geierstamm's novels. The other day one of them was lying on the table, and when her mother was out Hella had a hurried look at it and read the title The Power of Woman!!! When her mother had finished it, she watched to see where it was put in the bookcase, and now we are reading it. It's simply wonderful! It keeps me awake all night; Signe whom he is so passionately fond of and who deceives him. We cried so much that we could not go on reading. And Gretchen, the girl, to whom her father is everything; I can understand so well that she is always anxious lest her father should marry that horrid Frau Elise, although she has a husband already. And when she dies, oh, it's so horrible and so beautiful that we read it over three times in succession. The other day my eyes were quite red from crying, and Aunt said I must be working too hard; for she thinks that Hella and I are studying literature together. Oh dear, lessons are an awful nuisance when one has such books to read.

October 24th. When I look at Father I always think of the novel The Power of Woman; of course leaving Signe out of account. Hella hopes she'll be able to get hold of some other book, but it's not so easy to do without her mother finding it out, for she often lends books to her friends. Then there would be an awful row. We certainly don't want to read The Little Brother's Book, the title does

150

not attract us; but there's a novel called The Comedy of Marriage, it must be splendid; we must get that whatever happens.

October 26th. The Bruckners are going to keep on their flat, and Hella's grandmother will come and live there; only the Herr General!!! is going to C., and of course Hella's mother too. Lizzi will stay, for she is taking cooking lessons, since she is to be married in Mid-Lent.

October 31st. Hella's parents left to-day, she cried frightfully, for she did so want to go with them. Lizzi was quite unconcerned, for she is engaged already, and the Baron, her fiance, is coming at Christmas, either to Vienna or Cracow; he does not care which.

November 4th. Some of the girls in our class were furious in the German lesson to-day. One or two of the girls did not know the proper places for commas, and Prof. Fritsch hinted that we had learned nothing at all in previous years. We understood perfectly well that he was aiming at Frau Doktor M., whose German lessons were 10 times or rather 100 times better than Professor F.'s. And on this very matter of punctuation Frau Doktor M. took a tremendous lot of trouble and gave us lots of examples. Besides, whether one has a good style or not does not depend upon whether one puts a comma in the right place. The two Ehrenfelds, who towards the end were awfully fond of Frau Doktor M., say that we, who were Frau Doktor M.'s favourites, ought to write a composition without a single comma, just to show him. That's a splendid idea, and Hella and I will do it like a shot if only the others can be trusted to do it too.

November 6th. This year all the classes must have at least two outings every month, even in winter. If that had been decided in the last school year, when Frau Doktor M. was still there, I should certainly have gone every time. But this year, when she has left, we can't enjoy it. Frau Doktor St. is awfully nice, but not like Frau Doktor M. Besides, we go somewhere with Father every Sunday, Hella comes with us, and Lizzi if she likes. As soon as the snow comes we are going to have tobogganing parties at Hainfeld or Lilienfeld.

December 3rd. Nearly a whole month has passed without my writing, but I must write to-day! There's been such a row in the German lesson!! We got back the compositions in which Hella and I, the 2 Ehrenfelds, Brauner, Edith Bergler, and Kuhnelt, had not put a single comma. Nothing would have been found out had not that idiot Brauner put in commas first and then scratched them out. We had agreed that if the Prof. noticed anything we would say we had meant to go through them together before the lesson, and to decide where to put in commas, but that we had had no time. Now

151

the silly fool has given away the whole show. He is going to bring the matter before the staff meeting. But after all, it's simply impossible to give 6 girls out of 25 a bad conduct mark.

December 4th. The head mistress came to inspect the German lesson to-day. Afterwards she said that she expected us to make all the knowledge which Frau Doktor M. had instilled into us for 3 years, the firm foundation of our further development in the higher classes. In the English lesson she referred to the more restricted use of punctuation marks in English; and afterwards we 6 sinners were summoned to the office. The whole school knew about the trouble and was astonished at our courage, especially the lower classes; the Fifth and the Sixth were rather annoyed that we in the Fourth had dared to do it. The head gave us a terrible scolding, saying that it was an unexampled piece of impudence, and that we were not doing credit to Frau Doktor M. Then Hella said very modestly: "Frau Direktorin, will you please allow me to say a word in our defence?" Then she explained that Prof. Fritsch never missed a chance of casting a slur upon Frau Doktor M., not in plain words of course, but so that we could not fail to understand it, and that was why we acted as we did. The head answered we must certainly be mistaken, that no member of the staff could ever speak against another in such a way we had simply misunderstood Prof Fritsch! But we know perfectly well how often the Nutling used to say in the Maths lesson: "Don't you know that? Surely you must have been taught that." The emphasis does it!!!!! The staff meeting is to-morrow, and we were told to do our best to make amends before the meeting. The 2 Ehrenfelds suggested that we should write the compositions over again, of course with all the commas, and should place them on his desk to-morrow morning before the German lesson; but all the rest of us were against this, for we saw plainly that the head had changed colour when Hella said what she did. We shall make the corrections and then we shall all begin new copybooks.

December 8th. It is 3 days now since the staff meeting, but not a word has been said yet about our affair, and in the German lesson yesterday the Prof. gave out the subject for the third piece of home work without saying anything in particular. I think he is afraid to. Hella has saved us all, for everyone else would have been afraid to say what she did, even I. Hella said: "My dear Rita, I'm not an officer's daughter for nothing;" if I have not courage, who should have? The girls stare at us in the interval and whenever they meet us, though in the office the head said to us: "I do hope that this business will not be spread all over the school." But Brauner has a sister in the Second and Edith Bergler's sister is in the Fifth and through them all the classes have heard about it. I suppose nothing is going to be said to our parents or something would have happened already. Besides, to be on the safe side, I have already dropped a few hints at home. And since Dora, thank goodness, is no longer at the school, it is impossible that there can be much fuss. It was only at first that we were alarmed, but Hella was quite right when she said: "I'm sure nothing will happen to us, for we are in the right."

December 15th. A meeting with Viktor!!! Dora and I had gone to do our Christmas shopping, and we came across him just as we had turned into Tuchlauben. Dora got fiery red, and both their voices trembled. He does look fine, with his black moustache and his flashing eyes! And the green facings on his tunic suit him splendidly. He cleared his throat quickly to cover his embarrassment, and walked with us as far as the Upper Market-place; he has another six-months furlough because of throat trouble; so Dora can be quite easy in her mind in case she fancied that — — — —. When he said goodbye he kissed our hands, mine as well as Dora's, and smiled so sweetly, sadly and sweetly at the same time. Several times I wanted to turn the conversation upon him. But when Dora does not want a thing, you can do what you like and she won't budge; she's as obstinate as a mule! She's always been like that since she was quite a little girl, when she used to say: Dor not! That meant: Dora won't; little wretch! such a wilful little beast!

December 17th. Yesterday we had our first tobogganing party on the Anninger; it was glorious, we kept on tumbling into the snow; the snow lay fairly thick, especially up there, where hardly anyone comes. As we were going home such a ridiculous thing happened to Hella; she caught her foot on a snag and tore off the whole sole of a brand new shoe. She had to tie it on with a string, and even then she limped so badly that every one believed she had sprained her ankle tobogganing. Her grandmother was frightfully angry and said: "That comes of such unladylike amusements!" Aunt Dora was very much upset, for she had been with us, but Father said: Hella's grandmother is quite an old lady, and in her day people had very different views in this respect. I should say so, in this respect, Hella finds it out a dozen times a day, all the things she must not say and must not do, and all the things which are unsuitable for young girls! Her grandmother would like to keep her under a glass shade; but not a transparent one, for she must not be able to see out, and no one must be able to see in. (The last is the main point.)

December 20th. To-day was the last German lesson before Christmas, and not a word more has been said about our affair. Hella has proved splendidly right. Even Verbenowitsch, who curries favour with every member of the staff, has congratulated her, and so has Hammer, who is a newcomer and did not know Frau Doktor M. By the way, at 1 o'clock the other day we met Franke; she goes now to a school of dramatic art, and says that the whole tone of the place is utterly different, she is so glad to have done with the High School. She had heard of the affair with Prof. F. and she congratulated us upon our strength of character, especially Hella of course. She says that the matter is common talk in all the High Schools of Vienna, at least she heard of it from a girl at the High School for the Daughters of Civil Servants, a girl whose sister is at the School of Dramatic Art. She is very happy there, but she is annoyed that such an institution should still be called a school; it's not a school in the least; we would be astonished to see how free they all are. She is very pretty and has even more figure than she used to have. She speaks very prettily too, but rather too loudly, so that everyone turned round to look at us. She hopes that she will be able to invite us to see her debut in one year!!! I should never be able to stand on a stage before a lot of strangers, I know I would never be able to get a word out.

December 21st. Hella is awfully unlucky. The day before yesterday she got such bad influenza and sore throat that she can't go to Cracow. She says she is born to ill luck; this is the second Christmas that has been spoiled, two years ago the appendicitis operation, and now this wretched influenza. She hopes her mother will come to Vienna, but if so her father will be left quite alone. And how on earth shall we get on, Christmas without Mother, the first Christmas without Mother. I simply don't dare to think of it, for if I did it would make me cry. Dora says too that it can't be a proper Christmas without Mother. I wonder what Father will say when he sees Mother's portrait. I do hope the frame will be ready to-morrow. Hella is especially unhappy because she is not able to see Lajos. Besides, she is madly in love at the same time with a lieutenant of dragoons whom we meet every day and who is a count, and he is madly in love with her. He knows that her father is a general, for when her father went to kiss the Emperor's hand he took Hella part of the way with him in the motor, and she was introduced to the lieutenant then. So now he salutes her when they meet. He is tremendously tall and looks fearfully aristocratic. But what annoys me with Hella is that she invariably denies it when she is in love with anyone. I always tell her, or if she notices anything I don't deny it. What's the sense of it between friends? for example, the year before last she was certainly in love with the young doctor in the hospital. And in September when we came back from Theben with that magnificent lieutenant in the flying corps, I made no secret of the fact that I was frantically in love with him. But she did not believe me, and said: That is not real love, when people don't see one another for months and flirt with others between whiles. That was aimed at Hero Siegfried. Goodness me, at him!! it's really too absurd.

December 22nd. I am so delighted, Frau Doktor M., at least she is Frau Professor Theyer now, has written to me. I had sent her Christmas good wishes, and she sent a line to thank me, and at the same time she wished me a happy New Year, she took the lead in this; it was heavenly. I was frightfully annoyed because Dora said that she had done it only to save herself the trouble of writing again; I'm sure that's not true. Dora always says things like that simply to annoy me. But her sweet, her divine letter, I carry it about with me wherever I go, and her photograph too. She sent Hella only a card, naturally, for that was all Hella had sent her. I can quite well fancy Frau Doktor M. as a stepmother, that is, not quite well, but better than anyone else. She wrote so sweetly about Mother, saying that of course I should find this Christmas less happy than usual. She is certainly right there. We can none of us feel as if the day after to-morrow is to be Christmas Eve. The only thing that I really enjoy thinking of is the way Father will stare when he sees the portrait. But really in the first years after such a loss one ought not to keep Christmas, for on such days one feels one's sadness more than ever.

December 23rd. I have still a frightful lot to do for Christmas, but I must write to-day. There was a ring at the front door this morning at about half past 11. I thought it must be Hella come to fetch me, that she must be all right again, so I rushed out, tore the door open, prepared to greet Hella, and then I was simply kerblunxed, for there was a gentleman standing who asked most politely: Is anyone at home? I knew him in a moment, it was that Dr. Pruckmuller from Fieberbr. Meanwhile Dora had opened the drawing-room door, and now came the great proof of deceitfulness: She was not in the least surprised, but said: "Ah, Dr. Pruckmuller, I am so glad you have kept your word." So it was plain that he had promised her to come, and I am practically sure she knew he was coming to-day, for she was wearing her best black silk apron with the insertions, such as we only wear when visitors are expected. What a humbug she is! So I went into the drawing-room too. Then Aunt Dora came in and asked him to supper this evening. Then he went away. All the time he had not said a word to me, it seemed as if he had not even noticed that there was such a person as me in the world Not until he was actually leaving did he say: "Well; Fraulein, how are you?" "Oh well," said I, "I'm much as anyone can expect to be so soon after Mother's death." Dora got as red as fire, for she understood. I shall know how to treat him if he becomes my

155

brother-in-law. But that may be a long way off; for he lives in Innsbruck, and Father is not likely to allow Dora to marry away to Innsbruck. At dinner I hardly said a word, I was so enraged at this deceitfulness. But there is more to come. At 7, or whatever time it was, Dr. Pruckmuller turned up. Dora appeared in a white blouse with a black bow, and had remained in her room till the last minute so that I might not know what she was wearing. For I had believed she would wear her black dress with the insertions, and so I was wearing mine. Oh well, that did not matter. At supper he talked all the time to Dora, so I purposely talked to Oswald. Then he said that on March 1st he was going to be transferred to Vienna. Once more Dora was not in the least astonished, so she must have known all about it! But now I remember quite well that in October the postman handed me a letter for her with the Innsbruck postmark. So she was corresponding with him openly the whole time, less than 6 months after Mother's death. It really is too bad! But when I was chattering about the country, she kicked me under the table as a hint not to laugh so frightfully. And when my brother-in-law in spe, oh how it does make me laugh, two or three years ago, in Goisern I think it was, we used to call Dora Inspe, because she had said of Robert Warth and me: The bridal pair in spe! And now she is in the same position. When he went away in the evening I was trembling lest Father should invite him to the Christmas tree, but thank goodness when Father asked: "What are you doing with yourself to-morrow," he answered: "To-morrow I am spending the day with my sister's family, she is married to a captain out Wieden way." Thank goodness that came to nothing, for we are not at all in the mood for visitors, especially the first Christmas without Mother. And if she knew — — — I wish I knew what really happens to the soul. Of course I gave up believing in Heaven long ago; but the soul must go somewhere. There are so many riddles, and they make one so unhappy; in a newspaper feuilleton the other day I saw the title of a chapter: The Riddle of Love. But this riddle does not make people sad, as one can see by Dora. Anyhow, all girls, that is all elder sisters, seem alike in this respect. I remember what Hella told me about Lizzi's engagement. It is true, she had first made his acquaintance in London, not at home; but there was just the same deceitfulness. What on earth does it mean? Would it not be much more kindly and reasonable to tell your sister everything? Otherwise how can anyone expect one to be an ally. Oh well, I don't care, I'm not going to let my Christmas Eve be disturbed by a thing like that; if one can call it a Christmas Eve at all. On Boxing Day, when he is to spend the evening here, I shall tell Hella that I want to come to her and her grandmother. After all, I am glad she has stayed in Vienna.

December 25th. Christmas Eve was very melancholy. We all three got Mother's picture, life size in beautiful green frames, for our rooms. Dora sobbed out loud, and so I cried too and went up to Father and put my arms around him. His eyes were quite wet; for he adored Mother. Only Oswald did not actually cry, but he kept on biting his lips. I was so glad that Dr. P. was not there, for it is horribly disagreeable to cry before strangers. We both got lovely white guipure blouses, not lace blouses, then Aunt gave me a splendid album for 500 postcards, and she also gave me an anthology which I had asked for. Brahms' Hungarian Dances, because Dora would not lend me hers last year because she said they were too difficult for me; as if that were any business of hers; surely my music mistress is a better judge; then some writing paper with my monogram, a new en-tout-cas with everything complete, and hair ribbons and other trifles. Father was awfully delighted with Mother's portrait; of course we had not known that he was getting us life-size portraits of Mother, and from the last photograph of the winter before last we had quite a small likeness painted by Herr Milanowitz, who is a painter, and who knew Mother very well—in colour of course. And we got a lovely rococo frame to close up; when it is open it looks as if Mother were looking out of the window. That was my idea, and Herr Milanowitz thought it most original. Dora considered it very awkward that he would not take any money for it, but it made it possible for us to get a much more elegant frame. After Christmas; for New Year, we are going to send Herr M. some of the best cigars, bought with our own money, I wanted to send them for Christmas, but we don't know anything about cigars, and we did not want to tell anyone because one can never know whether one won't be betrayed and you will be told it is unintentional; but that is not true, for when one betrays anything one has always secretly intended to do so; and then one says it was a slip of the tongue; but one really knows all the time. I can't write down all the extra things that Dora got, only one of them: At 7 o'clock just when Father was lighting the candles on the tree, a commissionaire brought some lovely roses with two sprays of mistletoe interwoven and beneath a nosegay of violets — — — of course from Dr. P. with a card, but she would not let anyone read that. All she said was: "Dr. P. sends everyone Christmas greetings; I believe he had really written: Merry Christmas," but Dora did not dare to say that. Oh, and Hella gave me a bead bag, and I gave her a purse with the double eagle on it, for she wanted a purse that would have a military look. I never knew anyone with such an enthusiasm for the army as

157

Hella; certainly I think officers look awfully smart; but surely it's going too far when she feels that other men practically don't exist. The others have to learn a lot, for example doctors, lawyers, mining engineers, not to speak of students at the College of Agriculture, for perhaps these last "hardly count" (that's the phrase Hella is always using); but all of them have to learn a great deal more than officers do; Hella never will admit that, and always begins to talk of the officers of the general staff; as if they all belonged to the general staff! We have often argued about it. Still, I do hope she will get an officer for her husband, of course one who is well enough off to marry, for otherwise it's no go; for Father says the Bruckners have no private means. It's true he always says that of us too, but I don't believe it; we are not so to say rich, but I fancy we should both of us have enough money for an officer to be able to marry us. Anyhow, Dora voluntarily renounces that possibility, if she is really going to marry Dr. P.

27th. Well, I went to Hella's yesterday and stayed till 9, and on Christmas Day she was here. I see that I wrote above that the Bs. were not well off; it seems to me to be very much the reverse. We always get a great many things and very nice ones at Christmas and on our birthdays and name days (of course Protestants don't have these last), but we don't give one another such splendid things as the Bs. do. Hella had been given a piece of rose-coloured silk for a dress to wear at the dancing class which must have cost at least 50 crowns, and a lace collar and cuffs, which we had seen at the shop, and it had cost 24 crowns, then she had a gold ring with an emerald, and a number of smaller things which she never even looked at. And to see all the things her sister got, things for her trousseau! And the Bs. Christmas tree cost 12 crowns whilst ours cost only 7, though ours was just as good. So I think that the Bs. really have plenty of money, and I said to Hella: "You must be enormously rich." And she said: "Oh well, not so rich as all that; I must not expect to marry an officer on the general staff. Lizzi has done very well for herself for Paul is a baron and is very well off. He is frantically in love with her; queer taste, isn't it?" I quite agree, for Lizzi has not much to boast of in the way of looks, beautiful fair hair, but she is so awfully thin, not a trace of b — —, Hella has much more figure. And if one hasn't any by the time one is 20 one is not likely to get one.

Something awfully funny happened to-day. Hella asked me: "I say, what's the Christian name of that Dr. who is dangling after your sister?" Then it struck me for the first time that on his visiting card he only has Dr. jur. A. Pruckmuller, and then I remembered that last summer, when we first made his acquaintance, Dora said, It's a pity he's called August, the name does not suit him at all. Well, we

158

laughed till we felt quite ill, for of course Hella began to sing: "O du lieber Augustin," and then I thought of Der dumme August [clown's nickname in circus] and we wondered what Dora would call him. Gusti or Gustel, or Augi, my darling Augi, my beloved Gusterl, oh dear, we were in fits of laughter. Then we discussed what names we should like to have for our husbands, and I said: Ewald or Leo, and Hella said: Wouldn't you like Siegfried? But I put my hand on her mouth and said: "Shut up, or you will make me really angry, that is and must remain forgotten." She said what she would like best would be to have a husband called Peter or Thamian or Chrysostomus; then for a pet name she would use Dami or Sosti; and then she said quite seriously that she would only marry a man called Egon, or Alexander, or at least Georg. Just at that moment her mother came in to call us to tea, and she said: "What's an that about Alexander and Georg? You are such dreadful girls. If you are alone together for a couple of minutes (I had come at half past 2 and the Brs. have tea at 4, and that's what Hella's mother calls 2 minutes), you begin to talk of unsuitable things." Hella was afraid her mother would think God knows what, so she said: "Oh no, Mother, we were only discussing what names we should like our fiances to have." You ought to have seen how her mother went on. "That's just it, that when you are barely 15 (I'm not 15 yet) you should have nothing but such things in your heads!" Such things, how absurd. At tea it was almost as dull as it was the other evening at home; for the Herr Baron was there, that is, they all say Du to one another now, for the wedding is to be in February, as soon as it is settled whether the Baron is to stay in London or to be transferred to Berlin. It must be funny to say "Du" to a strange man. Hella says she soon got used to it, and that she likes Paul well enough. When he brings Lizzi sweets, when he is taking her to the theatre, he always gives Hella a box for herself. Other people would certainly not do that, and I know other people who wouldn't accept it. When I got home, Father said: Well, another time I think you'd better stay and sleep at the Brs., and I said: I did not want to be a killjoy here. And Oswald said: "What you need is a box on the ear," Father was luckily out of the room already and so I said: "Your children, if you ever have any, can be kept in order by boxing their ears till they are green and blue, but you have no rights over your sisters, Father told you so in Fieberbrunn." "Oh, I know Father always backs you two up, he has done so from the first." "Please don't draw me into your quarrels," said Dora, as if she had been something quite different from me. And then Aunt Dora said: "I do wish you would not keep on quarreling." "I didn't begin it," said I, and went away without saying goodnight; that is I went to Father's room to say goodnight to

159

him and I saw Aunt Dora in the hall, but I didn't say goodnight to Oswald and Dora, for I'm not going to put up with everything. And now it's half past 11 already, for I have been writing such a long time, and have cried such a lot, for I'm very unhappy. Even Hella doesn't know how unhappy I am. I must go to bed now; whether I shall sleep or not is another question. If I can possibly manage it, I shall go alone to the cemetery to-morrow.

31st. Hella and I went to the cemetery to-day. Her father and mother returned to Cracow yesterday evening, and she told her grandmother she was going to spend the morning with me, and I said I was going to the Brs., so we went alone to Potzleinsdorf. Hella went for a walk round the cemetery while I went to darling Mother's grave. I am so unhappy; Hella consoles me as much as she can, but even she can't understand.

January 1, 19—! Of course we did not keep New Year's Eve yesterday, but were quite alone and it was very melancholy. This morning Dr. P. brought Dora and Aunt Dora some roses and he gave me some lovely violets as a New Year's greeting. He is leaving on the 4th, so he is coming here on the evening of the 3rd. I can't say I look forward to it. To-morrow school begins thank goodness. I met a dust cart, that means good luck; Father says it is a scandal the way the dirt carts go on all through the day in Vienna, and that one should see one even on New Year's day at 2 in the afternoon. But still, if it means good luck!

January 2nd. The dust cart did bring good luck. We had a real piece of luck to-day! In the big interval I noticed a little knot of girls in the hall, and suddenly I felt as if my heart would stop beating. Frau Doktor M., I should say Frau Professor Theyer, was standing among them, she saw us directly and held out her hand to us so we kissed it. She has come to visit her parents and her husband is with her; since she did not know for certain whether she would be able to come to the school she had not written either to me or to Hella about it. She is so lovely and so entrancingly loveable. When the bell rang for class and Frau Doktor Dunker came in I saw that she was still standing outside. So I put my handkerchief up to my face as if my nose were bleeding, and rushed out to her. And because I slipped and nearly fell, she held out her arms to me. Hardly had I reached her, when Hella came out and said: "Of course I understood directly; I said you were awfully bad, so I must go and look after you." Then the Frau Professor laughed like anything and said: "You are such wicked little actresses; I must send you back immediately." But of course she did not but was frightfully sweet. Then we begged her to let us stay with her, but she said: "No, no, I've been your teacher here, and I must not encourage you in mischief. But here is

160

a better idea. Would you like to come and see me to-morrow?" "Rather," we both exclaimed. She said she was staying in a hotel, but we must not come alone to a hotel, so she would see us at her parents, in Schwindgasse, and we were to come there at 4 or half past. Then we kissed both her hands and were so happy! To-morrow at 4! Oh dear, a whole night more and nearly a whole day to wait. "If your parents allow you," she said; as if Father or even Hella's grandmother would not allow that! All Father said was: "All right Gretel, but don't go quite off your head first or you won't be able to find your way to Schwindgasse. Is Hella as crazy as you are?" Of course, how can one be otherwise?

January 3rd. Still 2 hours, it's awful, Hella is coming to fetch me at half past 3. In school to-day we kept on looking at one another, and all the other girls thought it must be something to do with a man. Goodness, what do we care about a man now! We had a splendid idea, that we had just time to make a memento for her, since she does not leave until the evening of the 5th. I am having traced on a piece of yellow silk for a book marker an edelweiss and her monogram E. T., the new one of course. Hella is painting a paperknife in imitation of tarsia mosaic. I would rather have done something of that sort too, but I have no patience for such work, so I often spoil it before I've finished. But one can't very well spoil a piece of embroidery. But I shan't get the tracing on the silk back from the shop until half past 3, so I shall have to work all night and the whole day to-morrow.

Evening. Thank goodness and confound it, whichever way you like to take it, the idiot at the shop had forgotten about the bookmarker and I shan't get it until to-morrow morning early. So I'm able to write now: It was heavenly! We had to walk up and down in front of her house for at least half an hour, until at last it was 5 minutes past 4. She was so sweet to us! She wanted to say Sie to us, but we simply would not have it, and so she said Du as she used to. We talked of all sorts of things, I don't know what, only that I suddenly burst out crying, and then she drew me to her b — —, no, I can't write that about her; she drew me to herself and than I felt her heart beating! and went almost crazy. Hella says that I put both my arms round her neck, but I'm sure that's all imagination, for I should never have dared. She has such fascinating hands, and the wedding ring glistens so on her divine ring finger. Of course we talked about the school, and then she suddenly said: Tell me what really happened about those compositions, when half the class deliberately refrained from putting any punctuation marks. "Oh," we said, "that is a frightful cram, it wasn't half the class, but only 6 of us who have a special veneration for you." Then we told her how

161

it all came about. She laughed a little, and said: "Well, girls, you did not do me any particular service. It really was a great piece of impertinence." But I said: "Prof. Fritsch's remarks were 10 times more impertinent, for they related to another member of the staff, and what was worse to you." Then she said: "My darling girls, that often happens in life, that the absent are given a bad reputation, whether justly or unjustly; one is liable to that in every profession." Hella said that the head mistress was not like that or there would have been a frightful row, since the matter had become known in all the High Schools of Vienna. Then Frau Doktor M. said: "Yes, the Frau Direktorin is really a splendid woman." Then there came something glorious, or really 2 glorious things: (1). She gave us some magnificent sweets, better than I have ever eaten before. Hella agrees, and we are really connoisseurs in the matter of sweets. The second thing, even more glorious, was this: after we had been there some time, there was a knock at the door and in came her husband, the Herr Prof., and said: "How are you my treasure?" and to us: "Goodday, young ladies." Then she introduced us, saying: "Two of my best-loved pupils and my most faithful adherents." Then the Herr Prof. laughed a great deal and said: "That can't be said of all pupils." So I said quickly: "Oh yes, it can be said of Frau Doktor, the whole class would go through fire for her." Then he went away, and she said: "Excuse me for a moment," and we could hear quite plainly that he kissed her in the next room, and then she said as she came in again: "Oh well, be off with you, Karl, goodbye." It's a pity his name is Karl, it's so prosaic, and he calls her Lise, and I expect when they are alone he calls her Lieschen, since he is a North German. I must go to bed, it's half past 11 already. To be continued to-morrow. Sleep well, my sweet glorious ecstatic golden and only treasure! God, I am so happy.

January 6th. Thank goodness to-day is a holiday, and we can't go tobogganing because Dora has a chill!!! I got the bookmarker on the 4th, worked at it all day and up till midnight, and yesterday I got up at half past 5, went on working the whole morning, and at 2 o'clock we took our mementoes to the house. Though we should have liked to give them to her ourselves, we didn't, but only gave them to the maid. She said: Shall I show you in? but Hella said: "No, thank you, we don't want to disturb Frau Theyer, and when I reproached her for this she said: Oh no, it was better not; you are quite upset anyhow, you know what she said: But my dear child, you will make yourself ill; you must not do that on my account!" Oh dear, I'm crying so that I can hardly write, but I must write, for there is still so much that's glorious to put down, things that I must never, never forget, even if it should take me a week to write. The great thing is that I shall simply live upon this memory, and the only thing I want in life is that I may see her once more. Of course we took her some flowers on Friday, I lilies of the valley with violets and tuberoses, and Hella Christmas roses. She was delighted, and went directly to fetch 2 vases which her mother brought in. She is as small as Frau Richter, and her hair is grey, she is charming; but she is not in the least like Frau Doktor M. When we said goodbye she offered us still more sweets, but since we were both nearly crying already we did not want to take any more, but she wrapped them nearly all up for us, saying: "To console you in your sorrow." From anyone else it might have sounded ironical, but from her it was simply lovely. There were 17 large sweets, and Hella gave me 9 of them and took only 8 for herself. I shall eat only one every day, so that they will last me 9 days. Joy and sorrow combined!! Hella is not so frightfully in love as I am, and yesterday she said, in joke of course: "It seems to me that your whole world is foundered; I must pull you out, or you'll be drowned." And then she asked me how I could have been so stupid as to use the word honeymoon to her, although she hemmed to warn me. She said it really was utterly idiotic of me, and that the Frau Prof. blushed. I did not notice it myself, but when her husband came in, she certainly did flush up like anything. Hella and I talked of quite a lot of other things of that sort. I should so much have liked to ask her whether she has given up going to church, for I think the Herr Prof. really is a Jew, though he does not look like one. For lots of other men wear black beards. But I did not venture to ask, and Hella thinks it is a very good thing I did not, for one does not talk about such things. I wonder whether she will have a baby? Oh, it would be horrible. Of course she may have entered into a marriage contract, that would have been the best way. However, Hella thinks that the professor would not have agreed to anything of the kind. But surely if he was frantically in love with her . . .

January 1 5th. The girls in our class are frantically jealous. We did not say in so many words that we, alone among them all, had been invited to see her, but Hella had brought one of the sweets she had given us and in the interval she said: This must be eaten reverently, and she cut it in two to give me half. The Ehrenfelds thought it must have been given by some acquaintance made at the skating rink, and Trude said: "Doubly sweetened, by chocolate and love." "Yes," said I, "but not in the sense you imagine." And since she said: "Oh, of course, I know all about that, but I don't want to be indiscreet," Hella said: "I may as well tell you that Frau Doktor M., or I should say the married Frau Prof. Theyer, gave us this sweet and a great many more on the day she had invited us to go and see her." Then they were all utterly kerblunxed and said: "Great Scott, what luck, but you always were Frau Doktor M.'s favourites, especially Lainer. But Lainer always courted Frau Doktor M."

January 17th. The whole school knows about our being invited to see her, the glorious one! I've just been reading it over, and I see that I have left a frightful lot out, especially about her father. When we were leaving, just outside the house door we burst out crying because as I opened the door I had said, For the last time! Just then an old gentleman came up and was about to go in, and when he saw that we were crying, though we were standing quite in the shadow, he came up to us and asked what was the matter. Then Hella said: "We have lost out best friend." Then the old gentleman looked at us for a tremendously long time and said: "I say, do you happen to be the two ardent admirers of Frau Doktor Mallburg? She is my daughter, you know. And then he said: But you really can't go through the streets bathed in tears like that. Come upstairs again with me and my daughter will console you." So we really did go upstairs again, and she was perfectly unique. Her father opened the door and called out: Lieserl, your admirers simply can't part from you, and I found them being washed out to sea in a river of tears. Then she came out wearing a rose-coloured dressing-gown!!! exquisite. And she led us into the room and said: "Girls, you must not look at me in this old rag, which is only fit to throw away." I should have liked to say: "Give it to me then." But of course I could not. And when we made our final goodbye, perhaps for ever, she kissed each of us twice over and said: Girls, I wish you all the happiness in the world!

January 18th. Hella invited me there to-day, to meet Lajos and Jeno. But I'm not going, for Jeno does not interest me in the very least. That was not a real love. I don't care for anyone in the whole world except her, my one and only! Even Hella can't understand that, in fact she thinks it dotty. Father wanted me to go to Hella's to change the current of my thoughts. Of course I hardly say a word about her to anyone, for no one understands me. But I never could have believed that Father would be just like anyone else. It's quite true that I'm getting thin. I'm so glad that we are not going tobogganing to-day because Dora has a chill, a real chill this time. So I am going to the church in Schwindgasse and shall walk up and down in front of her house; perhaps I shall meet her father or her mother. I wrote to her the day before yesterday.

January 24th. I am so happy. She wrote to me by return! This is the second letter I have had from her! At dinner to-day Father said: "Hullo, Gretel, why are you looking so happy to-day? I have not seen you with such a sunny face for a long time." So I answered in as few words as possible: "After dinner I will tell you why." For the others need not know anything about it. And when I told Father vaguely that Frau Prof. Th. had written to me, Father said: "Oh, is that what has pleased you so much. But I have something up my sleeve which will also please you. February 1st and 2nd are Sunday and Monday, you have 2 days free, and if you and Hella can get a day off from school on Saturday we might make an excursion to Mariazell. How does that strike you?" It would be glorious, if only Hella is allowed to come, for her grandmother imagines that the sore throat she had before Christmas was due to the tobogganing on the Anninger, where the sole was torn off her shoe! As if we could help that. Still, by good luck she may have forgotten it; she is 63 already, and one forgets a lot when one is that age.

Evening. Hella may come; it will be splendid! Perhaps we shall try a little skiing. But really Hella is a horrid pig; she said: "All right, I'll come, if you'll promise not to be continually talking about Frau Professor Th. I'm very fond of her too, but you are simply crazy about her." It's really too bad, and I shall never mention her name to the others any more. I am looking forward so to the tobogganing at Mariazell. We've never made any such excursion in winter before. Hurrah, it will be glorious! Oh I do wish the 31st of January were here; I'm frantically excited.

EDITOR'S NOTE

Rita's joyful expectations of tobogganing among glistening snow-clad hills, remained unfulfilled. The rude hand of fate was thrust into the lives of the two sisters. On January 29th their father, suddenly struck down with paralysis, was brought home in an ambulance, and died in a few hours without recovering consciousness.

Torn from the sheltering and affectionate atmosphere of home, separated from her most intimate friend, the young orphan had to struggle for peace of soul in the isolation of a provincial town
— — —